Re-Placing Women in Psychology
Readings Toward a More Inclusive History

Janis S. Bohan, PhD
Metropolitan State College of Denver

KENDALL/HUNT PUBLISHING COMPANY
2460 Kerper Boulevard P.O. Box 539 Dubuque, Iowa 52004-0539

Contents

Women have been present and active in psychology since its beginnings, but for a variety of reasons, they and their work have been largely invisible to psychology as a whole, and are therefore largely absent from the texts which chronicle psychology's emergence and growth as a discipline. The invisibility of women is a concern expressed in recent scholarship across the disciplines. The aim of this book is to provide a vehicle for making visible the women of psychology.

My own involvement in this topic emerged from a long-standing interest in psychology's history, combined with a growing awareness of the paucity of women included in traditional portrayal of that history. As I undertook to rectify this marginalization of women and their work, I expected a relatively straightforward task of locating and recording women's efforts. The project became, to my pleasure and occasional frustration, a major odyssey, leading me to a number of new and unanticipated understandings. I developed a deep appreciation for women's history in general; I came to a clearer recognition of the myriad factors that have inhibited women's full participation in and recognition by the discipline; I came to view psychology quite differently, as the invisibility of women highlighted for me assumptions within the field which need reconsideration; and I learned a great deal about what history is and is not.

This book is an outgrowth of that journey, and is intended to provide a vehicle by which faculty and students can achieve some of those same understandings without the necessity for so long and convoluted a process of discovery. The readings included in the book are selected to serve several purposes:

- To introduce students to recent scholarship stressing the role of context in the shaping of knowledge and of history
- To apply these principles in exploring the contextual forces which have shaped women's place in psychology
- To explore the process of integrating women into psychology's history, using illustrative recent writings in this area
- To raise the question of what impact this process of integrating women will have on psychology.

The book is primarily intended as a supplementary reader for courses in history and theories or history and systems of psychology. Texts in this area continue to follow long-standing assumptions about the appropriate format and content of such subject matter, assumptions which have acted to marginalize women and their work. Few texts include women's work at all; those that do, incorporate minimal discussion of a very few women's contributions. None directly addresses the complex reasons why this marginalization exists and persists. This book is designed to supplement standard texts in order to give students a deeper understanding of the issues involved in women's absence from psychology's histories, as well as to introduce them to the lives and work of some of psychology's women. The concepts presented and the illustrations used here would also offer useful supplementary material for courses in sex roles, psychology of women, or social psychology, as well as women's studies courses in history or sociology.

This book is the product of several years' work, during which my efforts have been supported and encouraged by many. My special thanks go to Imelda Mulholland, my "personal librarian" at the Auraria Higher Education Center Library, who has taught me what an invaluable and irreplaceable resource a good librarian is. I am indebted to the many students who have been excited by my work and whose enthusiasm has been my source of invigoration. I am grateful also to my colleagues, Lyn Wickelgren and Diane Grey, whose thoughtful reviews encouraged significant improvements in the book's content, and to two bright and conscientious students, Jeff Froyd and Carol Willmon, who provided me with an invaluable student's eye view of the book before I subjected other students to its vagaries.

On a more personal level, this book (and, indeed, all of my work) would not have come to fruition without the steadfast support of Ann Cook and Marjorie Leidig. Though neither has read the book, both are midwives to it.

To the Instructor

Despite considerable recent research directed at discovering and explicating the work of women in psychology, standard history and systems texts still treat this topic minimally, if at all. Faced with this dilemma, instructors seeking to teach a more inclusive history course have been forced to seek out scattered resources to support that effort in a widely dispersed and theoretically formless literature—a time-consuming and often frustrating task. The purpose of this book is to provide a single-source overview of major issues raised by attempts to develop a women-inclusive history of psychology, and to do so within the context of a theoretical framework that joins diverse works into a coherent whole.

This book is not a compendium of biographical information. There are too many women worthy of recognition, and the biographical literature is now too vast to sample adequately here. Instead, the book outlines a structure within which these women can be incorporated into course content in a manner that makes sense of their inclusion. An extensive bibliography is provided to facilitate further research into the lives and work of individual women, as well as the conceptual issues raised by the process of creating women-inclusive history.

The format of the book is designed to allow its ready use with any major history and systems text. The following outline suggests how the readings included here might be distributed across an academic term. In addition to recommendations for readings in this collection which parallel textbook topics, the chart below also indicates individual women whose work would be appropriate accompaniment to the topic under consideration. These suggestions might be utilized either by the instructor as a part of lecture material or by students as topics for papers or class presentations. The bio-bibliographic Appendix B cites resources for learning about these women and their work.

Selected Women of Psychology

TOPIC IN STANDARD TEXT	READINGS IN THIS BOOK	SELECTED WOMEN TO INCLUDE
INTRODUCTION: What is history, theory; Philosophical issues **PRE-PSYCHOLOGY:** Greek Thought Pre-Modern Thought Descartes to 19th Century Physiological influences	**SECTION I:** 1. Furumoto 2. Lerner 3. Bohan	*EDNA HEIDBREDDER;* History, Theory *MARY HENLE:* Historian *CHRISTINE LADD-FRANKLIN:* Color Vision
THE NEW PSYCHOLOGY: Wundt Structuralism Darwin/Evolution Functionalism	**SECTION I:** 1. Shields 2. Furumoto and Scarborough	*MARY CALKINS:* Word Association, Self Psychology *DOROTHEA DIX:* Mental Health Reform *JUNE DOWNEY:* Aesthetics, Personality *LETA HOLLINGWORTH:* Sex Differences, Giftedness *HELEN THOMPSON (WOOLLEY)* Sex Differences MARGARET WASHBURN: Comparative Psychology

LATER AMERICAN PSYCHOLOGY	SECTION II:	ANNE ANASTASI:
Psychometrics, Mental Testing	3. Russo and Denmark	Individual Differences
		LOIS MURPHY Child Development
Behaviorism	SECTION III:	CHARLOTTE BUHLER:
Gestalt, Field Theories	1. Lott	Humanistic Psychology
"Third Force": Humanism Existentialism		ELEANOR GIBSON: Experimental Psychology Perception
		FLORENCE GOODENOUGH: Child Development,
		EDNA HEIDBREDDER: Cognition
		MARY HENLE: Gestalt Psychology
		MARY COVER JONES: Behavior Therapy, Developmental Psychology
		GRACE KENT: Clinical Practice and Research
		MYRTLE MCGRAW: Child Development
		LOIS MURPHY: Child Development, Social Psychology
		JANET TAYLOR SPENCE: Experimental Psychology Gender
		LEONA TYLER: Individual Differences Clinical Psychology
		BLUMA ZEIGARNIK: Field Theory
PSYCHOANALYTIC APPROACHES (PSA)		NANCY CHODOROW: PSA and Gender
		HELENE DEUTSCH: PSA Psy of Women
		MARIE BONAPARTE: Traditional PSA

PSYCHOANALYTIC APPROACHES (PSA) (cont.)		*ANNA FREUD:*
		  PSA with Children
		  and Adolescents
		KAREN HORNEY:
		  Social PSA, Feminism
		MELANIE KLEIN:
		  Object Relations
		MARGARET MAHLER:
		  Object Relations

CONTEMPORARY PSYCHOLOGY, NEW DIRECTIONS
Applied Psychologies
Cognitive Psychology
Social Action
	SECTION III:
	
	2. Crawford and
	   Marecek
	3. Mednick
		SANDRA BEM:
		  Gender Roles/Cognition
		MAMIE PHIPPS CLARK:
		  Child Development,
		  Racism
		FLORENCE DENMARK:
		  Gender,
		  Feminist Psychology
		CAROL GILLIGAN:
		  Moral Development and
		  Gender
		BARBEL INHELDER:
		  Cognitive Development
		ELEANOR MACCOBY:
		  Child Development,
		  Gender
		MARTHA MEDNICK:
		  Social Psychology,
		  Gender
		JEAN BAKER MILLER:
		  Psychology of Women
		MARIA MONTESSORI:
		  Early Child Education
		ANNE ROE:
		  Occupational Psychology
		VIRGINIA SATIR:
		  Family Dynamics/Therapy

CONTEMPORARY PSYCHOLOGY, NEW DIRECTIONS (cont.)		*CAROLYN SHERIF:* Social Psychology, Feminist Psychology *BARBARA WALLSTON:* Social Psychology, Feminist Psychology

The book incorporates certain features which are intended to aid in the process of melding this material with more standard course content, and also to assist the instructor in assuring that students benefit from and integrate this material.

- Following each section of readings, a student evaluation form solicits input from students regarding the clarity, usefulness, and impact of the readings. When students submit this form (which is printed on perforated, removable pages), the instructor will have immediate feedback about students' reactions to the readings. This information should point up topics of particular interest, points of confusion or uncertainty, and conflicts perceived by students between these readings and text or lecture material. These forms can thus guide discussion of the readings.
- Each section of readings is also followed by a page of review questions, which focus students' attention both on the content of the articles and also on their relevance to broader course content. These pages are also perforated so that the instructor can request that students submit them as required assignments, for extra credit, or simply to encourage their attention to this information. These questions are ideal for essay questions on examinations or as items for take-home exams, extra-credit essays, or the more extensive papers these topics might generate.
- At the end of the book, Appendices provide extensive bibliographic resources dealing with both the broad philosophical issues and the pragmatic concerns of incorporating women into psychology's histories. Appendix A includes a broad range of resources addressing the theoretical and contextual issues presented only briefly in the readings and surrounding discussions. Appendix B includes a listing of selected women of psychology, followed by a bibliography of biographical resources, each keyed to indicate which woman or women it concerns. While this bibliography represents only a small sample of the proliferating biographical material now available, it will provide a basis for your own or students' further research into the lives and work of a number of important women psychologists. The pages of both Appendices are perforated to allow easy removal for further use and for easy filing.

My often frustrating research in this area has convinced me that the process of incorporating women and their work into standard curriculum is no easy task. The intent of this book is to ease that undertaking, and it is my hope that the pedagogical features described here will facilitate the smooth incorporation of this material into history and systems courses.

To the Student

In the past, students of the history of psychology have encountered a portrayal of the field's evolution largely devoid of women as contributors. This presentation of psychology's history has not seemed particularly startling to most of us. Histories in general (whether of societies or of academic disciplines) have included few women, and the resultant perception that women have contributed little of major significance to history did not seem problematic. In recent decades, however, a growing literature has documented not only the dearth of women in the histories of societies and of disciplines, but also the fact that women have indeed made major, if unrecognized contributions. Further efforts have analyzed the socio-historical forces which have created women's invisibility. Unfortunately, the awareness of the problem and attempts of scholars to address it have not led immediately to changes in textbooks, and so students are often left with the older, now-discredited view of a woman-less history of psychology.

The purpose of this book is to address this problem. Its aim is to explain women's place in psychology's history (including their invisibility) as an understandable product of how historical knowledge is developed. By reassessing the process of writing history, it becomes possible to recognize and incorporate women and their work as integral to psychology. This process of creating a history of psychology which includes women takes into account both the nature of what we term "knowledge" and the particular influences that have shaped psychology's histories in a manner that has rendered those histories largely blind to women and their contributions.

The book is organized so that the readings move systematically from a consideration of broader issues of the nature of psychological knowledge and history, through the application of these principles to women's place in the discipline, and finally to a discussion of the impact on psychology of this process of including women.

Unfortunately, a brief book of this sort cannot adequately present the lives and work of the many women who have contributed to psychology. The literature which introduces those women is now vast, and to pick a few of those articles would do injustice to the many. Accordingly, this book is not intended as a biographical compendium but as a tool for making sense of the process of creating an inclusive history of psychology.

Incorporated into the format of the book are several features which will help you derive maximum benefit from this organization, and also assist in coordinating this material with the information included in your regular text and your instructor's presentations:

- At the end of each section of readings you will find an evaluation form designed to allow you to comment on the readings. This form will provide specific feedback to your instructor to clarify the impact of the readings and to point up areas of confusion or conflicts with text or lecture material. Your submitting these forms will allow your instructor to incorporate student comments and concerns in class discussion. These forms are printed on perforated pages for easy removal.
- Also following each section of readings is a page of review questions designed to direct your thinking toward the meaning of these readings and their relation to the broader context of the task at hand. These questions may be assigned by your instructor or may serve to clarify and elaborate the material for your own understanding. These questions are also printed on perforated pages so that you can remove them easily for submission or to file with class notes.
- The Appendices provide extensive bibliographies to assist your further explorations of these topics. Included here are resources that elaborate on the conceptual issues raised by the readings (Appendix A), and also resources for biographical research on selected individual women of psychology (Appendix B). These readings will provide substantial support for term papers, class presentations, or other projects that move beyond the limited content of this brief reader. Again, the perforation of these pages allows you to remove them for easier use, or to file the bibliographies in a more compact and accessible form.

My hope is that the writings included in this book and the ancillary features described here will facilitate your understanding of women's place in the history of psychology. While this book can by no means fulfill the challenge of creating a history and systems course that is adequately inclusive of women, it offers a beginning for that process. It moves us to acknowledge the importance of addressing the issue of women's invisibility in psychology's histories, and it introduces a view of psychology which takes women as integral to what the field has been and is becoming.

Women's Invisibility: The Reasons, the Costs, the Alternative

> While the prevailing myth may be that female psychologists have been less accomplished and less productive than their male colleagues, the reality appears to be that their work has been disproportionately unnoticed, and as low-status members of the psychological community, their names, though not their contributions, have been largely lost to history. (Denmark, 1980, p. 1059)[1]

The use of the neologism "re-placing" in the title of this book is intended to convey a fundamental, if little-recognized fact about women's place in psychology. Women have in fact been present and active in psychology since its beginnings, but for a variety of reasons they and their work have been largely invisible to psychology as a whole, and therefore largely absent from the texts which chronicle the field's evolution. This exclusion of women and their work has been self-maintaining: the belief that women have not contributed significantly to psychology has led us to disregard their actual participation, thus reinforcing the initial belief that they have played no important role in psychology. In Denmark's (1980) words, "fictions that are held as truths function for future generations as if they were truths, and prophecies fulfill themselves" (p. 1059). The purpose of this book of readings is to confront the fiction that women have not been an integral part of psychology and to provide a framework through which women can be placed again, *re-placed,* in their rightful position in the histories of the discipline.

The reader might well question the necessity for or value of this project designed to re-place women in psychology. What impact, one might ask, would the presence or absence of women have on the field or its participants? Surely knowledge is gender-

---

1. All sources cited in the discussions surrounding the readings are included among the references in *Appendix A,* **Resources for Re-Placing Women in Psychology: History, Constructionism, and Gender Theory.**

neutral, it might be argued; whether women or men are included in histories is not as important as that crucial ideas (whoever their originator) are included. Further, insofar as history is a factual representation (re-presentation) of earlier events, women who have been important to psychology's past would surely be represented in historical research.

However, the reality is that the neglect of women is not an exclusion without consequence, nor is it an objectively supported depiction of psychology's history. Let me expand on these assertions.

The Importance of Models

One impact of women's invisibility derives from the function that history serves in our individual and collective intellectual development. History serves as a model. It is a model of reality, a portrayal of what has been and what is the human condition, what is and is not possible for us. The individuals that people our histories become models for our own strivings; the ideas deemed worthy of historical record become ideas worthy of notice; events as recorded in histories become predictors of the success or doom of our own efforts. Thus, a history which excludes the perspective of a particular group unavoidably misses a segment of the scope of psychological ideas. This constriction of vision leaves an impoverished range of possible scripts for individuals and for the discipline as a whole.

The invisibility of women also robs psychology of important personal and intellectual models, for women and men alike. As O'Connell & Russo (1980) pointed out, male students can take for granted the presence of eminent same-sex models in their chosen field, with consequent beneficial effects on their work and their aspirations. The absence of comparable models for women students must act to inhibit the efforts of women aspiring to a career in psychology, as well as women already in the field. The importance of models for achievement has been well-documented (e.g., Douvan, 1976; Goldstein, 1979; O'Connell, 1978), and in their absence women "often feel that they are competing against insurmountable odds and that they are competing alone" (O'Connell & Russo, 1980, p. 6). The need to provide models for women who aspire to careers in psychology seems particularly urgent, given recent data demonstrating that approximately two thirds of undergraduate and graduate students in psychology are women, and that women now earn over half of all doctorate degrees in psychology (Walker, 1991).

Men, too, are affected by the invisibility of women in psychology. When the consensus (Denmark's "fiction," discussed above) is that women have contributed little and have had no significant impact on the development of the discipline, the perspective of everyone—male and female—is narrowed. Not only do men lack access to the range of ideas offered by women, but they also lack the models that would demonstrate women's potential in the field. It must be difficult for men to take their women colleagues seriously when they are led by their reading to believe that women have little to offer. A striking illustration of this dynamic was offered by Bernstein and Russo (1974), who cited the following disturbing incident: Psychology graduate students at Cornell University requested that the department limit the admission of women to graduate study, arguing that women don't contribute significantly to psychology. This position seemed defensible to them in spite of the fact that one of their psychology professors was Eleanor Jack Gibson, widely acclaimed for her work, a future contributor to the respected series, *A History of Psychology in Autobiography,* one of the few women ever elected to the National Academy of Sciences, and a recipient of the American Psychological Association's prestigious Distinguished Scientific Contribution Award (Russo & O'Connell, 1980).

History: The Telling of Facts?

Still, one might argue, history is history. If women aren't included in major history of psychology texts, it must be that they have not in fact made significant contributions to the discipline. We could add some women, no doubt, women whose work may have been slighted; but history must necessarily be selective, and many men have been excluded, as well. The argument that women's absence from psychology's histories accurately reflects their contributions to the field is grounded in the **myth of meritocracy.** Meritocracy, in its genuine form, rewards merit, acknowledges excellence, grants prominence selectively to those who have earned it through exceptional work. If meritocracy in fact ruled and women's work had been of import, their work would be included in psychology's histories. The myth lies in the erroneous assumption that science (or psychology) operates in this logical and unbiased manner. In truth, people achieve positions of prestige for a variety of reasons, many of which have more to do with political realities, professional tradition, and social values than with the merit or excellence of their work. Many influences on recognition which are extraneous to merit will be addressed in the readings in this book.

As you will learn, women's invisibility in psychology reflects not the paucity or the inadequacy of their work but other factors which have shaped their experience and psychology's evaluation of their efforts. Women's invisibility is an understandable product of the contexts in which they have functioned and the forces (internal and external) that have framed the discipline. Re-placing women in psychology, then, demands attention to the contexts which have shaped their place (including their marginality) in psychology. Re-placing women in psychology's history requires more than adding a few names to the litany of psychology's great people. It requires viewing history from a new perspective, one that attends to the impact of context.

History and the Centrality of Context

In order to approach this process of integrating women into psychology's history, it is essential to recognize that history is not a straightforward presentation of unambiguous

3

events of the past. Rather, any history is a creation of a particular historian, who, in turn, is the product of personal experiences, of a socio-historical milieu, and of a particular professional environment. History is written within and is therefore unavoidably shaped by all these levels of context. What is presented as history, therefore, must be seen as simply one view of history, one perspective, one hypothesis about what happened, why it happened, which events were important, and what impact they had on future events. Any such portrayal is necessarily limited in scope and is inseparable from the contexts in which it is produced and disseminated. As you will see, women's substantial absence from psychology's histories is a product not of an objective rendering of psychology's past, which is impossible, but of a particular perspective grounded in contexts that act to marginalize women.

The readings that follow elaborate on these issues. In various ways, they demonstrate that the process of re-placing women in psychology's history requires a direct engagement with the assumption and practices that have acted to marginalize women's work in previous histories.

The Impact of Re-Placing Women

As further incentive for undertaking this project to re-place women, the incorporation of women and their work into psychology promises to raise provocative questions and to challenge earlier perspectives on the discipline. New questions arise, old models reveal their limitations, and exciting possibilities for the future of psychology emerge. A history of psychology that integrates women and their work will be a history expanded in important ways. It will not only incorporate more individuals and more ideas; it will also challenge us to consider new modes of understanding and new criteria for importance. Re-placing women in psychology will have consequences beyond the mere addition of names to our listings of eminent psychologists; it will reshape the discipline in a manner as yet unknown.

Organization of Readings

The readings in this book are intended to provide students with a beginning awareness of the issues raised above: appreciation for the impact of context on the construction of knowledge and of history; an understanding of the contextual forces which have shaped women's place in psychology, including their invisibility; and an indication of the potentially profound impact on psychology of women's integration into the discipline and its histories.

Readings in *Section I* introduce and expand upon the notion that "knowledge" is a product of context, is constructed rather than discovered, and that history reflects the inescapable imprint of the context in which it is written. These arguments coalesce to demonstrate how women's exclusion from history is a product not of lesser merit but of contextually-determined assumptions underlying psychology's self-definition and directing the writing of its history.

Section II includes readings which apply these concepts to the particular goal of re-placing women in the history of psychology. These articles ask what psychology would look like if women's perspective were respected rather than marginalized, if the history of psychology recognized as legitimate the context which has shaped women's place in the discipline.

Section III explores the impact on psychology of the process of integrating women and their perspective into our view of the field. Questions are asked here about how psychology has responded to the impact of changing social context (particularly the challenges raised by feminism) and how the incorporation of women's work can both contribute to and benefit from psychology's traditional perspectives. Also reiterated here is the determining salience of context: recent changes in psychology also reflect the particular political, social, and economic milieu in which they are occurring. This last section of readings thus completes the circle: women's work both shapes and is shaped by social context, exactly the central theme of the first section.

The *Conclusion* brings closure to the questions raised by the readings, and anticipates future directions in this process of understanding women's place in psychology. These comments are not definitive statements about the future of women in psychology but rather reflect emerging issues in this now burgeoning literature. Final answers to the challenges raised by this literature are not, of course, possible. For another psychologist working in a different network of contexts would necessarily construe both the questions and their answers differently than do I. But that is precisely the point. What we see as truth depends on the lens we use. Just as traditional histories looking from one perspective have seen a psychology largely absent women, so we can look again using a different angle of vision and find women central to psychology.

Finally, this closing discussion is followed by the *Appendices*, which are designed to support further reading and research. The readings included in this book have been selected to provide a conceptual framework for understanding women's place in the discipline and the importance and impact of their re-placement, rather than attempting to sample the now-vast biographical literature on individual women. Appendix A provides further resources for those interested in further exploration of the underpinnings of this approach, and includes readings on historiography, constructionism, and gender theory.

Recent years have witnessed a burgeoning literature identifying and exploring the contributions of individual women to psychology. For those interested in learning more about these women and their work, Appendix B provides a listing of selected women of psychology and a bibliography of further readings.

The Construction of Knowledge, the Construction of History

Historically, the discipline of psychology has been grounded in a philosophy of knowledge (an **epistemology**) termed positivism, which is based on the assumption that it is possible to discover reality or "truth" through the proper application of scientific methods. This approach to knowledge has underlain psychological scholarship in America since the discipline's inception just before the turn of the present century. From this perspective, reality exists independently of the knower, and the aim of science (psychology) is to create circumstances in which that reality can be systematically and objectively observed. The information thus developed is assumed to entail an accurate description of that reality. Knowledge, then, reflects truth as discovered. The accuracy of our rendition of reality depends on the care with which we apply our methods.

The Construction of Knowledge

Recent scholarship in epistemology, **historiography** (the study of how history is written) and the **sociology of knowledge** (the study of how social forces shape understanding) has brought into question these traditional conceptions of the validity of truth claims. Such scholarship suggests, in contrast to the traditional view, that so-called knowledge—or "what passes for knowledge", to borrow from Berger & Luckmann (1967)—is not a simple presentation of facts garnered through the objective observation of an independently existing reality. Rather, what we purport to know is in fact a "construction," a hypothesis about a presumed reality, inextricably intertwined with the socio-cultural and historical context within which we pursue knowledge.

This alternative perspective on knowledge has been dubbed **social constructionism** (e.g., Gergen, 1985). This term emphasizes two notions: 1) the assertion that so-called-knowledge is constructed rather than discovered, and 2) an insistence on the fundamentally social nature of this process of knowledge-construction. In order for an item to be deemed knowledge, it must be widely held as true, must be so thoroughly fixed as factual in the consciousness of the group holding it that its accuracy is taken for granted. From inside this social context, such a "truth" does not appear as constructed; rather, it appears as discovered, as an observed fact about an objective reality. It is precisely this imbeddedness in context which renders such a construction (apparently) self-evident.

Crucial to the constructionist view of knowledge is the recognition that our understanding is thoroughly framed by context; neither the knower nor the process of truth-seeking exists in isolation. The individual (here, the psychologist) searching for the truth of human experience unavoidably functions within an intricate web of influences—the contemporary socio-historical milieu, the structure and assumptions of the individual's profession, her or his own personal experiences and biases, and so forth. Further, the method employed, the very process of seeking psychological knowledge is also inescapably shaped by contextual forces: the discipline's preferred model of searching, the tools and measures available (and hence the sort of questions that can be asked and the form of answers that will result), the socio-political milieu of the discipline and its role in defining which questions are deemed important and which answers acceptable, and so forth.

Given this realization that both the knower and the process of knowing are inevitably circumscribed by context, the so-called knowledge that is generated must be acknowledged as inextricably bound up in these contexts. What is produced through such knowledge-seeking, then, is not a free-standing and revealed truth, but a best guess, based on selective vision, using limited tools, shaped by the contextual forces surrounding the search. It is not Truth; it is a historically and contextually situated understanding, a social construction (see Gergen, 1973, 1985; Lincoln & Guba, 1985; and Polkinghorne, 1983, for thorough discussions of these concepts).

As an illustration: turn-of-the-century psychologists concurred with and participated in the propagation of the belief that women were incapable of serious intellectual endeavor and risked sterility if they pursued higher education. While this notion seems absurd to us, situated in our own socio-historical context, it made perfect sense in the intellectual and social context of that time (which will be discussed in the readings to follow). It was taken not as a hypothesis, not as a social belief, but as a self-evident truth.

The Construction of History

If we apply this same epistemological analysis to the writing of histories, we can see that history, too, is a construction. From a constructionist perspective, the telling of history is not a simple representation (re-presentation) of past events. The initial impediment to history's being "factual" in this sense is that, by definition, we cannot know history directly; we know historical events only through the accounts of others who were present or by access to residual measures such as the concrete consequences of events (cf Nowell-Smith, 1977).

When we recognize that even those who witness historical events can only interpret rather than know what has occurred (for observation is always context-bound, as explained above), even the most direct of historical information—the eye-witness account—is seen to be constructed. As this initial interpretation is reported and interpreted through time and subsequent renderings, history becomes ever more distant from actual events, ever more influenced by the particular biases acting upon the procurement and analysis of historical "data." Historical accounts are inevitably influenced at every step by the personal and social contexts in which history is written (cf. Collingwood, 1946; Kuhn, 1977; Nowell-Smith, 1977; Stocking, 1965).

Among the forces framing historical writings are numerous tiers of context. First, the values of the society in which the historian works guide the selection, analysis, and evaluation of historical information; the **Zeitgeist** (or "spirit of the times," the view of reality held in this socio-historical frame) influences the particular interpretation of history offered and its acceptance by the larger community. More narrowly, the professional community within which a historian works directs and shapes how history is written through that discipline's definition of criteria for relevance, accuracy, and adequacy, as reflected in the profession's current world view or **paradigm** (Kuhn, 1970). Finally, the historian is an individual with individual values, expectations, and biases which influence her or his interests, judgments and emphases in writing history. What we have in recorded history, then, is a construction. A history is not objective knowledge about the past; it is "what passes for knowledge."

The readings in this section are rooted in these arguments regarding the nature of knowledge in general and the nature of historical knowledge in particular. The recurring theme is the centrality of context and the need to understand history as contextually grounded. The first paper by Laurel Furumoto presents "the new history of psychology," an approach to understanding psychology's past and re-evaluating its historical record through a contextual lens. In this paper, Furumoto offers an illustration of history constructed with an eye to context; her example is based upon her study of one of psychology's pioneer women, a fitting introduction to this book's overall aim. Gerda Lerner's contribution, the second paper, represents a more specific application of such a contextual approach. Lerner is explicitly interested in re-viewing history in such a way that women's experience is taken as valid in its own right, and her writings outline her model for this process. As the final paper in this section, my own article aims to merge these various perspectives—social constructionism, Furumoto's "new history," and Lerner's model for women-inclusive history—to approach the specific question of women's place in psychology. This synthesis presages subsequent readings, forming the linkage between the constructionist framework and its application to the task at hand: re-placing women in the history of psychology.

Summary

In combination, the readings included in this section suggest a new approach to understanding the chronicles of psychology's evolution, an approach which I suggest provides a framework for integrating women and their work. Briefly, the perspective provided by these readings can be summarized as follows:

Any rendition of the discipline's history is necessarily framed by a plethora of contextual forces, which collectively act to shape the description of psychology's evolution. The themes presented, the individuals selected as noteworthy, the connections drawn between earlier work and contemporary psychology all reflect the historian's and the discipline's current conceptions of what is important to an understanding of the history of psychology.

Histories as written to date have largely excluded or, at best, marginalized the women of psychology and their work. The invisibility of women is a product of certain contextual forces, both within society as a whole and in psychology itself, which have excluded women from these histories in two ways: First, social norms have minimized women's access to the opportunities which facilitate professional contributions; and, second, the work that women have performed has been adjudged by historians to be of little significance, because much of its is not in keeping with the dominant paradigm by which such work is evaluated (see Bohan, 1990a; 1990b for a detailed discussion of these issues).

The resultant invisibility of women in psychology has led to histories largely blind to the true rule of women in the discipline. An awareness of this marginalization and its sources leads us to the question explored in Section II: What would psychology look like if the contexts shaping women's participation were taken into account?

Laurel Furumoto

The New History of Psychology

Psychologists currently teaching the history of their discipline are unlikely to have had any instruction in the field other than a graduate level course introducing them to "great men" and "great ideas." This stands in marked contrast with psychologists teaching courses in areas such as personality, developmental, social, and experimental psychology, where prior training in research methods, as well as in the subject matter of the specialty, is the norm.

This lack of training in historiographical methods can be attributed to the fact that, up until approximately 20 years ago, history of psychology was a neglected research area. Recently, the situation has changed; we are now witnessing a surge of historical scholarship that deserves to be called "the new history of psychology." However, with a few exceptions (see Benjamin, 1988; Hilgard, 1987; Leahey, 1987), textbooks in the history of psychology have yet to reflect the advent of this new history, and most teachers of the history course, not trained as historians, are heavily dependent on such works for their approach to the topic.

An almost inevitable conclusion follows: The history of psychology as currently taught in the typical college and university classroom remains largely uninformed by the new history, a state of affairs that, in my view, affords our students an impoverished understanding of psychology's past. In this chapter, I want to argue for a change in the status quo by drawing the attention of teachers of the history course to the new history and by discussing its implications for transforming the traditional history of psychology course.

Rise of the New History

Within the discipline of history proper, the so-called "new history" is not all that new; in fact, it dates back at least to 1912. In that year, a collection of essays appeared by James Harvey Robinson (1912), professor of history at Columbia University, entitled *The New History*. In this volume, Robinson made a plea for the adoption of what he called "the modern historical outlook." Instead of "perpetuating the conception of history as a chronicle of heroic persons and romantic occurrences" (p. 10), which he dubbed the "epic poem approach," Robinson advocated the study of institutions as a surer route to historical understanding. Robinson considered institutions to be synonymous with national habits, and he defined them "in a very broad sense, to include the ways in which people have thought and acted in the past, their tastes and their achievements in many fields besides the political'' (p. 15).

In the ensuing three quarters of a century, the new history has become increasingly influential within the profession. It has also become increasingly diverse. The term ''new history'' as it is currently used refers to a variety of approaches, such as social history, psycho-history, and cliometrics, that are not necessarily consistent with one another, but which have in common the fact that they all represent a challenge to traditional history. The dominant place that the new history now occupies is testified to in a recent assessment of its status by Gertrude Himmelfarb (1987), a well-known historian who places herself in the camp of the old history. In fact, Himmelfarb claims that the new history has largely displaced the old, moving it from the center to the periphery of the profession.

The new history has long made its presence felt within the specialty area of history of science as well. Thomas Kuhn (1968) described how, over the course of the 20th century, historians of science gradually went through a reorientation in the way they viewed their subject matter. Efforts in the history of science were unevenly distributed, however, as Kuhn notes, and until fairly recently were almost exclusively confined to the physical and biological sciences. Thus, Kuhn could observe as late as 1968 that ''as yet, the new historiography has not touched the social sciences'' (p. 77).

In the mid-1970s, another historian of science, Stephen J. Brush (1974), published an article in the journal *Science* with the provocative title, ''Should the History of Science Be Rated X?'' At the outset, he acknowledged that the history he was referring to was primarily that of physics and early astronomy, as ''these subjects usually furnish the successful examples of the scientific approach to be emulated in other fields'' (p. 1164). Brush debated the pros and cons of teaching the new history of science to science students, indicating certain dilemmas that it posed for instructors who wanted to incorporate the historical perspective into their courses. For example, he pointed out that whereas traditional history portrayed the scientist as an objective fact finder and neutral observer, the new history emphasized the notion that scientists often operate in a subjective fashion, under the influence of a variety of extra-scientific factors. Also, Brush claimed, the new history rejected the traditional view of scientific activity as a continuous progression from error to truth, and opted instead for a model that depicts scientific change as a shift from one world view to another—world views that are linked to theoretical commitments involving esthetic as well as metaphysical considerations.

These aspects of the new history of science, Brush observed, fly in the face of the canons of scientific method as typically taught to science students and run counter to the beliefs of most of their science teachers as well. Teachers who want ''to indoctrinate students in the traditional role of the scientist as a neutral fact finder,'' he concludes, ''should not use historical materials of the kind now being prepared by historians of science'' (p. 1170) because they will not serve the purpose well.

If, as I have attempted to document thus far, history in general, including the subfield of history of science, has been profoundly altered by the new history's coming of age, what has its impact been within the history of psychology? As previously mentioned, just 20 years ago Kuhn (1968) could see no influence of the new historiography in the social sciences. At about the same time another historian of science, Robert Young (1966) published a lengthy paper evaluating the status of scholarship in the history of the behavioral sciences. Young had few kind words for and many criticisms of the work then being done in the history of psychology.

In particular, he took historians of psychology to task for stressing "the history of problems of current interest" and for then proceeding to write history "backwards from the viewpoint of the modern textbook" (p. 18). Young charged that historians of psychology in the mid-1960s remained largely unaware of the message of the new historiography of science and demonstrated "little grasp of the implications of the demand that we understand the past in its own terms before comparing it with our own vantage point" (p. 19).

Young also reviewed the history of psychology as written by psychologists in the previous four decades, pointing out its shortcomings. For one, the field appeared to him to be severely afflicted by what he termed "perseveration." As Young described it, "the number of subjects within the history of behavioural sciences which would repay intensive study, seems inexhaustible" (p. 26). Yet, he noted, the same stories are being told time and again. In addition to the shortcoming of perseveration, Young identified "three limitations from which the history of psychology suffered: great men (whom to worship?), great insights, and great dates" (p. 36). In spite of his predominantly negative assessment of the status of historical scholarship in psychology in the mid-1960s, Young's review concluded on an optimistic note. The appearance of the *Journal of the History of the Behavioral Sciences,* which had begun publication in 1965, he hailed as "the single most important development in the field, which gives hope for the future" (p. 36).

There were several other developments in 1965 and shortly thereafter that established the history of psychology as a legitimate subfield. See Watson (1975) for a detailed account of these events. In September 1965, the American Psychological Association's Council of Representatives approved the formation of the Division of the History of Psychology,

Division 26; and in November of that year, the Archives of the History of American Psychology were officially established at the University of Akron. In 1967, the first graduate program in the history of psychology was launched at the University of New Hampshire in the Department of Psychology under the direction of Robert I. Watson. The following year, New Hampshire hosted the first National Science Foundation institute on the teaching of history of psychology. The 6-week summer program brought together 30 participants and 7 lecturers and spawned an organization, Cheiron, the International Society for the History of the Behavioral and Social Sciences. Conceived in the summer of 1968 by the members of the institute as a means of perpetuating the group, the Cheiron society began its annual meetings in 1969.

The New History Comes to Psychology

For a decade or so following these events, work in the history of psychology was dominated by the traditional approach to the history of science. That is, history was written by practitioners of the discipline, who by and large viewed the history of science as a cumulative linear progression from error to truth and who tended to write history backwards from the present, concentrating on "great men" and "great ideas." The mid-1970s witnessed a change as the new history made its appearance within the history of psychology, challenging traditional scholarship. The challenge issued from some psychologists who had come to specialize in historical scholarship and some historians of science who had begun to study the social sciences.

The new history, known as "critical history" to some of its advocates, would perhaps be more accurately called new or critical *histories* in that it has assumed a variety of forms within intellectual as well as social history. One focus of the new scholarship in intellectual history has been a reexamination of the work of Wilhelm Wundt, the traditional founding father of experimental psychology. As the 1979 centennial of his Leipzig laboratory approached, historians of psychology began to read Wundt's works in the original, discovering, in the words of one historian (Ash, 1983), "a philosopher and scientist quite different from the one portrayed in standard histories" (p. 169). A leader in the reappraisal of Wundt's thought, cognitive psychologist Arthur L. Blumenthal (1975), observed that Wundt scholars in the 1970s were "in fair agreement that Wundt as portrayed today in many texts and courses is largely fictional and often bears little resemblance to the actual historical figure" (p. 1081). Nor, Blumenthal went on, was this "only the nit-picking of a few antiquarians obsessed with minor matters of interpretation" (p. 1081). On the contrary, he asserted, "these are claims about the very fundamentals of Wundt's work, often asserting the opposite of what has been a standard description prevailing over much of the past century" (p. 1081).

The revisionist Wundt scholars tend to consider the source of this pervasive misrepresentation of Wundt's thought to be his student E.B. Titchener (Blumenthal, 1975, 1980; Danziger, 1979, 1980; Leahey, 1981; Tweney & Yachanin, 1980). An explanation for the subsequent spread of the distorted view can be found in Kurt Danziger's (1979) observation that E.G. Boring's classic *A History of Experimental Psychology* (1950) fails utterly to convey Wundt's vision of psychology. Danziger notes that "it is very difficult to reconcile Boring's interpretation of Wundt's fundamental ideas with the original work, especially the larger and most important part of the original which remains untranslated. This is not really surprising. It is apparent that Boring took his admired teacher, E.B. Titchener as a guide in these matters, and Titchener practically made a career out of interpreting Wundt in his own highly idiosyncratic fashion" (Danziger, 1979, p. 206).

The work of such Wundt scholars represents part of a larger movement by intellectual historians of psychology toward meticulous investigation of original sources. An important institutional locus for this brand of new scholarship is the University of New Hampshire, where Robert I. Watson's successors, David E. Leary and William R. Woodward, carry out their own research and teach history of psychology to both graduate and undergraduate students. Woodward (1980) described the effort there as "a critical approach to knowledge—involving the pursuit of limited goals in keeping with modern historical scholarship, awareness of and compensation for sources of bias in the history of science, and a sensitivity to the social function of this young cross-disciplinary field, the history of psychology" (p. 52). One historian of science (Ash, 1983) characterized the New Hampshire program as "clearly not intended to radically alter psychology, but to help it enrich its knowledge of itself by professionalizing its historiography" (p. 172). Three recently published volumes, *A Century of Psychology as Science* (Leary & Koch, 1985), *The Problematic Science: Psychology in Nineteenth Century Thought* (Woodward & Ash, 1982), and *Psychology in Twentieth Century Thought and Society* (Ash & Woodward, 1987), testify to the steps the program is taking in this direction.

Another domain of scholarship in the new history of psychology, is that of social history. A focus for some of this work is the neglect of contributions made by groups other than White males in the history of psychology. Examples of this approach include Robert V. Guthrie's (1976) book *Even the Rat Was White,* which provides an account of Black psychologists in America; a paper by Maxine D. Bernstein and Nancy Felipe Russo (1974), calling attention to contributions of women psychologists; and an article that I published on the life and career of the first women president of the American Psychological Association, Mary Whiton Calkins (Furumoto, 1979).

Also fitting into the category of social history is a body of work that adopts a critical stance toward the discipline of psychology itself, rather than being primarily concerned with history's oversights; see, for instance, Buss (1979). An early, often-cited example of this genre is a paper by Franz Samelson (1974), a social psychologist, in which he called upon his colleagues to engage in a critical examination of their past. Samelson's paper debunked the notion conveyed by many recent social psychology textbooks that Auguste Comte was the founder of modern social psychology. Identifying Gordon Allport (1968) as the likely source of this idea, Samelson used Allport's presentation of Comte as "a strategically located example," going on "to open up some basic issues concerning the past and present history of social psychology, the treatment of history at the hands of psychologists, and the meanings and functions of such histories" (Samelson, 1974, p. 217).

Samelson argued that Allport was highly selective in his use of Comte's ideas, presenting those that appeared consonant with modern social psychology and disregarding the rest, many of which were incompatible or even antithetical to it. "Such treatment of history," Samelson concluded, "amounts not to a *critical examination* of the past, but to the creation of an origin myth" (pp. 222–223). The function of such origin myths, in Samelson's opinion, is to validate and legitimize present ideas by demonstrating their venerability. That is, if it can be shown that a great thinker held these views a hundred years ago, an impression of continuity and tradition accrues to the discipline. Samelson took pains to point out that it was not his objective "to attack Allport's integrity as a scholar, but to call attention to the naivete with which psychologist historians approached the history of their discipline" (p. 223).

Works in the history of psychology, Samelson charged, typically revealed a lack of any real awareness of recent developments in the field of history of science. This scholarly discipline, Samelson explained, no longer sees "its task as producing chronicles of scientific discoveries, or biographical accounts of its heroes, or the settling of priority claims. A new sensitivity for historical material has developed. It insists on respecting the integrity of the thought of past figures, on the need to understand them in their own terms, within their historical context, instead of mapping out straight lines of scientific progress or pointing to anticipations of the present" (Samelson, 1974, pp. 223–224).

Echoing Kuhn's (1968) and Young's (1966) verdicts, Samelson (1974) maintained that the new historiography of science had not reached the social sciences. He found it rather odd that psychologists, who were so proud of methodology in their own field, showed so little awareness of methodological issues in their approach to historical work. Issuing a warning that "a science without memory is at the mercy of the forces of the day," Samelson voiced the opinion that "the history of social psychology as a critical examination of the past, leading to a better understanding of the present, still remains to be written" (p. 229).

Samelson's (1974) appeal for a more critical history, which had appeared in an obscure journal, was answered in the principal professional journal of the American Psychological Association in the latter half of the 1970s. Several articles and commentaries bearing the stamp of this brand of critical history appeared in the *American Psycholo-*

gist between 1976 and 1980. They began with a series of two papers by another social psychologist, Lorenz J. Finison (1976, 1978) discussing the impact and consequences of unemployment among psychologists during the Depression. Drawing on interviews and archival materials, Finison reconstructed attempts by psychologists to alleviate the unemployment situation. He focused on two organizations that resulted from these attempts, the Society for the Psychological Study of Social Issues and the Psychologists League, carefully placing them in their historical and sociopolitical context.

Two more critical history papers, one by Ben Harris, a social personality psychologist, and another by a historian of science, John O'Donnell, appeared in 1979. Harris' paper was a reexamination of John B. Watson and Rosalie Rayner's (1920) classic study of conditioned emotional responses in the infant Albert B. The attempt to condition little Albert, Harris observed, was widely used in undergraduate textbooks "to illustrate the applicability of classical conditioning to the development and modification of human emotional behavior" (Harris, 1979, p. 151). However, a careful reading of these accounts, Harris noted, reveals extensive distortion and misrepresentation of the original experiment. This, combined with the fact that the Albert study, due to its many methodological flaws, was not very convincing proof of classical conditioning of emotional behavior, raises the question of what function the story serves.

Harris sees the Albert study as another example of what Samelson, in discussing Comte as the alleged father of social psychology, called an origin myth. And speaking more generally, he argued that "modern citations of classic studies can often be seen as attempts by current theorists to build a false sense of continuity into the history of psychology" (p. 157). This myth-making process, Harris emphasized, is not a con-

scious attempt to defraud. Rather, it stems from the attempt to build historical support for new theoretical perspectives. As for the problem with such reevaluations, Harris, in agreement with Samelson, concluded that "they obscure the actual factors that determine the course of scientific research" (p. 157).

The paper by O'Donnell (1979) is an account of historian of psychology E.G. Boring, focusing on the 1920s and examining "the extent to which Boring's professional concerns affected his historical vision" (p. 289). O'Donnell portrayed Boring as "a staunch experimentalist," dedicated to the ideal of pure research, who became increasingly disturbed by "what he perceived to be a pernicious tendency toward applied psychology after World War I" (p. 289). In fact, O'Donnell observed, "power had shifted significantly to the proponents of applied psychology after the war" (p. 289). This, coupled with dwindling institutional support for psychological laboratories, inability to attract and place future experimentalists, and established experimentalists going over to applied work, "fortified Boring's fears for the future of psychological research in America and fueled his resentment of applied psychology" (p. 292).

O'Donnell contends that if Boring had not considered history a forceful persuader, he would not have absented himself from the laboratory to take up historical work during what was potentially the most productive period of his career. And, he asserts, "for Boring, history was not merely a matter of describing the past but of altering the future" (p. 289). O'Donnell suggests that Boring's intent in writing *A History of Experimental Psychology* (1929) was to make experimentalism more visible while downplaying the impact of applied concerns in the development of the discipline. O'Donnell characterizes the resulting history as one that delineates "the intellectual *content* but not the social *function* of psychology in America" (p. 289). Maintaining that, in this respect, subsequent historiography of psychology has followed Boring's lead, O'Donnell calls for a change: "beneficiaries of Boring's immense erudition, we must not remain prisoners of his perspective" (p. 294).

In 1980, additional discussion of the historiography of psychology made its way into the pages of the *American Psychologist*. Several reactions to Harris' little Albert paper (1979) appeared in the comment section (Cornwell, Hobbs, & Prytula, 1980; Church, 1980; Murray, 1980; Seligman, 1980) together with a reply from the author. Harris (1980) began his remarks by addressing various issues raised in the published responses to his paper and concluded by drawing a distinction between what he called "ceremonial" and "critical" history, urging historians of psychology to do less of the former and more of the latter. Harris defined ceremonial history as "accounts without a critical focus, stories (or cautionary tales) that have a symbolic function but do not help us understand the social forces with which we interact daily" (p. 219). By contrast, a "socially informed, critical history of psychology," Harris argued, is a better method, which instead of focusing on the personal characteristics and intentions of historical figures, such as J.B. Watson, for example, asks "*historical* questions about subjects such as Watson's career, the acceptance of behaviorism in American psychology, and its subsequent institutionalization" (p. 219). Fortunately, Harris noted, workers in the history of psychology were beginning to address the issue of "what constitutes a good historical question" (p. 219).

One of these workers, Franz Samelson, whose call as early as 1974 for a more critical history of psychology has already been discussed, was the author of another paper on the topic that appeared in the *American Psychologist* in 1980. Samelson cited Harris' recently published paper on little Albert, juxtaposing Watson and Rayner's study (1920) with the identical-twin study of English psychologist Cyril Burt (1966) "in order to raise some questions about their status and treatment in the social process of (psychological) science" (Samelson, 1980, p. 619). Observing that "serious historical research may have unexpected outcomes" (p. 622), Samelson pointed to L.S. Hearnshaw's study of Burt. Hearnshaw (1981) writes in the preface to his biography that when he agreed to undertake it, it had never occurred to him to suspect Burt's integrity; yet, by the time the book was completed, Hearnshaw was convinced that the charges of fraud made against Burt after his death in 1971 were true.

Thus Samelson (1980) notes, with a touch of irony, that in 1979, as the Wundt and Watson centennials were showing "the ceremonial function of history at its best" (p. 622), historical work in a more critical vein was calling into question the scientific bases of two major opposing psychological paradigms. On one hand, there was the charge that Burt had falsified data on identical twins reared apart, evidence that had been used in arguments for the heritability of intelligence. On the other hand, there was the claim that there were serious methodological flaws in Watson's study of little Albert, "the textbook exemplar for human conditioning" (Samelson, 1980, p. 622).

"What are we to make of such allegations?" (p. 622), Samelson asks. Noting that it would be easy to focus on the actors and their intentions in fashioning an explanation (e.g., Watson was more a propagandist than a scientist), Samelson argues that ultimately this approach amounts to an evasion. The real question, in Samelson's view, is why it took so long for this public criticism to surface when "anybody who read Watson's accounts carefully and critically, could not fail to see some problems," and "anybody reading through Burt's papers in similar manner could not fail but be struck by the implausibility of some of his stories'' (p. 623). Could it be, Samelson asks, that there "is a shared hesitancy to look back at what we are really doing, an attitude of encouraging public criticism to go only so far and not to touch fundamentals?'' (p. 624). Admitting that an answer to this question was clearly beyond the scope of his paper, Samelson noted that the mere fact that it presents itself "indicates at least the need for a more critical understanding of our history and, more generally, for a more reflexive and self-critical attitude toward our activities'' (p. 624).

Whereas the decade of the 1970s witnessed the stirring of the new history of psychology, the 1980s has seen an outpouring of the new scholarship (e.g., Ash & Woodward, 1987; Burnham, 1988; Capshew & Lazlo, 1986; Danziger, 1985; Finison, 1986; Harris, Unger, & Stagner, 1986; Leary, 1987; Leary & Koch, 1985; Morawski, 1986, 1988; Napoli, 1981; O'Donnell, 1985; Pauly, 1986; Samelson, 1985; Scarborough & Furumoto, 1987; Sokal, 1987; Walsh, 1985; Woodward & Ash, 1982). What can be said in general about the characteristics of this new history and how it differs from the old? I see at least five noteworthy aspects: The new history tends to be critical rather than ceremonial, contextual rather than simply the history of ideas, and more inclusive, going beyond the study of "great men." The new history utilizes primary sources and archival documents rather than relying on secondary sources, which can lead to the passing down of anecdotes and myths from one generation of textbook writers to the next. And finally, the new history tries to get inside the thought of a period to see issues as they appeared at the time, instead of looking for antecedents of current ideas or writing history backwards from the present content of the field.

My Encounter With the New History

To illustrate in concrete terms how the traditional and the new history differ, I want to describe to you my own experience in teaching and doing research in the history of psychology, and more specifically my intellectual pilgrimage from the old to the new history of psychology. This personal case study extends back over more than 25 years to the time when I was a graduate student. In the early 1960s, while completing a PhD in experimental psychology at Harvard, I learned about psychology's "great men" and their "great ideas" from both R. J. Herrnstein and emeritus professor E.G. Boring.

My first step away from this traditional approach consisted of looking beyond "great men" to the "great women" in the history of psychology. In the decade of the 1970s, my initial research in history focused on rediscovering Mary Whiton Calkins, a predecessor of mine at Wellesley College, and forgotten fourteenth president of the APA back in 1905. In addition to reintroducing Calkins to late twentieth-century psychologists by giving talks and publishing accounts of her life and career, I called attention to her contributions, most notably the invention of the paired-associate technique for the study of memory, and a system of self-psychology.

A further departure from traditional history has characterized my research efforts in the 1980s. At the beginning of this decade, I broadened my inquiry from Calkins to the first generation of American women psychologists, who entered the field around the turn of the century. I collaborated on this project with Elizabeth Scarborough, another psychologist with training and interest in the history of psychology. The research focus also shifted away from discovering women psychologists and their contributions. This is reflected in the text of a talk that I gave at the Fifth Berkshire Conference on the history of women, held at Vassar College in June, 1981. There I outlined work in progress, in collaboration with Elizabeth Scarborough, describing it as an attempt to reconstruct the lives and experiences of the first generation of women psychologists in the United States, paying attention to a set of problems that they faced as women seeking higher education and employment in a newly emerging discipline. The emphasis in that 1981 talk was no longer on specific individual women and their contributions, but rather on the shared experience of a generation of women.

As this shift of emphasis was occurring in my historical research, I started teaching a seminar in history that concentrated on women psychologists. After offering the seminar for three consecutive years, I described my approach and the outcome in an article published in *Teaching of Psychology* (Furumoto, 1985). I began by expressing my surprise that nowhere in the many articles on the history course published in the pages of *Teaching of Psychology* in the previous decade had anyone voiced concern over the fact that typically women psychologists are made invisible in such courses. As the course is traditionally taught, I maintained, students come away believing that women have played little or no role in the discipline, whereas, in fact, women's participation and contribution to the discipline in the United States goes back almost 100 years. Noting that absence or invisibility of women is not unique to the history of psychology, I observed that it has, until quite recently, been true of historical accounts in general. I went on to discuss the relatively new field of women's history and its implications for teaching the history of psychology.

Women's History

Spurred by the women's movement of the late 1960s, a body of scholarship has grown up in the past twenty years that is called "women's history." American historian Gerda Lerner, a central figure in this field, has articulated a model for understanding the enterprise that has relevance for the history of psychology. She presented her model in a collection of essays (Lerner, 1979), written in the 1970s, in which she explains her views on women's history, why it is important, and how it differs from standard history.

Lerner observed that women, who represent half of human experience, have been largely excluded from history. In fact, she maintained that history, as traditionally written, can properly be thought of as the "history of men." What are her recommendations for beginning to place women in history? Lerner sees a starting point in what she calls "compensatory history," an approach in which the historian searches the past to find lost or overlooked women and uses them to fill up the empty niches in traditional history. Other names that have been applied to this brand of scholarship are the "history of women worthies" and the "add-women-and-stir approach." The next stage of women's history proposed by Lerner is what she terms "contribution history." Here, it is a movement which is of primary concern (e.g., the Progressive movement), and women are important or of interest only in terms of their contributions to that movement—contributions evaluated according to standards set by men.

Compensatory and contribution history do answer the questions "Who were the women in history?" and "What did they contribute?" and Lerner acknowledges them as necessary first steps. Yet, in her view, they do not in themselves provide an adequate women's history. She sees part of their deficiency rooted in the fact that most history has been written by men, and a history of women as written by men has "a special character, a built-in distortion: it comes to us refracted through the lens of men's observations; refracted again through values which consider man the measure" (p. 160). Arguing that women's "culturally determined and psychologically internalized marginality. . . makes their historical experience essentially different from men" (p. xxxi), Lerner describes the past as gendered. Therefore, in order to tap women's experience, the scholar must "ask what would history be like if it were seen through the eyes of women and ordered by values they define?" (p. 178).

What is the relevance of Lerner's analysis for teaching the history of psychology? It suggests that although placing women in the traditional course may very well begin with the discovery of lost women and their contributions to the discipline, it should not end there. An adequate history of women in the discipline needs to reconstruct the experience of those women as they lived their lives and as they worked to establish their professional identities. This approach to including women in the history of psychology course does not dismiss or deny the importance of history of ideas and systems in psychology or the life histories of the men in the discipline. It does maintain that even when all of those have been taken into consideration, something remains missing from the account. That something is the women's story: who they were, what they contributed, and what their experience was.

How does Lerner's model and, more generally, women's history relate to the new history outlined in the first part of this chapter? Women's history is typically viewed as one variety of the new history (Himmelfarb, 1987; Norton, 1986), presenting a challenge to the traditional approach which with its concentration on politics, economics, and diplomacy virtually excludes women from historical consideration. Within women's his-

tory itself, one is confronted with myriad points of view (Berkin & Norton, 1979; Cott & Pleck, 1979; Kerber, 1988; Scott, 1983). Lerner's model encompasses three of these, two of which—compensatory and contribution— have, aside from their focus on women, much in common with the old history of men. The other, which asserts that the past is gendered or, in other words, that the experience of men and women is and has been so different that each requires its own historical account, is a more radical departure from traditional history.

While not denying the importance of gender-specific experience, there are women's historians who, uneasy with the separation and even isolation of women that this approach fosters, have recently been charting other courses for their scholarship. Some are seeking to understand gender as a "socially constructed category of behavior that affects both sexes," while others, seeing pitfalls in an exclusive preoccupation with "women and their own perceptions of themselves and their struggles," are trying to situate women's experience within the broader political or economic context (Norton, 1986, p. 41).

Seminar on Early
Women Psychologists

To give history of psychology instructors a concrete example of how women might be incorporated into the course, my *Teaching of Psychology* article (Furumoto, 1985) also contained a description of a seminar I had taught. The students were women undergraduates, most of whom were psychology majors planning careers in psychology or related fields. As I have already indicated, the focus of the seminar was my own research interest, women in the history of American psychology.

At the beginning of the term, I asked my students to choose a women psychologist from the group of over 50 that appear in the first three editions of *American Men of Science* (Cattell, 1906; Cattell, 1910; and Cattell & Brimhall, 1921). Each then carried out research on her psychologist that formed the basis for writing a biographical essay. In the second half of the term, prior to writing the essay, each student reported to the seminar on the progress she was making in reconstructing the life of her psychologist. In the biographical essay, I asked for a description of the origins, educational experience, and career pattern of the women psychologist studied. The students were also to discuss the school or system with which the woman psychologist was associated and to situate her in a historical context that reached beyond the discipline of psychology.

Students in the seminar read a standard history of psychology textbook, supplemented by selected papers on historiography of psychology and topics in the history of psychology, as well as by lectures, slides, films, class discussions, and short writing assignments. Throughout the term I tried to integrate learning about the history of psychology with reading, lectures, and discussion on women's history and the history of women in psychology. We dealt primarily with the period from 1890 to 1920, when American psychology was emerging and becoming established as a discipline and a profession.

My goal, in taking this approach, was to involve students in the experience of one woman psychologist and in the concrete details of that individual's life. They were asked to document that life as extensively as possible, and then to try to view it in the context of what was happening in American psychology in the late nineteenth and early twentieth centuries. Finally, students were instructed to relate their psychologist's life to what they had learned about the life experiences of American women from similar class and ethnic backgrounds during the same historical period.

In most respects the seminar was rewarding to students and instructor, and over the three years I taught it, student evaluations were quite positive. Many students remarked that the seminar was significant to them in that for the first time they became aware of the substantial number of women in the history of American psychology. Further, they came to appreciate the circumstances of these women's lives and to see how they contributed to the early development of the discipline. Some students commented that they found the seminar to be a new kind of learning experience in which individual projects and collective group work were closely integrated.

While the seminar was successful overall, it was not without problems. Some students became frustrated in their search for archival materials and information on their women psychologists, and at least one questioned whether it was worth the effort. Others had difficulty developing a historical perspective on the material. Some students were dismayed when, in the course of their research, they discovered the many compromises that these early psychologists were compelled to make. For example, they encountered some women who had been derailed from their careers because they chose to marry and others who managed to forage careers, only to be perceived as deviant and sometimes as social isolates. Few of the women psychologists, if any, managed to have it all.

Two students wrote an account of the seminar that appeared in the Undergraduate Update section of the APA *Monitor*. The article, by Natalie Golden and Christina Van Horn (1984), Wellesley College Class of 1983, began: "Ten undergraduate students majoring in various fields encountered excitement, satisfaction and frustration when they entered the world of historical research. . . . We quickly learned that doing primary research meant that we had to become detectives, searching through a historical maze that often yielded its clues only reluctantly" (p. 31).

Golden and Van Horn also described the research process as it unfolded during the semester: "Our principal task was to obtain whatever primary source material was available for a biographical essay. . . .Our searches led us to archivists (some more cooperative than others), family members, small town officials, colleagues and friends of the person we came to think of as 'my psychologist,' and in two cases, to the actual psychologist. Despite the differences among the psychologists, our discussions revealed many similar themes in the private and professional lives of these women." Summarizing the seminar, they characterized it as "a shared quest that gave each of us recognition and the entire group satisfaction and stimulation" (p. 31).

Beyond Compensatory and Contribution History

Teaching the seminar and writing an article on it resulted in an unanticipated fringe benefit. Namely, it helped me clarify my thinking about the nature and direction of my research in history. Returning to Lerner's (1979) model of women's history, it was clear that in my study of Mary Calkins I had begun with compensatory and contribution history. Although this approach is different from traditional history in the sense that it is concerned with a women rather than a man, I concur with Lerner's assessment that it does not represent a serious challenge to traditional history.

In the early 1980s, persuaded by Lerner's arguments regarding the necessity to move beyond compensatory and contribution history, I began to attempt the reconstruction of women's experience. This was to become a central focus of the work com-

pleted by Elizabeth Scarborough and myself in subsequent years—work that resulted, in part, in an article (Furumoto & Scarborough, 1986) in the *American Psychologist* and a book (Scarborough & Furumoto, 1987), both concerned with the first generation of American women psychologists. This recent work reflects increased sensitivity to the major dimensions of the new history that I mentioned previously. Specifically, in contrast with traditional history, it is more contextual, more critical, more inclusive, more archival, and more past-minded. To illustrate concretely these differences between the new and the old history, I will offer you an example from my own work, contrasting my earlier more traditional scholarship with my later work that reflects the influence of the new history.

Perusing my earlier work on Calkins, you will find a traditional biographical account; the following is a sample of that genre:

Mary Calkins was born in 1863, the eldest of five children, and grew up in Buffalo, New York, where her father was a Protestant minister. In 1881, the family moved to Newton, Massachusetts, a city about 12 miles west of Boston, where The Reverend Wolcott Calkins had accepted the pastorate of a Congregational church. After completing high school in Newton, Mary Calkins went to Smith College, where she graduated in 1885.

Shortly after completing her undergraduate study at Smith, Calkins accompanied her family to Europe, where they traveled for more than a year. Upon their return to New England in fall 1887, Calkins was offered a job teaching Greek at Wellesley College, a woman's college located just a few miles from her family home in Newton. She accepted the position and thus began a more than 40-year association with that institution, where she was to spend her entire career.

After having been at Wellesley little over a year, Calkins' talent as a teacher and her interest in philosophy prompted a professor in the philosophy department to recommend to the college president that Calkins be appointed to a newly created position in experimental psychology. The appointment was made contingent upon Calkins' studying the subject for a year, an undertaking that required petitions and special arrangements since neither Clark University, where she was tutored by E.C. Sanford, nor Harvard, where she had attended the seminars of William James and Josiah Royce, was willing to admit women as students at that time. Upon her return to Wellesley in the autumn of 1891, Calkins established a psychological laboratory and introduced the new scientific psychology into the curriculum.

A year later, feeling the need for additional study, Calkins returned to Harvard to work in the psychological laboratory of Hugo Münsterberg. There, pursuing research on factors influencing memory, she invented what has come to be known as the paired-associate technique. Although by the fall of 1849 she had completed all the requirements for the PhD and her Harvard professors enthusiastically recommended that it be awarded to her, the institutional authorities refused because she was a woman.

Calkins, as mentioned earlier, spent her entire career at Wellesley College, teaching, developing a system of self-psychology, publishing prolifically in both psychology and philosophy, and achieving recognition in both fields. She was the first woman to be elected president of the American Psychological Association in 1905, and of the American Philosophical Association in 1918. Honorary degrees were bestowed on Calkins by Columbia University in 1909 and her alma mater, Smith, in 1910, and she was elected to honorary membership in the British Psychological Association in 1928.

This brief account of Calkins' life and career is characteristic of the approach I took in my early work and can be appropriately labeled compensatory and contribution history. In order to move beyond these initial forms of women's history to an inquiry that illuminates Calkins' experience requires adopting a stance that I have called "past-mindedness." It is similar to an approach labeled "historicism" (Stocking, 1965) originally articulated by Butterfield (1931/1959), a historian who argued in favor of "trying to understand the past for the sake of the past" rather than "studying the past for the sake of the present" (p. 16). That is, historical understanding should be sought by attempting to place oneself in the past and seeing things through the eyes of the actors at that time. The vehicle for achieving this perspective is serious and sustained immersion in published and unpublished documents of the time and in the relevant historical scholarship.

In the early 1980s, Elizabeth Scarborough and I took on this task for Calkins and the two dozen or so other women we called "the first generation of American women psychologists." It led us to archives large and small throughout the United States, from

Berkeley to Columbia, from Akron to Chicago. It involved us with work of women's historians, educational historians, and historians of science. And eventually it paid off. We began to feel our way into the concrete reality of the early women psychologists' lives and to detect certain recurrent gender-specific themes that we took as a framework for the section of our book called "The Difference Being a Woman Made" (Scarborough & Furumoto, 1987). These themes were barriers to graduate education, the family claim, the marriage versus career dilemma, uncollegiality of male colleagues, and the myth of meritocracy.

In five separate chapters (one for each theme), we told the story of a woman psychologist whose life experience provided a vivid example of that theme. If we explore Calkins' life in terms of these themes, we have a markedly different account from the one yielded by compensatory and contribution history. Take for example, the family claim and the marriage-versus-career dilemma. Our research unearthed convincing evidence, corroborated by other scholarship in women's history, that in the late nineteenth century, women, unlike men, were required to choose between pursuing an academic career and marriage. In our group about half the women eventually married, and it was clear that a woman who chose to marry in that era sabotaged her career in academic psychology, which at the time was just about all of psychology. We also became aware of a phenomenon that the founder of Hull House, Jane Addams, had termed, "the family claim." The family claim referred to the fact that a middle-class daughter, and especially an unmarried one, had numerous obligations to her family members, and the responsibilities these entailed were expected to take precedence over her vocational interests and aspirations.

Both of these themes, the marriage-versus-career dilemma and the family claim,
were salient features of Calkins' experience. Never married, she lived in her parents' home for her entire life, and as their sole surviving daughter, she, rather than her three brothers, took on increasing responsibility for her aging parents' welfare. In her notes for an address to a group of women students at Bryn Mawr College (1911), Calkins mused over the hardships of the life of the woman scholar, particularly those of not being able to marry and have a family of her own and of having to bear heavy responsibility for her parents' care.

Speaking of adjustments necessitated by "the often conflicting claims of scholarship and life in its social relations," Calkins observed that while this adjustment is "seldom easy for anyone," it "is particularly difficult in the lives of most women." In support of this claim, she pointed to the acceptance of the view, "that a woman has more exacting social and especially family obligations than a man." Maintaining that these norms affected not only "the woman who is a mother" but the unmarried woman as well, Calkins noted "the chances are, for example, that the unmarried daughter rather than the unmarried son, if a choice becomes necessary, should undertake the responsibility of their parents' home."

I have tried to illustrate by this discussion of gender-specific themes in relation to Calkins that in reconstructing the experience of actors in the past, we reveal dimensions of their lives undisclosed by a more traditional approach to history. Furthermore, being aware of these dimensions can sometimes help us understand why their careers as psychologists assumed the particular shapes they did. For example, realizing the potency of the family claim makes intelligible Calkins' decision to decline a joint Columbia-Barnard professorship offered by James McKeen Cattell in 1905.

As she wrote to her mentor Hugo Münsterberg, in part she had reservations about the kind of work the position might entail, but she also disclosed to him that she was held back by her sense of responsibility to her parents. Describing the position to Münsterberg, Calkins wrote, "I think that Barnard needs and desires someone to start a small undergraduate psychological laboratory, and that I have no wish to do. Nor did I see any good chance for me to do the work, on that faculty, which I am best fitted to do; for the field is already well occupied. This is my professional consolation for the decision with which, personally, I am well content. I think I shall teach subjects which better suit my capacity, and accordingly that I shall write more and better, at Wellesley than Barnard-Columbia."

The personal consideration that Calkins told Münsterberg was the deciding factor had to do with her parents. "I was unwilling to leave my home, both because I find in it my deepest happiness and because I feel that I add to the happiness of my mother's and father's lives. They would have considered transferring the house to New York, but I became convinced that it would be distinctly hurtful to them to do so" (Calkins, 1905, June 18).

In a more candid letter written to her younger brother Raymond, Mary Calkins revealed that concern for the welfare of her ailing 74-year-old father precluded her from even seriously considering the job in New York City. As Calkins explained to her brother, "I have decided as you thought I would not to go to New York. The deciding factor was my certainty that father ought to stay here. To be sure on this point, I consulted Dr. Blake who said that father ought not to have the nervous strain accompanying a complete readjustment of his life. This settled the matter beyond hesitation. I am not sure how I should have decided without this" (Calkins, 1905, June 8).

Sometimes a richly detailed reconstruction of past experience may even provide insight into the source of a psychologist's theoretical orientation not available through other means. This is precisely what happened to me recently as, in the process of writing an address on Calkins, I pondered a question that has puzzled me for many years: Why was Calkins so firmly committed to self-psychology in an era of militant behaviorism? What now seems to me to be a very plausible answer lies in the particular institutional context of Wellesley College in the late 19th and early 20th centuries, when Calkins was formulating her system of self-psychology.

Educational historian Patricia A. Palmieri (1983), who has recently completed a study of the early faculty at Wellesley, found an atmosphere there dramatically different from that existing in male-dominated institutions of the day. Wellesley, with its all-female all-single professoriate, formed a close-knit women's community in which deeply felt and long-lasting relationships flourished. Palmieri characterized the group of 53 academic women who formed the basis of her study as "strikingly homogeneous in terms of social and geographic origins, upbringing, and sociocultural world-view" (p. 197).

Explaining what life was like in this community of academic women who had so much in common, Palmieri described it as "very much like an extended family. Its members, with shared backgrounds and tastes, shared visions of life and work, and often shared bonds of family or prior friendship, could hardly but produce an extraordinary community. In this milieu, no one was isolated, no one forgotten" (p. 203). Palmieri observes that in contrast to our contemporary society where "occupational and private selves rarely meet, the academic women of Wellesley conjoined public and private spheres" and became "not merely professional associates but astoundingly good friends" (p. 203).

Wellesley's institutional context stands in marked contrast to the university settings where most male psychologists were developing their theories and carrying out their research. Of Johns Hopkins in that same period, historian Hugh Hawkins (1960) noted the unbreachable gulf that existed between isolated specialized researchers, and how extremely difficult the men found it to get to know fellow faculty. One senior professor at Johns Hopkins pictured the situation thus: "we only get glimpses of what is going forward in the minds and hearts of our colleagues. We are like trains moving on parallel tracks. We catch sight of some face, some form that appeals to us and it is gone" (p. 237).

Returning to the question of why Mary Calkins became so intensely committed to conceiving the subject matter of psychology as the self, and more specifically interacting social selves, in the heyday of behaviorism, once one appreciates the Wellesley context of her era, the answer seems almost embarrassingly obvious. From the time she entered the Wellesley community in 1887 until her death in 1930, her personal and professional lives were closely intertwined with those of her Wellesley friends and colleagues. Although trained in the mainstream academic, laboratory psychology of the 1890s by her male professors at Harvard and Clark, she soon thereafter came to question the atomistic, impersonal conception of the subject matter characteristic of this approach, and still later, she rejected it outright.

As Edna Heidbreder put it in a paper on the topic of Calkins' self psychology, Calkins came to see "the classical experimental psychologists as out of touch. . .with important portions of. . .[the] subject matter [of psychology] as it presents itself in ordinary experience as she herself observed it and as she believed, by checking with others, that they too observed it" (Heidbreder, 1972, p. 63). It is worth noting here that the classi-

cal experimental psychologists referred to were for the most part male psychologists, in university environments, whose experience as isolated specialists was vastly different from that of Calkins. It is not surprising then that the alternative to the classical experimental view espoused by Calkins concerned itself with something of the utmost significance to her and to the other women with whom she shared her Wellesley world, namely the reality and importance of selves in everyday experience.

Conclusion

I have tried to convey to you in this chapter how the new history of psychology differs from the old and to describe some ways in which the new history can enhance our understanding of the past. In conclusion, I want to consider briefly the implications of the new history for teaching the history of psychology.

First and foremost, the new history alerts us to the need to move beyond traditional textbook history of psychology. Much has been written about the problematic nature of textbook history in science, in general, as well as in psychology, in particular. In his classic work, *The Structure of Scientific Revolutions*, Thomas Kuhn (1970) observed that textbooks in science and the historical tradition they supply are rewritten after every scientific revolution. In these texts, Kuhn says, "partly by selection and partly by distortion, the scientists of earlier ages are implicitly represented as having worked on the same set of fixed problems, and in accordance with the same set of fixed canons that the most recent revolution in scientific theory and method has made seem scientific" (p. 138). What is accomplished by the portrayal of a discipline's past as developing linearly and cumulatively toward its present vantage, according to Kuhn, is that "both students and professionals come to feel like participants in a long-standing historical tradition" (p. 138). However, Kuhn warns, this rewriting of history backward from the present also serves to truncate scientists' sense of their discipline's history.

Kuhn's view (1968) in regard to textbook history of science in general had been voiced in the 1980s with respect to textbook history of psychology in particular. Historian of science Mitchell G. Ash (1983) has advanced the claim that a particularly important function of the history of psychology as practiced in the United States has been what he calls "pedagogical self-presentation." That is, textbook history aimed at beginning and advanced students that portrays psychology as a science and as descended from an ancient tradition of knowledge has served the discipline as a legitimation strategy. Ash distinguishes between such textbook history and historical scholarship in psychology, noting that the recent scholarship is currently yielding results that may not be compatible with textbook versions of psychology's past. The recent scholarship that Ash refers to is what I have described as the new history of psychology, and I concur with his assertion that this work poses a challenge to much of what appears in textbook accounts. Given this state of affairs, what is the teacher of the history course to do?

My recommendation is that we move beyond textbook history into the new history of psychology posthaste. This will mean teaching a history that is more contextual, more critical, more archival, more inclusive, and more past-minded. Above all, it will require a change in emphasis from the way in which we psychologists have traditionally approached the history of our discipline. This change involves a shift from focusing on great men and their ideas to reconstructing particular sociohistorical contexts.

Charles Rosenberg (1987) described these differing emphases succinctly in a re-

cent editorial in the history of science journal *Isis* that commented on the history, current status, and future of that field as the journal approached its 75th anniversary. In the early years of the journal, Rosenberg noted, work in the history of science was carried on by scientists and scholars who were practitioners of other disciplines. In contrast, most of the work currently published in *Isis* is by professional historians of science.

Those past generations of historians who were practitioners of other disciplines often neglected what, in Rosenberg's view, is a fundamental aspect of the current historian's task. He urges contemporary historians of science not to be guilty of the same oversight. I believe that his words of advice to historians are also an appropriate exhortation to teachers of the history of psychology, and I offer them to you in conclusion: "We must strive to understand the richness and relatedness of past experience. The scientist has been an actor in specific historical settings, not simply a solver of cognitive dilemmas" (p. 517).

References

Allport, G. (1968). The historical background of modern social psychology. In G. Lindzey & E. Aronson (Eds.), *The handbook of social psychology, Vol. 1* (2nd ed.), (pp. 1–80). Reading, MA: Addison Wesley.

Ash, M. G. (1983). The self-presentation of discipline: History of psychology in the United States between pedagogy and scholarship. In L. Graham, W. Lepenies, & P. Weingart (Eds.), *Functions and uses of disciplinary histories, Vol. 7* (pp. 143–189). Dordrecht, Holland: D. Reidel.

Ash, M. G., & Woodward, W. R. (Eds.). (1987). *Psychology in twentieth-century thought and society.* New York: Cambridge University Press.

Benjamin, L. T., Jr. (Ed.). (1988). *A history of psychology: Original sources and contemporary research.* New York: McGraw-Hill.

Berkin, C. R., & Norton, M. B. (Eds.). (1979). *Women of America: A history.* Boston: Houghton Mifflin.

Bernstein, M. D., & Russo, N. F. (1974). The history of psychology revisited, or up with our foremothers. *America Psychologist, 29,* 130–134.

Blumenthal, A. L. (1975), A reappraisal of Wilhelm Wundt. *American Psychologist, 30,* 1081–1086.

Blumenthal, A. L. (1980). Wilhelm Wundt and early American psychology: A clash of cultures. In R. W. Rieber (Ed.), *Wilhelm Wundt and the making of a scientific psychology* (pp. 117–135). New York: Plenum.

Boring, E. G. (1929). *A history of experimental psychology.* New York: The Century Co.

Boring, E. G. (1950). *A history of experimental psychology* (2nd ed.). New York: Appleton-Century-Crofts.

Brush, S. G. (1974). Should the history of science be rated X? *Science, 183,* 1164–1172.

Burnham, J. C. (1988). *Paths into American culture: Psychology, medicine, and morals.* Philadelphia: Temple University Press.

Burt, C. (1966). The genetic determination of differences in intelligence. *British Journal of Psychology, 57,* 137–153.

Buss, A. R. (Ed.). (1979). *Psychology in social context.* New York: Irvington.

Butterfield, H. (1959). *The Whig interpretation of history.* London: G. Bell and Sons. (Original work published 1931).

Calkins, M. W. (1905, June 8). Letter to R. Calkins. (From papers held by the Calkins family).

Calkins, M. W. (1905, June 18). Letter to H. Münsterberg. (From the Hugo Münsterberg Papers, Boston Public Library, Boston, MA).

Calkins, M. W. (1911). Notes for "The place of scholarship in life." (From the Wellesley College Archives, Wellesley, MA).

Capshew, J. H., & Lazlo, A. C. (1986). "We would not take no for an answer": Women psychologists and gender politics during World War II. *Journal of Social Issues, 42,* 157–180.

Cattell, J. McK. (Ed.). (1906). *American men of science.* New York: The Science Press.

Cattell, J. McK. (Ed.). (1910). *American men of science* (2nd ed.). New York: The Science Press.

Cattell, J. McK., & Brimhall, D. R. (Eds.). (1921). *American men of science* (3rd ed.). Garrison, NY: The Science Press.

Church, R. M. (1980). The Albert study: Illustration vs. evidence. *American Psychologist, 35,* 215–216.

Cornwell, D., Hobbs, S., & Prytula, R. (1980). Little Albert rides again. *American Psychologist, 35,* 216–217.

Cott, N. F., & Pleck, E. H. (Eds.). (1979). *A heritage of her own: Toward a new social history of American women.* New York: Simon and Schuster.

Danziger, K. (1979). The positivist repudiation of Wundt. *Journal of the History of the Behavioral Sciences, 15,* 205–230.

Danziger, K. (1980). Wundt and the two traditions of psychology. In R. W. Rieber (Ed.), *Wilhelm Wundt and the making of a scientific psychology* (pp. 73–87). New York: Plenum.

Danziger, K. (1985). The origins of the psychological experiment as a social institution. *American Psychologist, 40,* 133–140.

Finison, L. J. (1976). Unemployment, politics, and the history of organized psychology. *American Psychologist, 31,* 747–755.

Finison, L. J. (1978). Unemployment, politics, and the history of organized psychology, II: The Psychologists League, the WPA, and the National Health Program. *American Psychologist, 33,* 471–477.

Finison, L. J. (1986). The psychological insurgency, 1936–1945. *Journal of Social Issues, 42,* 21–35.

Furumoto, L. (1979). Mary Whiton Calkins (1863–1930): Fourteenth president of the American Psychological Association. *Journal of the History of the Behavioral Sciences, 15,* 346–356.

Furumoto, L. (1981, June). *First generation of U.S. women in psychology.* Paper presented at the Fifth Berkshire Conference on the History of Women, Vassar College, Poughkeepsie, NY.

Furumoto, L. (1985). Placing women in the history of psychology. *Teaching of Psychology, 12,* 203–206.

Furumoto, L., & Scarborough, E. (1986). Placing women in the history of psychology: The first American women psychologists. *American Psychologist, 41*, 35–42.

Golden, N., & Van Horn, C. (1984, February). Seminar focuses on early women leaders. *APA Monitor*, p. 31.

Guthrie, R. V. (1976). *Even the rat was white: A historical view of psychology*. New York: Harper & Row.

Harris, B. (1979). Whatever happened to little Albert? *American Psychologist, 34*, 151–160.

Harris, B. (1980). Ceremonial versus critical history of psychology. *American Psychologist, 35*, 218–219.

Harris, B., Unger, R. K., & Stagner, R. (Eds.), (1986). 50 years of psychology and social issues. *Journal of Social Issues, 42(1)*.

Hawkins, H. (1960). *Pioneer: A history of the Johns Hopkins University, 1874–1889*. Ithaca, NY: Cornell University Press.

Hearnshaw, L. S. (1981). *Cyril Burt: Psychologist*. New York: Vintage Books. (Originally published by Cornell University Press, 1979).

Heidbreder, E. (1972). Mary Whiton Calkins: A discussion. *Journal of the History of the Behavior Sciences, 8*, 56–68.

Hilgard, E. R. (1987). *Psychology in America: A historical survey*. San Diego: Harcourt Brace Jovanovich.

Himmelfarb, G. (1987). *The new history and the old*. Cambridge, MA: Harvard University Press.

Kerber, L. K. (1988). Separate spheres, female worlds, woman's place: The rhetoric of women's history. *The Journal of American History, 75*, 9–39.

Kuhn, T. S. (1968). The history of science. In D. L. Sills (Ed.), *International Encyclopedia of the Social Sciences, Vol. 14* (pp. 74–83).

Kuhn, T. S. (1970). *The structure of scientific revolutions* (2nd ed.). Chicago: University of Chicago Press.

Leahey, T. H. (1981). The mistaken mirror: On Wundt's and Titchener's psychologies. *Journal of the History of the Behavioral Sciences, 17*, 273–282.

Leahey, T. H. (1987). *A history of psychology: Main currents in psychological thought* (2nd ed.). Englewood Cliffs, NJ: Prentice-Hall.

Leary, D. E. (1987). Telling likely stories: The rhetoric of the new psychology, 1880–1920. *Journal of the History of the Behavioral Sciences, 23*, 315–331.

Leary, D. E., & Koch, S. (Eds.). (1985). *A century of psychology as science*. New York: McGraw-Hill.

Lerner, G. (1979). *The majority finds its past: Placing women in history*. New York: Oxford University Press.

Morawski, J. G. (1986). Organizing knowledge and behavior at Yale's Institute of Human Relations. *Isis, 77*, 219–242.

Morawski, J. G. (Ed.). (1988). *The rise of experimentation in American psychology*. New Haven: Yale University Press.

Murray, F. S. (1980). Search for Albert. *American Psychologist, 35*, 217.

Napoli, D. S. (1981). *Architects of adjustment: The history of the psychological profession in the United States*. Port Washington, NY: Kennikat Press.

Norton, M. B. (1986, April 13). Is Clio a feminist? The new history. *New York Times*, pp. 1, 40–41.

O'Donnell, J. M. (1979). The crisis of experimentalism in the 1920s: E. G. Boring and his uses of history. *American Psychologist, 34*, 289–295.

O'Donnell, J. M. (1985). *The origins of behaviorism: American Psychology, 1870–1920*. New York: New York University Press.

Palmieri, P. A. (1983). Here was fellowship: A social portrait of academic women at Wellesley College, 1895–1920. *History of Education Quarterly, 23*, 195–214.

Pauly, P. J. (1986). G. Stanley Hall and his successors: A history of the first half century of psychology at Johns Hopkins. In S. H. Hulse & B. F. Green, Jr. (Eds.), *One hundred years of psychological research in America: G. Stanley Hall and the Johns Hopkins tradition* (pp. 21–51). Baltimore: Johns Hopkins University Press.

Robinson, J. H. (1912). *The new history*. New York: Macmillan.

Rosenberg, C. (1987). *Isis* at seventy-five [Editorial]. *Isis, 78*, 515–517.

Samelson, F. (1974). History, origin myth and ideology: "Discovery" of social psychology.

Journal for the Theory of Social Behaviour, 4, 217–231.

Samelson, F. (1980). J. B. Watson's little Albert, Cyril Burt's twins, and the need for a critical science. *American Psychologist, 35*, 619–625.

Samelson, F. (1985). Organizing for the kingdom of behavior: Academic battles and organizational policies in the twenties. *Journal of the History of the Behavioral Sciences, 21*, 33–47.

Scarborough, E., & Furumoto, L. (1987). *Untold lives: The first generation of American women psychologists*. New York: Columbia University Press.

Scott, J. W. (1983). Women in history: The modern period. *Past and Present, 101*, 141–157.

Seligman, M. E. P. (1980). Harris on selective misrepresentation: A selective misrepresentation of Seligman. *American Psychologist, 35*, 214–215.

Sokal, M. M. (Ed.). (1987). *Psychological testing and American society, 1890–1930*. New Brunswick, NJ: Rutgers University Press.

Stocking, G. W., Jr. (1965). On the limits of "presentism" and "historicism" in the historiography of the behavioral sciences [Editorial]. *Journal of the History of the Behavioral Sciences, 1*, 211–218.

Tweney, R. D., & Yachanin, S. A. (1980). Titchener's Wundt. In W. G. Bringmann & R. D. Tweney (Eds.), *Wundt studies: A centennial collection* (pp. 380–395). Toronto: C. J. Hogrefe.

Walsh, M. R. (1985). Academic professional women organizing for change: The struggle in psychology. *Journal of Social Issues, 41*, 17–27.

Watson, J. B., & Rayner, R. (1920). Conditioned emotional reactions. *Journal of Experimental Psychology, 3*, 1–14.

Watson, R. I. (1975). The history of psychology as a specialty: A personal view of its first 15 years. *Journal of the History of the Behavioral Sciences, 11*, 5–14.

Woodward, W. R. (1980). Toward a critical historiography of psychology. In J. Brozek & L. J. Pongratz (Eds.). *Historiography of modern psychology* (pp. 29–67). Toronto: Hogrefe.

Woodward, W. R., & Ash, M. G. (Eds.). (1982). *The problematic science: Psychology in nineteenth-century thought*. New York: Praeger.

Young, R. M. (1966). Scholarship and the history of the behavioural sciences. *History of Science, 5*, 1–51.

Gerda Lerner

Placing Women in History: Definitions and Challenges[1]

I n the brief span of five years in which American historians have begun to develop women's history as an independent field, they have sought to find a conceptual framework and a methodology appropriate to the task.

The first level at which historians, trained in traditional history, approach women's history is by writing the history of "women worthies" or "compensatory history." Who are the women missing from history? Who are the women of achievement and what did they achieve? The resulting history of "notable women" does not tell us much about those activities in which most women engaged, nor does it tell us about the significance of women's activities to society as a whole. The history of notable women is the history of exceptional, even deviant women, and does not describe the experience and history of the mass of women. This insight is a refinement of an awareness of class differences in history: Women of different classes have different historical experiences. To comprehend the full complexity of society at a given stage of its development, it is essential to take account of such differences.

Women also have a different experience with respect to consciousness, depending on whether their work, their expression, their activity is male-defined or woman-oriented. Women, like men, are indoctrinated in a male-defined value system and conduct their lives accordingly. Thus, colonial and early 19th-century female reformers directed their activities into channels which were merely an extension of their domestic concerns and traditional roles. They taught school, cared for the poor, the sick, the aged. As their consciousness developed, they turned their attention toward the needs of women. Becoming woman-oriented, they began to "uplift" prostitutes, organize women for abolition or temperance, and sought to upgrade female education, but only in order to equip women better for their traditional roles. Only at a later stage, growing out of the recognition of the separate interests of women as a group, and of their subordinate place in society, did their

From: *The Majority Finds its Past: Placing Women in History* (New York: Oxford University Press, 1979). Copyright Gerda Lerner, 1979. Reprinted by permission of Gerda Lerner and International Creative Management, Inc.

1. This essay, in an earlier version, was presented at the panel, "Effects of Women's History Upon Traditional Concepts of Historiography" at the Second Berkshire Conference on the History of Women, Cambridge, Mass., October 25–27, 1974. It was, in revised form, presented as a paper at the Sarah Lawrence College Workshop-Symposium, March 15, 1975. I have greatly benefitted from discussion with my co-panelists Renate Bridenthal and Joan Kelly-Gadol, and from the comments and critique of audience participants at both conferences. It was revised and published in *Feminist Studies,* Vol. III, Nos. 1–2 (Fall 1975), 5–14.

consciousness become woman-defined. Feminist thought starts at this level and encompasses the active assertion of the rights and grievances of women. These various stages of female consciousness need to be considered in historical analysis.

The next level of conceptualizing women's history has been "contribution history": describing women's contribution to, their status in, and their oppression by male-defined society. Under this category we find a variety of questions being asked: What have women contributed to abolition, to reform, to the Progressive movement, to the labor movement, to the New Deal? The movement in question stands in the foreground of inquiry; women made a "contribution" to it; the contribution is judged first of all with respect to its effect on that movement and secondly by standards appropriate to men.

The ways in which women were aided and affected by the work of these "great women," the ways in which they themselves grew into feminist awareness, are ignored. Jane Addams' enormous contribution in creating a female support network and new structures for living are subordinated to her role as a Progressive, or to an interpretation which regards her as merely representative of a group of frustrated college-trained women with no place to go. In other words, a deviant from male-defined norms. Margaret Sanger is seen merely as the founder of the birth-control movement, not as a woman raising a revolutionary challenge to the centuries-old practice by which the bodies and lives of women are dominated and ruled by man-made laws. In the labor movement, women are described as "also there" or as problems. Their essential role on behalf of themselves and of other women is seldom considered a central theme in writing their history. Women are the outgroup, Simone de Beauvoir's "Other."

Another set of questions concerns oppression and its opposite, the struggle for woman's rights. Who oppressed women and how were they oppressed? How did they respond to such oppression?

Such questions have yielded detailed and very valuable accounts of economic or social oppression, and of the various organizational, political ways in which women as a group have fought such oppression. Judging from the results, it is clear that to ask the question—why and how were women victimized—has its usefulness. We learn what society or individuals or classes of people have done to women, and we learn how women themselves have reacted to conditions imposed upon them. While inferior status and oppressive restraints were no doubt aspects of women's historical experience, and should be so recorded, the limitation of this approach is that it makes it appear either that women were largely passive or that, at the most, they reacted to male pressures or to the restraints of patriarchal society. Such inquiry fails to elicit the positive and essential way in which women have functioned in history. Mary Beard was the first to point out that the ongoing and continuing contribution of women to the development of human culture cannot be found by treating them only as victims of oppression. It is far more useful to deal with this question as one aspect of women's history, but never to regard it as the *central* aspect of women's history. Essentially, treating women as victims of oppression once again places them in a male-defined conceptual framework: oppressed, victimized by standards and values established by men. The true history of women is the history of their ongoing functioning in that male-defined world *on their own terms*. The question of oppression does not elicit that story, and is therefore a tool of limited usefulness to the historian.

A major focus of women's history has been on women's-rights struggles, especially the winning of suffrage, on organizational and institutional history of the women's movements, and on its leaders. This, again, is an important aspect of women's history, but it cannot and should not be its central concern.

Some recent literature has dealt with marriage and divorce, with educational opportunities, and with the economic struggles of working women. Much of recent work has been concerned with the image of women and "women's sphere," with the educational ideals of society, the values to which women are indoctrinated, and with gender role acculturation as seen in historical perspective. A separate field of study has examined the ideals, values, and prescriptions concerning sexuality, especially female sexuality. Ron Walters and Ben Barker-Benfield have tended to confirm traditional stereotypes concerning Victorian sexuality, the double standard, and the subordinate position of women. Much of this material is based on the study of such readily available sources as sermons, educational tracts, women's magazines, and medical textbooks. The pitfall in such interpretation, as Carl Degler has pointed out is the tendency to confuse prescriptive literature with actual behavior. In fact, what we are learning from most of these monographs is not what women did, felt, or experienced, but what men in the past thought women should do, Charles Rosenberg, Carroll Smith-Rosenberg, and Carl Degler have shown how to approach the same material and interpret it from the new perspective of women's history. They have sharply distinguished between prescription and behavior, between myth and reality.

Other attempts to deduce women's status from popular literature and ideology demonstrate similar difficulties. Barbara Welter, in an early and highly influential article, found the emergence of "the cult of true womanhood" in sermons and periodicals of the Jacksonian era. Many historians, feminists among them, have deduced from this that Victorian ideals of woman's place pervaded the society and were representative of its realities. More detailed analysis reveals that this mass-media concern with woman's domesticity was, in fact, a response to the opposite trend in society. Lower-class women were entering the factories, middle-class women were discontented with their accustomed roles, and the family, as an institution, was experiencing turmoil and crisis. Idealization is very frequently a defensive ideology and an expression of tension within society. To use ideology as a measure of the shifting status of women, it must be set against a careful analysis of social structure, economic conditions, institutional changes, and popular values. With this caution society's attitudes toward women and toward gender-role indoctrination can be usefully analyzed as manifestations of a shifting value system and of tensions within patriarchal society.

"Contribution" history is an important stage in the creation of a true history of women. The monographic work which such inquiries produce is essential to the development of more complex and sophisticated questions, but it is well to keep the limitations of such inquiry in mind. When all is said and done, what we have mostly done in writing contribution history is to describe what men in the past told women to do and what men in the past thought women should be. This is just another way of saying that historians of women's history have so far used a traditional conceptual framework. Essentially, they have applied questions from traditional history to women, and tried to fit women's past into the empty spaces of historical scholarship. The limitation of such work is that it deals with women in male-defined society and tries to fit them into the categories and value systems which consider *man* the measure of significance. Perhaps it would be useful to refer to this level of work as "transitional women's history," seeing it as an inevitable step in the development of new criteria and concepts.

Another methodological question which arises frequently concerns the connection between women's history and other recently emerging fields. Why is women's history not simply an aspect of "good" social history? Are women not part of the anonymous in history? Are they not oppressed in the same way as racial or class or ethnic groups have been oppressed? Are they not marginal and akin in most respects to minorities? The answers to these questions are not simple. It is obvious that there has already been rich cross-fertilization between the new social history and women's history, but it has not been nor should it be a case of subsuming women's history under the larger and already respectable field of social history.

Yes, women are part of the anonymous in history, but, unlike them, they are also and always have been part of the ruling elite. They are oppressed, but not quite like either racial or ethnic groups, though some of them are. They are subordinate and exploited, but not quite like lower classes, though some of them are. We have not yet really solved the problems of definition, but it can be suggested that the key to understanding women's history is in accepting—painful though that may be—that it is the history of the *majority* of humankind[†]. Women are essentially different from all the above categories, because they are the majority now and always have been at least half of humankind, and because their subjection to patriarchal institutions antedates all other oppression and has outlasted all economic and social changes in recorded history.

†I was quite unaware, in 1974–75, at the time of writing and at the first publication of this article that I used the word "mankind," subsuming women under the term "man." A student brought this to my attention, and I have ever since used the term "humankind." The shift in consciousness this semantic shift caused is astonishing.

Social history methodology is very useful for women's history, but it must be placed within a different conceptual framework. Historians working in family history ask a great many questions pertaining to women, but family history is not in itself women's history. It is no longer sufficient to view women mainly as members of families. Family history has neglected by and large to deal with unmarried and widowed women. In its applications to specific monographic studies, such as the work of Philip Greven, family history has been used to describe the relationships of fathers and sons and the property arrangements between them. The relationships of fathers to daughters and mothers to their children have been ignored. The complex family-support patterns, for example, whereby the work and wages of daughters are used to support the education of brothers and to maintain aged parents, while that of sons is not so used, have been ignored.

Another way in which family history has been interpreted within the context of patriarchal assumptions is by using a vaguely defined "domestic power" of women, power within the family, as a measure of the societal status of women. In a methodologically highly sophisticated article, Daniel Scott Smith discovered in the 19th century the rise of something called "domestic feminism," expressed in a lowered birth rate from which he deduced an increasing control of women over their reproductive lives. One might, from similar figures, as easily deduce a desire on the part of men to curb their offspring due to the demands of a developing industrial system for a more highly educated labor force, hence for fewer children per family. Demographic data can indeed tell us something about female as well as male status in society, but only in the context of an economic and sociological analysis. Further, the status of women within the family is something quite different and distinct from their status in the society in general.

In studying the history of black women and the black family one can see that relatively high status for women within the family does not signify "matriarchy" or "power for women," since black women are not only members of families, but persons functioning in a larger society. The status of persons is determined not in one area of their functioning, such as within the family, but in several. The decisive historical fact about women is that the *areas* of their functioning, not only their status *within* those areas, have been determined by men. The effect on the consciousness of women has been pervasive. It is one of the decisive aspects of their history, and any analysis which does not take this complexity into consideration must be inadequate.

Then there is the impact of demographic techniques, the study of large aggregates of anonymous people by computer technology based on census data, public documents, property records. Demographic techniques have led to insights which are very useful for women's history. They have yielded revealing data on fertility fluctuations, on changes in illegitimacy patterns and sex ratios, and aggregate studies of life cycles. The latter work has been done very successfully by Joseph Kett, Robert Wells, Peter Lalett, and Kenneth Keniston. The field has in the United States been largely dominated by male historians, mostly through self-imposed sex-role stereotyping by women historians who have shared a prejudice against the computer and statistics. However, a group of younger scholars, trained in demographic techniques, has begun to research and publish material concerning working-class women. Alice Harris, Virginia McLaughlin, Judith and Daniel Walkowitz, Susan Kleinberg, and Tamara Hareven are among those who have elicited woman-oriented interpretations from aggregate data. They have demonstrated that social history can be enriched by combining cliometrics with sophisticated humanistic and feminist interpretations. They have added "gender" as a factor for analysis to such familiar concepts as class, race, and ethnicity.

The compensatory questions raised by women's history specialists are proving interesting and valuable in a variety of fields. It is perfectly understandable that, after centuries of neglect of the role of women in history, compensatory questions and those concerning woman's contribution will and must be asked. In the process of answering such questions it is important to keep in mind the inevitable limitation of the answers they yield. Not the least of these limitations is that this approach tends to separate the work and activities of women from those of men, even where they were essentially connected. As yet, synthesis is lacking. For example, the rich history of the abolition movement has been told as though women played a marginal, auxiliary, and at times mainly disruptive role in it. Yet female anti-slavery societies outnumbered male societies; women abolitionists largely financed the movement with their fund-rasing activities, did much of the work of propaganda-writing in and distribution of newspapers and magazines. The enormous political significance of women-organized petition campaigns remains unrecorded. Most importantly, no historical work has as yet taken the organizational work of female abolitionists seriously as an integral part of the antislavery movement.

Slowly, as the field has matured, historians of women's history have become dissatisfied with old questions and old methods, and have come up with new ways of approaching historical material. They have, for example, begun to ask about the actual *experience* of women in the past. This is obviously different from a description of the condition of women written from the perspective of male sources, and leads one to the use of women's letters, diaries, autobiographies, and oral history sources. This shift from male-oriented to female-oriented consciousness is most important and leads to challenging new interpretations. Historians of women's history have studied female sexuality and its regulation from the female point of view, making imaginative use of such sources as medical textbooks, diaries, and case histories of hospital patients. Questions concerning women's experience have led to studies of birth control, as it affects women and as an issue expressing cultural and symbolic values; of the physical conditions to which women are prone, such as menarche and pregnancy and women's ailments; of customs, attitudes, and fashions affecting women's health and women's life experience. Historians are now exploring the impact of female bonding, of female friendship and homosexual relations, and the experience of women in groups, such as women in utopian communities, in women's clubs and settlement houses. There has been an interest in the possibility that women's century-long preoccupation with birth and with the care of the sick and dying have led to some specific female rituals.

Women's history has already presented a challenge to some basic assumptions historians make. While most historians are aware of the fact that their findings are not value-free and are trained to check their biases by a variety of methods, they are as yet quite unaware of their own sexist bias and, more importantly, of the sexist bias which pervades the value system, the culture, and the very language within which they work.

Women's history presents a challenge to the periodization of traditional history. The periods in which basic changes occur in society and which historians have commonly regarded as turning points for all historical development, are not necessarily the same for men as for women. This is not surprising when we consider that the traditional time frame in history has been derived from political history. Women have been the one group in history longest excluded from political power and they have, by and large, been excluded from military decision-making. Thus the irrelevance of periodization based on military and political developments to their historical experience should have been predictable.

Renate Bridenthal's and Joan Kelly-Gadol's work confirms that the history of women demands different periodization than does political history. Neither the Renaissance, it appears, nor the period during which women's suffrage was won, were periods in which women experienced an advance in their status. Recent work of American historians, such as Linda Kerber's and Joan Hoff Wilson's work on the American Revolution and my own work, confirms this conclusion. For example, neither during nor after the American Revolution nor in the age of Jackson did women share the historical experience of men. On the contrary, they experienced in both periods a loss of status, a restriction of options as to occupations and role choices, and certainly in Jacksonian America, there were restrictions imposed upon their sexuality, at least in prescriptive behavior. If one applies to both of these cases the kind of sophisticated and detailed analysis Kelly-Gadol attempts—that is, differentiations between women of different classes and comparisons between the status of men of a given class and women of that class—one finds the picture further complicated. Status loss in one area—social production—may be offset by status gain in another—access to education.

What kind of periodization might be substituted for the periodization of traditional history in order for it to be applicable to women? The answer depends largely on the conceptual framework in which the historian works. Many historians of women's history, in their search for a unifying framework, have tended to use the Marxist or neo-Marxist model supplied by Juliet Mitchell and recently elaborated by Sheila Rowbotham. The important fact, says Mitchell, which distinguished the past of women from that of men is precisely that until very recently sexuality and reproduction were inevitably linked for women, while they were not so linked for men. Similarly, child-bearing and child-rearing were inevitably linked for women and still are so linked. Women's freedom depends on breaking those links. Using Mitchell's categories we can and should ask of each historical period: What happened to the link between sexuality and reproduction? What happened to the link between child-bearing and child-rearing? Important changes in the status of women occur when it becomes possible through the availability of birth-control information and technology to sever sexuality from inevitable motherhood. It may be the case, however, that it is not the availability and distribution of birth control information and technology so much as the level of medical and health care which is the determinant of change. That is, when infant morality decreases, so that raising every child to adulthood becomes the normal expectation of parents, family size declines.

The above case illustrates the difficulty that has vexed historians of women's history in trying to locate a periodization more appropriate to women. Working in different fields and specialities, many historians have observed that the transition from agricultural to industrializing society and then again the transition to fully developed industrial society entails important changes affecting women and the family. Changes in relations of production affect women's status as family members and as workers. Later, shifts in the mode of production affect the kinds of occupations women can enter and their status within them. Major shifts in health care and technological development, related to indus-

trialization, also affect the lives of women. It is not too difficult to discern such patterns and to conclude that there must be a causal relationship between changes in the mode of production and the status of women. Here, the Marxist model seems to offer an immediately satisfying solution, especially if, following Mitchell, "sexuality" as a factor is added to such factors as class. But in the case of women, just as in the case of racial castes, ideology and prescription internalized by both women and men seem to be as much a causative factor as are material changes in production relations. Does the entry of lower-class women into industrial production really bring them closer to "liberation"? In the absence of institutional changes such as the right to abortion and safe contraception, altered child-rearing arrangements, and varied options for sexual expression, changes in economic relations may become oppressive. Unless such changes are accompanied by changes in consciousness, which in turn result in institutional changes, they do not favorably affect the lives of women.

Is smaller family size the result of "domestic freedom" of choice exercised by women, the freedom of choice exercised by men, the ideologically buttressed coercion of institutions in the service of an economic class? Is it liberating for women, for men, or for corporations? This raises another difficult question: What about the relationship of upper-class to lower-class women? To what extent is the relative advance in the status of upper-class women predicated on the status loss of lower-class women? Examples of this are: the liberation of the middle-class American housewife in the mid-19th century through the availability of cheap black or immigrant domestic workers: the liberation of the 20th-century housewife from incessant drudgery in the home through agricultural stoop labor and the food-processing industry, both employing low-paid female workers.

Is periodization then dependent as much on class as on gender? This question is just one of several which challenge the universalist assumptions of all previous historical categories. There is no ready answer, but I think the questions themselves point us in the right direction.

All conceptual models of history hitherto developed have only limited usefulness for women's history, since all are based on the assumptions of a patriarchal ordering of values. The structural-functionalist framework leaves out class and sex factors, the traditional Marxist framework leaves out sex and race factors as *essentials,* admitting them only as marginal factors. Mitchell's neo-Marxist model includes these but slights ideas, values, and psychological factors. Still, her four-structures model and the refinements of it proposed by Bridenthal are an excellent addition to the conceptual working tools of the historian of women's history. They should be tried out, discussed, refined. But they are not, in my opinion, the whole answer.

Kelly-Gadol offers the useful suggestion that attitudes toward sexuality should be studied in each historical period. She considers the constraints upon women's sexuality imposed by society a useful measure of women's true status. This approach would necessitate comparisons between prescribed behavior for women and men as well as indications of their actual sexual behavior at any given time. This challenging method can be used with great effectiveness for certain periods of history and especially for upper- and middle-class women. It is doubtful whether it can be usefully employed as a general criterion, because of the difficulty of finding substantiating evidence, especially as it pertains to lower classes.

I raised the question of a conceptual framework for dealing with women's history in 1969, reasoning from the assumption that women were a subgroup in history. Neither caste, class, nor race quite fits the model for describing us. I have now come to the conclusion that the idea that women are some kind of subgroup or particular is wrong. It will not do—there are just too many of us. No single framework, no single factor, four-factor or eight-factor explanation can serve to contain all that the history of women is. Picture, if you can, an attempt to organize the history of men by using four factors. It will not work; neither will it work for women.

Women are and always have been at least half of humankind, and most of the time have been the majority. Their culturally determined and psychologically internalized marginality seems to be what makes their historical experience essentially different from that of men. But men have defined their experience as history and have left women out. At this time, as during earlier periods of feminist activity, women are urged to fit into the empty spaces, assuming their traditional marginal, "subgroup" status. But the truth is that history, as written and perceived up to now, is the history of a minority, who may well turn out to be the "subgroup." In order to write a new history worthy of the name, we will have to recognize that no single methodology and conceptual framework can fit the complexities of the historical experience of all women.

The first stage of "transitional history" may be to add some new categories to the general categories by which historians organize their material: Sexuality, reproduction, the link between child-bearing and child-rearing; role indoctrination, sexual values and myths: female consciousness. Further, all of these need to be analyzed, taking factors of race, class, ethnicity, and, possibly, religion into consideration. What we have here is not a single framework for dealing with women in history, but new questions to all of history.

The next stage may be to explore the possibility that what we call women's history may actually be the study of a separate women's culture. Such a culture would include not only the separate occupations, status, experiences, and rituals of women but also their consciousness, which internalizes patriarchal assumptions. In some cases, it would include the tensions created in the culture between the prescribed patriarchal assumptions and women's efforts to attain autonomy and emancipation.

The questions asked about the past of women may demand interdisciplinary approaches. They also may demand broadly conceived group research projects that end up giving functional answers; answers that deal not with a functioning organism, a functioning whole, the society in which both men and women live.

A following stage may develop a synthesis: a history of the dialectic, the tensions between the two cultures, male and female. Such a synthesis could be based on close comparative study of given periods in which the historical experience of men is compared with that of women, their tensions and interactions being as much the subject of study as their differences. Only after a series of such detailed studies can we hope to find the parameters by which to define the new universal history. My guess is that no one conceptual framework will fit so complex a subject.

Methods are tools for analysis—some of us will stick with one tool, some of us will reach for different tools as we need them. For women, the problem really is that we must acquire not only the confidence needed for using tools, but for making new ones to fit our needs. We should do so relying on our learned skills and our rational skepticism of handed-down doctrine. The recognition that we had been denied our history came to many of us as a staggering flash of insight, which altered our consciousness irretrievably. We have come a long way since then. The next step is to face, once and for all and with all its complex consequences, that women are the majority of humankind and have been essential to the making of history. Thus, all history as we now know it, is, for women, merely prehistory.

The Majority Finds Its Past[2]

Women's experience encompasses all that is human; they share—and always have shared—the world equally with men. Equally in the sense that half, at least, of all the world's experience has been theirs, half of the world's work and many of its products. In one sense, then, to write the history of women means documenting all of history: women have always been making history, living it and shaping it. But the history of women has a special character, a built-in distortion: it comes to us refracted through the lens of men's observations; refracted again through values which consider man the measure. What we know of the past experience of women has been transmitted to us largely through the reflections of men: how we see and interpret what we know about women has been shaped for us through a value system defined by men. And so, to construct a new history that will with true equality reflect the dual nature of humankind—its male and female aspect—we must first pause to reconstruct the missing half—the female experience: women's history.

Women's history must contain not only the activities and events in which women participated, but the record of changes and shifts in their perception of themselves and their roles. Historically, women began their

2. This essay first appeared in *Current History*, Vol. 70, No. 416 (May 1976), 193–96, 231.

public activities by extending their concerns from home and family to the larger community. With this broadening of female concerns came the questioning of tradition, often followed by tentative steps in new directions: Anne Hutchinson holding weekly meetings for men and women in which she, not the male clergy, commented on the Bible; Frances Wright daring to assert women's freedom of sexual choice; Margaret Sanger discovering in one moment of insight and empathy that societally enforced motherhood was a wrong no longer to be tolerated.

Then came the reaching out toward other women: sewing circles and female clubs; women workers organizing themselves; women's rights conventions; the building of mass movements of women. By such steps women became "woman-oriented." Out of such activities grew a new self-consciousness, based on the recognition of the separate interests of women as a group. Out of communality and collectivity emerged feminist consciousness—a system of ideas that not only challenged patriarchal values and assumptions, but attempted to substitute for them a feminist system of values and ideas.

The most advanced conceptual level by which women's history can now be defined must include an account of the female experience as it changes over time and should include the development of feminist consciousness as an essential aspect of women's historical past. This past includes the quest for rights, equality, and justice which can be subsumed under "women's rights," i.e., the civil rights of women. But the quest for female emancipation from patriarchally determined subordination encompasses more than the striving for equality and rights. It can be defined best as the quest for autonomy. Autonomy means women defining themselves and the values by which they will live, and beginning to think of institutional arrangements that will order their environment in line with their needs. It means to some the evolution of practical programs, to others the reforming of existing social arrangements, to still others the building of new institutions. Autonomy for women means moving out from a world in which one is born to marginality, bound to a past without meaning, and prepared for a future determined by others. It means moving into a world in which one acts and chooses, aware of a meaningful past and free to shape one's future.

The central question raised by women's history is: what would history be like if it were seen through the eyes of women and ordered by values they define?

Is one justified in speaking of a female historical experience different from that of men? To find an answer to this basic question, it is useful to examine the life cycles and the turning points in individual lives of men and women of the past. Are there significant differences in childhood, education, maturity? Are social expectations different for boys and girls? Taking full cognizance of the wide range of variations, are there any universals by which we can define the female past? Material for answering such questions as far as they pertain to women can be found in many primary sources, some virtually untapped, other familiar. Autobiographical letters and diaries, even those frequently used, yield new information if approached with these questions and rearranged from the female point of view.

There are basic differences in the way boys and girls now and in the past experienced the world and, more important, the social roles they were trained to fulfill. From childhood on, the talents and drives of girls were channeled into different directions from those of boys. For boys, the family was the place from which one sprang and to which one returned for comfort and support, but the field of action was the larger world of wilderness, adventure, industry, labor, and politics. For girls, the family was to be the world, their field of action was the domestic circle. He was to express himself in his work, and through it and social action help to transform his environment; her individual growth and choices were restricted to lead her to express herself through love, wifehood, and motherhood—through the support and nurturance of others who would act for her. The ways in which these gender-differentiated patterns would find expression would change in the course of historical development; the differences in the function assigned to the sexes might widen or narrow, but the fact of different sex role indoctrination remained.

Throughout most of America's past, life was experienced at a different rhythm by men and women. For a boy, education was directed toward a vocational or professional goal, his life ideally moved upward and outward in a straight line until it reached a plateau of fulfillment; the girl's education was sporadic and often interrupted: it did not lead to the fulfillment of her life role, but rather competed with it. Her development was dependent on her relationship to others and was often determined by them; it moved in wave-like, circuitous motion. In the boy's case, life crises were connected to vocational goals: separation from the family for purposes of greater educational opportunity; success or failures in achievement and career; economic decisions or setbacks. For the girl, such crises were more closely connected to stages in her biological life: the transition from childhood to adolescence, and then to marriage, which usually meant, in the past, greater restraint rather than the broadening out which it meant for the boy. Love and marriage for her implied a shifting of domesticity from one household to another, and the onset of her serious responsibilities: childbirth, childrearing, and the nurture of the family. Finally came the crisis of widowhood and bereavement which could, depending on her economic circumstances, mean increasing freedom and autonomy or a difficult struggle for economic survival.

All people, in every society, are assigned specific roles and indoctrinated to perform to the expectations and values of that society. But for women this has always meant social indoctrination to a value system that imposed upon them greater restrictions of the range of choices than those of men. During much of the historic past, some of these restrictions were based on women's function as childbearers and the necessity of their bearing many children in order to guarantee the survival of some. With a declining infant mortality rate and advances in medical knowledge that made widely accessible birth-control methods possible, the gender-based role indoctrination of women was no longer functional but anachronistic. Women's indoctrination to motherhood as their primary and life-long function became oppressive, a patriarchal cultural myth. Additionally, even after educational restrictions were removed, women have been trained to fit into institutions shaped, determined, and ruled by men. As a result, their definitions of selfhood and self-fulfillment have remained subordinated to those of others.

American women have always shared in the economic life of the nation: in agriculture as equal partners performing separate, but essential work; in industry usually as low-paid unskilled workers; and in the professions overcoming barriers formed by educational discrimination and traditional male dominance. Although the majority of women have always worked for the same reasons as men—self-support and the support of dependents—their work has been characterized by marginality, temporariness, and low status. Typically, they have moved into the male-defined work world as outsiders, often treated as intruders. Thus, after each of the major wars in which the nation engaged, women who during wartime did all essential work and services, were at war's end shunted back to their traditional jobs. As workers, women have been handicapped by direct discrimination in hiring, training, and advancement, and, more profoundly, by their sex-role indoctrination that made them consider any work they did as subsidiary to their main job: wife and motherhood.

Thus, women often participated in their own subordination by internalizing the ideology and values that oppressed them and by passing these on to their children. Yet they were not *passive* victims; they always involved themselves actively in the world in their own way. Starting on a stage defined by their life cycle, they often rebelled against and defied societal indoctrination, developed their own definitions of community, and built their own female culture.

In addition to their participation in the economic life of society, women have shaped history through community-building and participation in politics. American women built community life as members of families, as carriers of cultural and religious values, as founders and supporters of organizations and institutions. So far, historians have taken notice mostly of the first of these functions and of the organizational work of women only insofar as they ''contributed'' to social reforms. Women's political work has been recognized only as it pertains to women's rights and woman suffrage.

Historical interpretation of the community-building work of women is urgently needed. The voluminous national and local records that document the network of community institutions founded and maintained by women are available. They should be studied against the traditional record of institution-building, which focuses on the activities of men. The research and the monographic work that form the essential groundwork for such interpretations have yet to be done.

The history of women's struggles for the ballot has received a good deal of attention by historians, but this narrow focus has led to the impression that the main political activity in which women engaged in the past was working for woman suffrage. While the importance of that issue is undeniable, it is impossible to understand the involvement of American women in every aspect of the nation's life, if their political activity is so narrowly defined. Women were involved in most of the political struggles of the 19th century, but the form of their participation and their activities were different from those of men. It is one of the urgent and as yet unfulfilled tasks of women's history to study the ways in which women influenced and participated in political events, directly or through the mass organizations they built.

The involvement of American women in the important events of American history—the political and electoral crises, the wars, expansion, diplomacy—is overshadowed by the fact of the exclusion of women from political power throughout 300 years of the nation's life. Thus women, half of the nation, are cast in the marginal role of a powerless minority—acted upon, but not acting. That this impression of the female past is a distortion is by now obvious. It is premature to attempt a critical evaluation or synthesis of the role women played in the building of American society. It is not premature to suggest that the fact of the exclusion of women from all those institutions that make essential decisions for the nation is itself an important aspect of the nation's past. In short, what needs to be explained is not why women were so little evident in American history as currently recorded, but why and how patriarchal values affected that history.

The steps by which women moved toward self-respect, self-definition, a recognition of their true position and from there toward a sense of sisterhood are tentative and varied and have occurred throughout our history. Exceptional women often defied traditional roles, at times explicitly, at other times simply by expressing their individuality to its fullest. The creation of new role models for women included the development of the professional woman, the political leader, the executive, as well as the anonymous working woman, the club woman, the trade unionist. These types were created in the process of changing social activities, but they also were the elements that helped to create a new feminists consciousness. The emergence of feminist consciousness as a historical phenomenon is an essential part of the history of women.

The process of creating a theory of female emancipation is still under way. The challenges of modern American women are grounded in past experience, in the buried and neglected female past. Women have always made history as much as men have, not "contributed" to it, only they did not know what they have made and had no tools to interpret their own experience. What is new at this time, is that women are fully claiming their past and shaping the tools by means of which they can interpret it.

Women are not a marginal "minority," and women's history is not a collection of "missing facts and views" to be incorporated into traditional categories. Women are at least half and often a majority of all Americans and are distributed through all classes and categories of American society. Their history inevitably reflects variations in economic class, race, religion, and ethnicity. But the overriding fact is that women's history is the history of the *majority* of humankind.

Janis S. Bohan

Contextual History: A Framework for Re-Placing Women in the History of Psychology*

The absence of women from published histories of psychology is addressed from a perspective that makes sense of women's place in the history of psychology, including their participation, their exclusion, and their invisibility. This approach is based on principles of social constructionism and on a contextual approach to history that seeks to understand women's place in psychology as a product of socially constructed notions of gender, psychology, and history. The article suggests that an awareness of the context created by these constructions explains women's role in psychology to date and holds promise for their meaningful inclusion in the future.

From: *Psychology of Women Quarterly*, 1990, *14*, pp. 213–228. Copyright (c) 1990 Division 35, American Psychological Association. Reproduced with the permission of Cambridge University Press.

*A version of this article was presented at the annual meetings of the Association for Women in Psychology, Newport, RI, March 1989. The author gratefully acknowledges the assistance of Todd Coffey, Barbara Gagliardi, and Pam Moke, who read earlier forms of this article, and the students in the Advanced Seminar, where these ideas were piloted and refined.

Address reprint requests to: Janis S. Bohan, Box 54, Metropolitan State College, Denver, CO 80204.

Imagine yourself living in a society where the genius of science implores a receptive public to understand "truths" such as these:

The chief distinction in the intellectual powers of the two sexes is shown by man's attaining to a higher eminence, in whatever he takes up, than can woman. (Darwin, 1871, pp. 326–327)

Identical education of the sexes is a crime before God and humanity, that physiology protests against and that experience weeps over. (Clarke, 1873, p. 127)

All that is distinctly human is man; all that is truly woman is merely reproductive. (Grant, 1889, p. 263)

Deficiency in reproductive power . . . can be reasonably attributed to the overtaxing of [women's] brains. (Spencer, 1867, p. 485)

The "woman's rights movement" is an attempt to rear, by the process of "unnatural selection," a race of monstrosities—hostile alike to men, to normal women, to human society, and to the future development of our race. (Bagehut, 1879, p. 213)

Imagine these snippets of scientific wisdom reinforced by the lay press, where the *Saturday Review* describes educated women as "defeminated," a "species of vermin," "one of the most intolerable monsters of creation" (cited in Delamont & Duffin, 1978, p. 180). Imagine that *The Mothers Magazine* condemns those who speak for an improvement in women's lot in these less-than-gentle terms: "These Amazonians are their own executioners. They have unsexed themselves in public estimation, and there is no fear that they will perpetuate their race" ("Female orators," 1838, p. 27).

If you lived in such a society, would you even contemplate abdicating children and domestic life for a professional career? Would you dare to undertake a course of action that would do irreversible damage to your reproductive capabilities? Would you consign yourself to the social rejection reserved for those selfish women who put their own wishes above the species, who "unsex" themselves in the name of women's rights?

These comments are illustrative of the beliefs prevalent when psychology emerged in America; they reflect how American society at that time understood the inherent "nature" and thus the proper place of women. In the terms to be utilized in this discussion, they illustrate how society constructed gender. The construction of gender formed one element of the sociohistorical background against which psychology began; subsequent constructions of gender have likewise contributed to the context within which the discipline has matured. These constructions have shaped women's participation in psychology, including their invisibility in psychology's histories.

In the discussion that follows, I will use the term *re-placing* women to depict the process by which women can assume their rightful place in the history of the field. To *place* women in psychology would be a misnomer, as they were never without a place in the discipline. Women have been largely excluded from psychology's recorded histories, a fact recently addressed by a growing literature (e.g., Bernstein & Russo, 1974; O'Connell & Russo, 1980, 1983, 1988; Scarborough & Furumoto, 1987; Stevens & Gardner, 1982). Women have often been invisible, have often confronted exclusionary practices and structures, have occasionally been misrepresented or denied acknowledgment, have frequently been trivialized. But women have not, despite all this, been absent.

Historian Gerda Lerner (1979) delineated three stages in the placement (or replacement) of women in history. In the first two stages, which Lerner dubs "compensatory" and "contribution" history, women's inclusion in history is predicated upon their relationship to dominant (male-defined) conceptions of what is important. Thus, these "add women and stir" approaches homogenize women and their work into the existent blend of historical discussion.

To appreciate fully women's role in history, Lerner suggests, we must move to another level; we must view history from the base of women's distinctive experience. Commensurate with Lerner's model, Furumoto (1988b) urged that histories of psychology become more inclusive, incorporating participants other than white men, and that they relinquish the traditional view of history as an unbiased reporting of events for a recognition of the contextual nature of historical constructions.

In response to Lerner's and Furumoto's challenges, the present article attempts to address the task of re-placing women in the history of psychology by granting legitimacy to women's experience as a significant contextual force in the determination of their place in the field. My aim is to demonstrate that women's place in the history of psychology (including their invisibility) makes sense. That sense derives from an awareness that knowledge and history are always a product of the context in which they are created, and that women's experience has formed a unique context for their relationship to psychology.

Social Constructionism and Contextual History

The argument that women can be sensibly re-placed in psychology's history is grounded in current challenges to the epistemological and historiographic bases of psychology (as of other disciplines). A cursory review of such challenges will offer a foundation for understanding their relevance to re-placing women.

Observation is not a certain route to truth. Nineteenth-century science was grounded in a philosophy of knowledge termed positivism, an epistemology that asserts that scientific observation is the only sure route to knowledge. Psychology embraced positivism, captured in its self-conscious attempt to ally itself with the natural sciences and thus to share in their expanding prestige. Ironically, while most disciplines have abandoned this single-minded reliance on positivism, recognizing the inadequacies of this position to be delineated here (Koch, 1959; Lincoln & Guba, 1985), psychology has clung steadfastly to the positivist paradigm.

Positivism restricts psychology's vision. By adhering to the positivist stance, psychology has severely limited its scope, selecting as topics for investigation only those that are amenable to atomistic analysis and direct observation, where salient variables can be operationally defined and controlled, and where

results of such manipulations can be expressed in quantitative terms. Much of the potential subject matter of a thoroughgoing study of human experience is necessarily excluded by such limitations. Complex issues such as the impact on behavior of social context, for instance, are clearly not readily amenable to such analysis.

Science is not value-free. Science (particularly social science) cannot be value-free. The very act of asking certain questions and not others implies value judgments. Further, psychology's methodological commitment to positivism itself reveals implicit assumptions about human experience; atomistic analysis and mechanistic explanations of human behavior, quantitative descriptions of complex social interactions, and context-stripping that minimizes, rather than focuses on, relevant context all reveal the biases inherent in a positivist view of reality.

In addition, psychological description and prescription are inextricably intertwined by virtue of the valuational connotations of psychological constructs. Gender-related terms, illustratively, clearly evidence this descriptive-prescriptive confusion—consider constructs such as androgyny, locus of control, field-dependence versus field-independence.

The human sciences cannot be objective. The assumption of subject-object duality which underlies the positivist conception of objectivity simply cannot be upheld in psychology; the ultimate reflectivity and mutuality of human experience are unavoidable adjuncts to psychological research. Psychologists are perforce both the subject and the object of their own observations. Conversely, human subjects are aware both of their place as objects of study and of their reciprocal relationship with the researcher. As a case in point, to view gender objectively is patently impossible. Neither men nor women can be objective about (separated from) the reality and the impact of gender.

"Knowledge" is socially constructed. Social constructionism represents an alternative to positivism as a conceptualization of the source of knowledge (e.g., Gergen, 1985). This perspective argues that reality cannot be directly apprehended and contends that we make sense of experience by constructing models of reality that we then agree through social interchange to accept as truth. Thus, knowledge—or what passes for knowledge—is socially constructed (rather than discovered), is validated only by its congruence with shared understanding, and is inevitably influenced by the social context within which it is derived, including the inevitable values and subjectivity of those involved.

At least two levels of context frame the definition of what will pass for knowledge. First, the construction of knowledge is influenced by the widely held attitudes and assumptions of the society in which it is developed. Second, what will be accepted as knowledge is constrained by the current paradigm(s) of the professional community from which such knowledge takes its legitimacy (Kuhn, 1970).[1] As we shall see, the construction of women's place in psychology reflects both levels of this two-tiered context: the beliefs of the broader society and the methods and mores of psychology as a discipline.

These principles can be applied to history as to other forms of knowledge. The historian is an individual with individual values; she or he is also a participant in a series of social and professional contexts each of which exerts an influence on the construction of history. Further, the subject matter described in historical narratives is itself a composite of constructions; the history of psychology is a history not of facts, but of ideas constructed in context. Far from being an objective telling of events, history is thus an aggregate of hypotheses whose content and explanatory structure are unavoidably value-laden and subjective (cf. Nowell-Smith, 1977). Thus, women's absence from psychology's historical narratives does not reflect facts about psychology's past, but is rather a product of hypotheses about (constructions of) selected elements (themselves constructions) of that past.

Constructing Women's Context

Moving from this constructionist perspective, an understanding of women's experience provides the crucial context within which to view their place in the evolution of the discipline. Two general domains of information are directly relevant. The first has to do with psychology's beginnings and the question of women's place there, as these events formed a backdrop for later developments. The second addresses events subsequent to those early years, as well as qualities endemic to psychology which have had a continuing impact on women's participation.

Psychology's Beginnings: Where Were the Women?

Women's place in society. The "doctrine of spheres" prevalent in 19th-century America decreed that the "true woman" should demonstrate certain cardinal virtues: piety, purity, submissiveness, and domesticity (Welter, 1966). That women were ill-represented in the professions during this era is at least in part a consequence of these terribly limiting prescriptions. Paradoxically, these same attributions also provided entry for women into the public sphere as nurturant and morally gifted caregivers for society. Barely disguised, they have defined the directions women have been allowed within psychology throughout its history.

Justification for women's confinement to this domestic sphere had previously come from religion and custom. In the late 19th century, reverence for science encouraged the application of scientific expertise to the "woman problem." The conclusions reached by science regarding women's nature and the evident differences between the sexes mirrored the beliefs of the time. The presumed scientific basis of assertions, such as those presented earlier, simply gave added credibility to ideas already firmly entrenched in social attitudes—a straightforward manifestation of social construction at work.

Women in education. Resistance to women's participation in academia had dual and profound effects on their presence in psychology. First, psychology's striving for academic and scientific credibility and for professionalization made the PhD a prerequisite for participation in the profession. Yet, women confronted major resistance to their entry into higher education, further opposition to their admission to graduate work, and exclusionary practices which even denied them graduate degrees duly earned (Rosenberg, 1982; Solomon, 1985). Second, because of psychology's academic nature, nearly all positions in the field were concentrated in academia. But women, even those with the requisite education, found employment opportunities scarce within academia, and largely nonexistent elsewhere (Bernard, 1964; Solomon, 1985).

This resistance to women's involvement in academia derived, predictably, from dominant societal attitudes, once again reinforced by science. Justification for this exclusion included items such as what follows.

The so-called variability hypothesis argued that women as a group demonstrate a narrower range of mental abilities than do men and are therefore unable to perform at the highest levels of academic and professional achievement (Darwin, 1871; Spencer, 1867). Further, women's brains were said to be less evolved and their intellectual skills

therefore more primitive (Bagehut, 1879; Spencer, 1867, 1874). In addition, women were believed to be inherently frail, their reproductive systems being especially vulnerable. The rigors of education thus represented a grave threat to women's reproductive capability and thus to the species (Bagehut, 1879; Clarke, 1873; Spencer, 1867).

Women in science. Because the new psychology strove to portray itself as a natural science, women who would enter psychology faced the biases that excluded women from science. At the most basic level, women were faced with the argument that science and femininity are incongruent—that "woman scientist" is, in Rossiter's (1982, p. xv) words, a "contradiction in terms." The woman who chose a career in science was therefore violating the culture's dictates for properly feminine behavior.

Women scientists found structural barriers, as well. Forced to operate with limited resources, women did not have access to the facilities and support that would encourage maximal productivity (Bernard, 1964; Harris, 1978). Further, women found themselves unwelcome in both formal and informal exchanges among colleagues and were thus excluded from the collegial networks that underpin professional growth (Furumoto, 1988a). Finally, the self-conscious process of professionalization within the sciences often served to exclude women from professional organizations (Furumoto, 1987; Rossiter, 1982).

Women in psychology. Regrettably, psychology harbored proponents of these misogynist notions. G. Stanley Hall (1903, 1906) insisted that the "best" women were obliged to reproduce or risk "race suicide." Hall also argued that women's primitive mental development would preclude significant achievement. Edward Thorndike (1906) insisted on the mediocrity of women's intellectual potential, and on that basis urged restrictions in their education.

James Cattell (1909) attributed the declining birth rate directly to the expansion of education for women and also opposed women academicians' promotion to professional rank (Rosenberg, 1982). Edward Titchener explicitly prohibited women from his prestigious professional network, The Society of Experimental Psychologists (Boring, 1967).[2]

In sum, the manner of women's entry into the new psychology was shaped by the social construction of gender at that time. That construction was in turn superimposed upon psychology by the individuals and institutions representing the emerging discipline.

Beyond the Beginnings

Sociohistorical context. Throughout psychology's history, women's place has continued to be socially constructed from beliefs about gender differences, the needs of society at large, and the changing self-definition of the field as it has responded to this societal context. A few illustrations will demonstrate this point.

The testing movement, spawned by the demands of World War I, provided opportunities for women as testing was delegated to lower status and lower salaried psychologists, primarily women. The child development and progressive education movements, also byproducts of World War I, offered openings (typically less well-paid and of lower prestige) for women, precisely because such work was deemed appropriate to women's natural abilities (O'Connell & Russo, 1983).

Applied psychology flourished after World War I and further since World War II, and women have come to be disproportionately represented among the applied specialities, particularly in areas dealing with children and families, a fact again in keeping with their presumed natural proclivities for caregiving. The continuing dominance of psychology by academia (where men predominate), however, has reinforced women's subordinate position throughout the discipline (Furumoto, 1987; Scarborough & Furumoto, 1987). In addition, because few women psychologists were enlisted in the armed services, many wartime training opportunities in areas of personnel and organizational psychology were largely unavailable to women; further, postwar clinical training programs focused on the need to provide services largely to adult male clients, often in hospital settings, and thus attracted primarily male trainees. The effect of these constraints was to restrict women's participation in many areas of psychology's rapid post-war expansion and also to exclude them from the professional networks that evolved from these activities (Furumoto, 1987).

Thus, psychology has been characterized by both horizontal segregation, with women concentrated in subfields deemed appropriate to their presumed nature, and hierarchical segregation, with women occupying positions of lesser status, with lower incomes and fewer opportunities for advancement. In brief, women's work in psychology has been shaped by the social construction of their proper role in society and by psychology's translation of that role to the field's own activities.

Within the space thus created for women in psychology, distinctively women's issues have been subordinated to other concerns. Women have engaged in the breadth of activities and interests that have characterized the expanding field, their efforts largely directed toward earning and justifying their positions through work compatible with the expectations and paradigmatic models of the discipline. Thus, for most of psychology's history, both women's concerns and individual women have been invisible and largely indistinguishable components of the field of psychology.

During the 1960s and 1970s the new context provided by the impact of the nascent women's movement generated a growing awareness of the potential role of psychology in addressing women's issues. This awareness has both generated and been informed by a burgeoning body of research and has challenged long-held conceptions of psychology's purpose as well as its methods. Once again, these developments within psychology reflect changes in the cultural construction of gender and, by extension, in psychology's construction of women's place in the discipline. As is typical of the dialectic that characterizes the construction of knowledge, these changes in psychology are both a product of and a stimulant to changes in the broader social context.

Women's place in the community of psychology. Women's place in psychology is measured in part by their invisibility, a product of the criteria used by the discipline as measures of eminence. The determination of eminence in psychology rests largely on research and publication, with such visibility being is own best sustenance. For myriad reasons, women have been less able to enter into this spiralling progress toward eminence. Because histories of psychology record the ideas of those deemed eminent, these impediments have effectively screened a large body of women's work from such histories.

First, much of women's work is concentrated in fields and topic areas that are less prestigious and less central to the discipline's self-definition than is the work more common to men (Scarborough & Furumoto, 1987). This is true of most applied psychologies; it is also true of topics clearly designated as women's issues. Stated simply, "women who are psychologists are not the kind of psychologists who get cited in the scientific literature" (Stevens & Gardner, 1982, Vol. I, p. 9). Furthermore, even where the work of women meshes with the research orientation of the field, their efforts often go unrecognized. The following factors contribute to this neglect.

Social Custom

Women's subordinate position in society is mirrored in psychology. The have often been research assistants and junior authors; their efforts have frequently received only footnote acknowledgment; their work has been misattributed; they have found less advocacy within professional circles (O'Connell & Russo, 1983; Scarborough & Furumoto, 1987; Stevens & Gardner, 1982). Also, women's traditional role within the family creates a handicap, for women who seek advancement are competing with colleagues who are able to devote greater time and energy to professional activities (Bryan & Boring, 1947; O'Connell & Russo, 1980; Simeone, 1987).

Names and Citations

Conventions in the use of names have proven detrimental to women's prestige. The practice of changing one's name at marriage sacrifices the continuity of career visibility. Further, the joint work of wife and husband psychologists—and even the woman's independent work—may be identified with a name, and the name with the man of the pair. Importantly, the APA citation format utilizing only initials of first names makes it impossible to identify women's work. This fact may have the insidious effect of supporting a presumption of male authorship; unless women are specifically identified, culturally-induced assumptions may result in a perception that all work is the work of men (Bernstein & Russo, 1974; Stevens & Gardner, 1982).[3]

Collegial Expectations

Finally, women's work has not achieved visibility commensurate with its worth precisely because psychology has failed to recognize and acknowledge women as significant contributors to the field. Members of the discipline are largely unaware of women's contributions to psychology (Brodsky, Nevill, & Kimmel, 1976; Simeone, 1987). Women's consequent invisibility serves to reinforce the notion that women contribute little of consequence, women's actual work is then trivialized, and so the cycle continues.

Re-Constructing Psychology, Re-Placing Women

The ideas proposed here suggest a means for making sense of women's historical invisibility in psychology and of the necessity for re-placing women in the field. This sense is based on the foundational awareness that what passes for knowledge is constructed; it is derived from agreements as to how we will interpret and respond to what we agree to take as reality. Our understanding of women has been constructed in a manner that leads to invisibility in history as history is usually written. When we look at the stultifying constructions of women's sphere at psychology's beginnings, it is not surprising to find women scarce there. If we consider how gender has been constructed throughout the evolution of the discipline, it is not surprising to discover women selectively shunted into particular subfields and devalued positions within psychology, nor to find them largely invisible to the discipline as a whole. And, when we view history as constructed, its construction based on the dominant world view of the society (including its construction of gender) and the reigning paradigm of the discipline (including its gendered components, both obvious and implicit), it is not surprising to find women largely absent from the histories of psychology.

Knowledge is fundamentally a set of agreements; such agreements are negotiable. Gender is constructed; psychology is constructed; history is constructed. Clearly, then, the place of women in the history of psychology is available for re-construction. If we take this as our charge, the reconstruction of psychology's history to re-place women, what novel frameworks might be entailed in the effort?

First, in one sense this new construction is already underway. Feminist critiques of science represent a first step in the reconstruction of psychology. Feminist analysis illuminates a number of problems inherent in the application of positivism to psychology and may thereby serve as a catalyst to the paradigm shift portended by widespread discontent with psychology's positivist model. The points raised in the constructionist criticism of psychology's commitment to positivism find striking parallels in feminist writings across the disciplines: the awareness of context, the acknowledgement of the inevitable valuing in human science, the inadequacy of dualistic models which revere objectivity as separation (e.g., Harding & Hintikka, 1983; Harding & O'Barr, 1987; Langland & Gove, 1981). This initial replacement of women's perspective, thus, already promises to contribute importantly to the dynamic of psychology's evolution.

Second, all manner of topics can be revisioned through this process of re-creating a place for women in psychology. What better example can one offer of knowledge as contextual than the outrageous (but socially fitting) notions about the inevitable damage done by education to women's reproductive capacity? What clearer illustration of science as lacking in objectivity is there than scientific proof that women are less variable than men, conveniently turned into its opposite when greater variability was deemed inferior (Shields, 1975)? The re-placement of women can thus serve as a prototype for the self-reflection that every discipline needs regularly to undergo.

Third, this goal of re-construction suggests a major task for those persuaded of its merits. We are charged to be cognizant of critiques of positivism, to be well-versed in the arguments of constructionism, alert to the nature of women's experience vis-à-vis the field of psychology, and to undertake to apply that awareness to research, to teaching, and to practice.

Re-viewing research. Re-constructionist research reflects a sensitivity to the inadequacy of the positivist model and an openness to alternative conceptualizations of subject matter and method. While feminist journals (such as *Psychology of Women Quarterly*) reflect a commitment to such alternative perspectives, mainstream journals have not yet evidenced similar openness (Lykes & Stewart, 1986). Yet, the credibility of alternative approaches (and of those espousing them) must rest on their widespread dissemination and the gradual acknowledgment of their merit outside feminist circles. Therefore, because publication in mainstream journals relies, at least for the time being, on review by gatekeepers who are likely to be representatives of the dominant (positivist) view, doing research from an alternative model requires not only familiarity with the issues involved but also a willingness to face the frustration of having ones work judged by criteria appropriate to another world view. This means publishing both in journals sympathetic to new perspectives and in mainstream journals, creating work that challenges established approaches while yet conscientiously meeting demands for scholarly excellence. Only by pursuing new models and achieving meaningful results that are persistently put before the psychological community will we be able to win acceptance for such alternatives.

Re-shaping teaching. Our teaching, too, should incorporate challenges to the traditional model of psychology's subject matter and method. Courses in research methods are obvious candidates for such revision, as are others that include material on research techniques. The history and systems course seems clearly inadequate without a discussion of the issues raised by social constructionism, and my own teaching experience has convinced me of the pedagogical merits of a constructionist model for replacing women in history. By first building an understanding of constructionism, it is possible to incorporate women and women's perspectives without their seeming in any sense after-thoughts or ancillary (although most textbooks still convey this impression). A constructionist view of the history of psychology makes women's inclusion a meaningful matter of course; the same might be said of other courses.

Re-considering practice. A view of women's place as constructed suggests several directions for psychological practice. First, certain alternatives to positivist epistemology have particular relevance for practice. Most notably, hermeneutics (e.g., Bowles, 1984) offers an exciting interpretation of communication in the clinical setting. Second, the recognition that our understanding is constructed challenges practitioners to step back from the ideas they take as facts in order to assess the bases from which those supposed truths were constructed. Practitioners' understandings of clients are complex constructions, as are clients' gradual creations of self-understanding. Both must be deconstructed to reveal the assumptions underlying them if practice is to remain open to the variety of re-constructions which might best serve clients' needs (cf. Hare-Mustin & Maracek, 1988).

Re-educating colleagues. Beyond our own work we need to be attentive to the contextual consciousness of our colleagues. Because of the filtering function of paradigmatic commitments (Kuhn, 1970), mainstream psychology and mainstream psychologist may be unaware of these issues.

Numerous avenues hold promise for bringing these ideas to colleagues' attention. In my own efforts toward this end, I have shared bibliographies, notified other faculty of resources on hand, introduced in department meetings the need for curriculum revision to address these topics, and rewritten syllabi to incorporate discussion of social constructionism, using it as a means for re-placing women. Additional opportunities might include informal discussions among colleagues, articles in in-house publications, formal meetings and symposia, presentations at professional conferences, and publication in mainstream journals. Knowledge is constructed in all of these forums; the goal is always to encourage the construction of knowledge that incorporates women.

Resources for Re-Construction

A plethora of existing resources are available for this effort, representing a variety of applications of constructionist perspectives to these concerns. As regards methodological issues, Bleir (1984) and Keller (1985) provided useful introductions to the challenges raised by feminist critiques of science. Lincoln and Guba (1985) presented a thorough discussion of alternatives to traditional methods that, while not explicitly feminist or constructionist in orientation, is much in keeping with the point of view suggested here. In psychology specifically, the work of Lott (1985), Scarr (1985), Unger (1983, 1985), Wallston and Grady (1985), and Wittig (1985) illustrated a variety of approaches to methodological concerns. Fine (1985) and Lykes and Stewart (1986) conducted self-reflective analyses of psychology's success in addressing these issues.

In a historical vein, Shields (1975) provided an informative study of the impact of societal belief and scientific bias on early psychology's view of women. Shields and Mallory (1987) also offered insight into the contextual forces that shaped early psychology, with particular emphasis on the effects of (and response to) women's presence in the discipline. Furumoto (1988b) used examples of her own work toward re-placing women as illustrations of a contextual approach to history.

As regards constructionist approaches to psychological constructs, Morawski (1988) neatly demonstrated how methods as well as constructs are products of the contexts in which they are derived, as well as pointing up the often ignored gendered nature of such contexts. In a disquieting article, Mednick (1989) argued that political and social context, rather than conceptual or scientific merit, determine the popularity of psychological (specifically, feminist) constructs. Hare-Mustin and Maracek (1988) applied a constructionist model to psychology's penchant for focusing on, alternatively, the existence or the absence of gender differences; they also discussed the implications of these two biases for psychological research and practice. Crawford and Maracek (1989) offered what amounts to a constructionist review of psychology's study of women, including commentary on and illustrations of new directions in research.

The idea of re-placing women is not, of course, new. What the framework here offers is not a new goal, but a means to approach that goal. If a constructionist model explains why women have been largely invisible to the field of psychology, then the framework can equally well be applied to the process of re-placing women and women's perspectives in their proper place in psychology.

Notes

1. While some, including Kuhn (1970) himself, have questioned whether psychology can be viewed as paradigmatic, others suggest that

psychology's allegiance to positivism represents an implicit paradigmatic commitment (e.g., Buss, 1978; Gergen, 1985). I concur with the latter judgment, and certain arguments in this article are based on that assumption.

2. Ironically, these same men were responsible for the education of and advocacy for some of psychology's pioneer women. Diehl (1986) offered an analysis of this paradox, specifically as relates to Hall; similar arguments might apply to the others, as well. This apparent discrepancy between espoused beliefs and actual behavior is a fascinating study in social constructionism.

3. References in this article include full first names of authors in an attempt to address this problem, if only on a small scale.

References

Bagehut, Walter. (1879). Biology and "women's rights." *Popular Science Monthly, 14,* 207.

Bernard, Jessie. (1964). *Academic woman.* Cleveland, OH: World Publishing.

Bernstein, Maxine D., & Russo, Nancy F. (1974). The history of psychology revisited: Or up with our foremothers. *American Psychologist, 29,* 130–134.

Bleir, Ruth. (1984). *Science and gender: A critique of biology and its theories on women.* Elmsford, NY: Pergamon.

Boring, Edwin G. (1967). Titchener's experimentalists. *Journal of the History of the Behavioral Sciences, 3,* 315–325.

Bowles, Gloria. (1984). The use of hermeneutics for feminist scholarship. *Women's Studies International Forum, 7,* 185–188.

Brodsky, Annette A., Nevill, Dorothy, & Kimmel, Ellen. (1976). A progress report on the Visiting Woman Psychologist Program. *Professional Psychology, 7*(20), 214–221.

Bryan, Alice I., & Boring, Edwin G. (1947). Women in American psychology: Factors affecting their careers. *American Psychologist, 2,* 3–20.

Buss, Alan R. (1978). The structure of psychological revolutions. *Journal of the History of the Behavioral Sciences, 14,* 57–64.

Cattell, James M. (1909). The school and the family. *Popular Science Monthly, 74, 74,* 91–92.

Clarke, Edward H. (1873). *Sex and education: Or, a fair chance for the girls.* Boston: J. R. Osgood.

Crawford, Mary, & Maracek, Jeanne. (1989). Psychology reconstructs the female, 1968–1988. *Psychology of Women Quarterly, 13,* 147–165.

Darwin, Charles. (1871). *The descent of man and selection in relation to sex.* London: John Murray.

Delamont, Sara, & Duffin, Lorna. (Eds.). (1978). *The nineteenth-century woman.* New York: Barnes & Noble.

Diehl, Lesley A. (1986). The paradox of G. Stanley Hall: Foe of co-education and educator of women. *American Psychologist, 41*(8), 868–878.

Female orators. (1938). *The Mothers Magazine,* VI, p. 27.

Fine, Michelle. (1985). Reflections on a feminist psychology of women. *Psychology of Women Quarterly, 9,* 167–183.

Furumoto, Laurel. (1987). On the margins: Women and the professionalization of psychology in the United States, 1890–1940. In Mitchell Ash & William Woodward (Eds.), *Psychology in twentieth century thought and society* (pp. 93–113). Cambridge: Cambridge University Press.

Furumoto, Laurel. (1988a). Shared knowledge: The experimentalists 1904–1929. In Jill G. Morawski (Ed.), *The risk of experimentalism in American psychology* (pp. 94–113). New Haven, CT: Yale University Press.

Furumoto, Laurel, (1988b, August). *The new history of psychology.* G. Stanley Hall Lecture, American Psychological Association, Atlanta, GA.

Gergen, Kenneth J. (1985). The social constructionist movement in psychology. *American Psychologist, 40,* 266–275.

Grant, Allen. (1889). Woman's place in nature. *Forum, 7,* 258–263.

Hall, G. Stanley, (1903). Coeducation in the high school. *Proceedings of the National Education Association,* 446–460.

Hall, G. Stanley, (1906). The question of coeducation. *Munsey's Magazine, 34,* 588–592.

Harding, Sandra, & Hintikka, Merrill. (Eds.). (1983). *Discovering reality: Feminist perspectives on metaphysics, epistemology, methodology and the philosophy of science.* Boston, MA: D. Reidel.

Harding, Sandra, & O'Barr, Jean. (1987). *Sex and social inquiry.* Chicago: University of Chicago Press.

Hare-Mustin, Rachel T., & Maracek, Jeanne. (1988). The meaning of difference: Gender theory, post-modernism, and psychology. *American Psychologist, 43,* 455–464.

Harris, Barbara J. (1978). *Beyond her sphere: Women and the professions in American history.* Westport, CT: Greenwood.

Keller, Evelyn Fox. (1985). *Reflections on gender and science.* New Haven, CT: Yale University Press.

Koch, Sigmund. (1959). Epilogue. In Sigmund Koch (Ed.), *Psychology: The study of a science* (Vol III, pp. 729–788). New York: McGraw-Hill.

Kuhn, Thomas S. (1970). *The structure of scientific revolutions* (2nd ed.). Chicago: University of Chicago Press.

Langland, Elizabeth, & Gove, Walter. (Eds.). (1981). *A feminist perspective in the academy: The difference it makes.* Chicago: University of Chicago Press.

Lerner, Gerda. (1979). *The majority finds its past: Placing women in history.* New York: Oxford University Press.

Lincoln, Yvonna, & Guba, Egon. (1985). *Naturalistic inquiry.* Beverly Hills, CA: Sage.

Lott, Bernice. (1985). The potential enrichment of social/personality psychology through feminist research and vice versa. *American Psychologist, 40,* 155–164.

Lykes, M. Brinton, & Stewart, Abigail J. (1986). Evaluating the feminist challenge to research in personality and social psychology: 1963–1983. *Psychology of Women Quarterly, 10,* 393–412.

Mednick, Martha T. (1989). On the politics of psychological constructs: Stop the bandwagon, I want to get off. *American Psychologist, 44,* 1118–1123.

Morawski, Jill G. (1988). Impossible experiments and practical constructions: The social bases of psychologists' work. In Jill G. Morawski (Ed.), *The rise of experimentalism in American psychology* (pp. 72–93). New Haven, CT: Yale University Press.

Nowell-Smith, P. H. (1977). The constructionist theory of history. *History & Theory, Studies in the Philosophy of History, 16,* 1–28.

O'Connell, Agnes N., & Russo, Nancy F. (Eds.). (1980). Eminent women in psychology: Models of achievement. *Psychology of Women Quarterly, 5* [Special Issue].

O'Connell, Agnes N., & Russo, Nancy Felipe. (1983). *Models of achievement: Reflections of eminent women in psychology.* New York: Columbia University Press.

O'Connell, Agnes N., & Russo, Nancy F. (1988). *Models of achievement: Reflections of eminent women in psychology* (Vol. II). Hillsdale, NJ: Erlbaum.

Rosenberg, Rosalind. (1982). *Beyond separate spheres: Intellectual roots of modern feminism.* New Haven, CT: Yale University Press.

Rossiter, Margaret W. (1982). *Women scientists in America Struggles and strategies to 1940.* Baltimore, MD: The Johns Hopkins University Press.

Scarborough, Elizabeth, & Furumoto, Laurel. (1987). *Untold lives: The first generation of America women psychologists.* New York: Columbia University Press.

Scarr, Sandra. (1985). Constructing psychology: Making facts and fables for our time. *American Psychologist, 40,* 499–512.

Shields, Stephanie A. (1975). Functionalism, Darwinism and the psychology of women: A study in social myth. *American Psychologist, 30,* 739–753.

Shields, Stephanie A., & Mallory, Mary E. (1987). Leta Stetter Hollingworth speaks on ''Columbia's Legacy.'' *Psychology of Women Quarterly, 11,* 285–300.

Simeone, Angela. (1987). *Academic women: Working towards equality.* South Hadley, MA: Bergin & Garvey.

Solomon, Barbara Miller. (1985). *In the company of educated women: A history of women and higher education in America.* New Haven, CT: Yale University Press.

Spencer, Herbert. (1867). *The principles of biology.* New York: Appleton.

Spencer, Herbert. (1874). Psychology of the sexes. *Popular Science Monthly, 4,* 32.

Stevens, Gwendolyn, & Gardner, Sheldon. (1982). *The women of psychology* (Vols. I & II). Cambridge, MA: Schenkman.

Thorndike, Edward L. (1906). Sex in education. *Bookman, 23,* 211–214.

Unger, Rhoda K. (1983). Through the looking glass: No wonderland yet! (The reciprocal relationship between methodology and models of reality). *Psychology of Women Quarterly, 8,* 9–32.

Unger, Rhoda K. (1985). Epistemological consistency and its scientific implications. *American Psychologist, 40,* 1413–1414.

Wallston, Barbara S., & Grady, Kathleen. (1985). Integrating the feminist critique and the crisis in social psychology: Another look at research methods. In Virgina E. O'Leary, Rhoda K. Unger, & Barbara S. Wallston (Eds.), *Women, gender, and social psychology* (pp. 7–33). Hillsdale, NJ: Erlbaum.

Welter, Barbara. (1966). The cult of true womanhood. *American Quarterly. 18,* 151–174.

Wittig, Michele A. (1985). Metatheoretical dilemmas in the psychology of gender. *American Psychologist, 40,* 800–811.

STUDENT EVALUATION OF READINGS

The following items are intended to provide feedback about the value of the *Introduction* and the readings in *Section I* in achieving the book's desired goal: creating a framework for the meaningful inclusion of women in the history of psychology. Your replies to these questions will serve two purposes: First, they will provide information about the usefulness of the articles; and second, they will give your instructor an idea of how well the articles are understood and received by students. Your answers will help your instructor to make optimal use of this book, and will also serve future students by guiding revisions of the book. Your thoughtful replies will be appreciated.

1. **Please rate each of the readings from 1 to 5 on the following dimensions:**
   (1 = poor; 3 = average; 5 = exceptional)

		Intro.	Furumoto	Lerner	Bohan
a.	Clearly written, readable	____	____	____	____
b.	Presents new information I'd not found elsewhere	____	____	____	____
c.	Stimulated my interest in topics it raised	____	____	____	____
d.	Caused me to re-think ideas I'd held previously	____	____	____	____

2. **To what extent do these readings fulfill the following aims:** (1 = not helpful; 3 = moderately helpful; 5 = extremely helpful)

		Intro.	Furumoto	Lerner	Bohan
a.	Helps to clarify how histories are shaped by context	____	____	____	____
b.	Helps to explain women's invisibility in histories of psychology	____	____	____	____
c.	Is helpful as a basis for re-placing women in psychology	____	____	____	____

3. **Briefly explain what you believe is the strongest point of each reading:**

   Introduction:

   Furumoto:

   Lerner:

   Bohan:

4. **Briefly explain what you believe is the greatest shortcoming of each reading:**

Introduction:

Furumoto:

Lerner:

Bohan:

5. **Are there any areas where you see conflicts or disagreements between readings and material presented in your text or in lectures?**

6. **Do you have any other comments about these readings?**

Review Questions

The following questions are intended to stimulate thought and discussion about the issues raised by readings in the *Introduction* and *Section I*. The questions are not mutually exclusive, so that it is possible to approach a given theme from several directions. The student who thoroughly answers all of these questions will be well-prepared to discuss and apply the notions raised here.

I. Discuss why it is important to incorporate women and their work into psychology's histories.

II. Define the following terms, and given an illustration of each from the readings included here or from your text:
   a. epistemology
   b. Zeitgeist
   c. historiography
   d. paradigm
   e. sociology of knowledge
   f. meritocracy, the myth of meritocracy

III. On social constructionism and women's place in psychology:
   a. What does it mean to say that "knowledge" is constructed?
   b. How does this contrast with our traditional view of knowledge and how it is attained?
   c. How does the constructionist view apply to history?
   d. How can a constructionist perspective on knowledge and history serve as a basis for re-placing women in psychology's histories?

IV. Regarding re-constructing psychology to re-place women:
   a. What factors have made women's work largely invisible in traditional histories of psychology?
   b. How do the factors discussed in "a" reflect:
      1) the social construction of gender
      2) the construction (i.e., the self-definition) or psychology—its subject matter, acceptable methods, the criteria for merit, etc?

V. Furumoto argues for the need for a different approach to doing history in psychology.
   a. What does she believe are the deficits in traditional histories? What examples of such problems can you detect in your text or in other histories you have read?
   b. What are the elements of Furumoto's "new history?" Explain how this model might provide a basis for overcoming the neglect of women and their work.

VI. Lerner argues that history as traditionally written excludes women and is really a history of only a segment of humanity.
   a. Give an example of how traditional methods of researching and defining history might exclude women. How does this notion relate to the social construction of knowledge?

b. What does Lerner mean by "compensatory" and "contribution" history? What is her recommended approach to adding women?

c. How would this approach apply specifically to the neglect of women in psychology's histories?

VII. Furumoto, Lerner, and Bohan all argue that it is possible to view history differently and thereby integrate women.

a. What relationship do you see between Furumoto's "new history" and Lerner's transitional stage in the process of incorporating women into history?

b. Briefly summarize Bohan's synthesis of constructionism, "new history" (Furumoto), and "transitional" history (Lerner).

c. If we apply this (contextual) approach to the history of psychology in general (rather than women's place specifically), how would our histories be different? Select an item (a theory, a person, an event) from your text and explain how you would address it from a contextual stance.

Re-constructing the History of Psychology: Re-Placing Women

If we are to re-place women as visible participants in psychology's history, it is essential to look carefully at the contexts that have defined women's place to date. This analysis must deal with two constructions of "truth." On the one hand is the societal understanding (the social construction) of gender, of women's proper place in the scheme of things. This construction determines which activities, opportunities, work, goals are available to women. On the other hand is psychology's own self-definition, its collective agreement about the nature of the discipline, what is important to its understanding, and what should be granted recognition in its histories. Where these two constructions intersect, the construction of gender and the construction of psychology, we find women's place in psychology.

As you will learn, women in psychology have largely assumed the roles which the confluence of society's beliefs about gender and psychology's self-definition have granted them. These roles are generally invisible in traditional histories, for women's place has been in precisely those parts of psychology which do not mesh with the criteria for eminence and visibility. To incorporate these women into our histories will require that we challenge both constructions. We must take into account the constructions of gender and its impact on women's experience. And we must take into account psychology's self-definition and its exclusionary implications.

Undertaking this re-constructive effort raises an intriguing question: What would the history of psychology look like if it were written in this way? What would we find if we re-viewed psychology's past, especially the place of women in that past, from this contextual perspective? The articles in this section address this question.

The first article in this section, by Stephanie Shields, represents a contextual analysis of a particular theme prevalent in early American psychology: the question of sex differences, often termed the "woman problem." In keeping with a "new history" approach to the topic, Shields goes beyond simply reporting the ideas of the time and the personages responsible for them. She looks further into societal beliefs (the construction of gender) and how such beliefs shaped the process and outcome even of supposedly objective and unbiased scientific work. Her discussion of how these ideas coincided with then-dominant interpretations of Darwin's work also illustrates the directing and constraining impact of paradigms.

The other two articles both present a contextual analysis of the lives and work of important women in psychology's history, women whose work has been largely invisible to date. Furumoto and Scarborough analyze the experiences of several first generation American women psychologists, unravelling the societal and personal themes which shaped their participation in psychology. The article by Russo and Denmark undertakes a similar analysis of a broader historical spectrum, discussing how social and historical forces (both in society as a whole and in psychology in particular) have acted to define the paths that psychology's women would take. In addition, Russo and Denmark draw out in some detail the depth and scope of women's activities in and influence on psychology. In doing so, they illuminate important work which has traditionally gone unacknowledged in history and systems texts.

Russo and Denmark also point out that women (especially of late) have shaped as well as been shaped by the contexts of their work. This notion is clearly in keeping with the constructionist perspective, for the very presence and recognition of women changes the context of psychology and challenges its traditional self-definition. The final section of readings will address this theme more fully, asking what is the impact on psychology of women's growing visibility in the field.

Summary

The articles in this section represent applications of the constructionist view of knowledge to the specific question of women's position in psychology and in histories of the field. These readings demonstrate that the role of women in psychology has been and continues to be shaped by context. The interaction of the social construction of gender with psychology's definition of its domain and purpose has defined women's place in the discipline and has shaped history's recognition of women and their work. In the next section, we will turn to the question of how women's changing role in psychology has, in turn, contributed to a reconstruction of psychology and social institutions related to gender.

Stephanie A. Shields

Functionalism, Darwinism, and the Psychology of Women: *A Study in Social Myth**

T he psychology of women is acquiring the character of an academic entity as witnessed by the proliferation of research on sex differences, the appearance of textbooks devoted to the psychology of women, and the formation of a separate APA division, Psychology of Women. Nevertheless, there is almost universal ignorance of the psychology of women as it existed prior to its incorporation into psychoanalytic theory. If the maxim "A nation without a history is like a man without a memory" can be applied, then it would behoove the amnesiacs interested in female psychology to investigate its pre-Freudian past.

This article focuses on one period of that past (from the latter half of the 19th century to the first third of the 20th) in order to clarify the important issues of the time and trace their development to the position they occupy in current psychological theory.

Stephanie Shields, "Functionalism, Darwinism and the psychology of women: A study in social myth." *American Psychologist*, 1975, *30*, pp. 739–753. Copyright (c) 1975 by the American Psychological Association. Reprinted by permission.

*The author would like to thank Judith Abplanalp, Carolyn Sherif, and Dale Harris for helpful comments concerning earlier drafts of this manuscript.

Requests for reprints should be sent to Stephanie Shields, Department of Psychology, Pennsylvania State University, University Park, Pennsylvania 16802.

Even a limited overview leads the reader to appreciate Helen Thompson Woolley's (1910) early appraisal of the quality of the research on sex differences:

> There is perhaps no field aspiring to be scientific where flagrant personal bias, logic martyred in the cause of supporting a prejudice, unfounded assertions, and even sentimental rot and drivel, have run riot to such an extent as here. (p. 340)

The Functionalist Milieu

Although the nature of woman had been an academic and social concern of philosopher psychologists throughout the ages, formal psychology (its inception usually dated 1879) was relatively slow to take up the topic of female psychology. The "woman question" was a social one, and social problems did not fall within the sharply defined limits of Wundt's "new" psychology. The business of psychology was the description of the "generalized adult mind," and it is not at all clear whether "adult" was meant to include both sexes. When the students of German psychology did venture outside of the laboratory, however, there is no evidence that they were sympathetic to those defending the equality of male and female ability (cf. Wundt, 1901).

It was the functionalist movement in the United States that fostered academic psychology's study of sex differences and, by extension, a prototypic psychology of women. The incorporation of evolutionary theory into the practice of psychology made the study of the female legitimate, if not imperative. It would be incorrect to assume that the psychology of women existed as a separate specialty within the discipline. The female was discussed only in relation to the male, and the function of the female was thought to be distinctly different from and complementary to the function of the male. The leitmotif of evolutionary theory as it came to be applied to the social sciences was the evolutionary supremacy of the Caucasian male. The notion of the supplementary, subordinate role of the female was ancillary to the development of that theme.

The influence of evolutionary theory on the psychology of women can be traced along two major conceptual lines: (a) by emphasizing the biological foundations of temperament, evolutionary theory led to serious academic discussion of maternal instinct (as one facet of the general topic of instinct); and (b) by proving a theoretical justification of the study of individual differences, evolutionary theory opened the door to the study of sex differences in sensory, motor, and intellectual abilities. As a whole, the concept of evolution with its concomitant emphasis on biological determinism provided ample "scientific" reason for cataloging the "innate" differences in male and female nature.

This article examines three topics that were of special significance to the psychology of women during the functionalist era: (a) structural differences in the brains of males and females and the implications of these differences for intelligence and temperament, (b) the hypothesis of greater male variability and its relation to social and educational issues, and (c) maternal instinct and its meaning for a psychology of female "nature." As the functionalist paradigm gave way to behaviorism and psychoanalytic theory, the definition and "meaning" of each of these issues changed to fit the times. When issues faded in importance, it was not because they were resolved but because they ceased to serve as viable scientific milieu. As the times change, so must the myths change.

The Female Brain

The topic of female intelligence came to 19th-century psychology via phrenology and the neuroanatomists. Philosophers of the time (e.g., Hegel, Kant, Schopenhauer) had demonstrated, to their satisfaction, the justice of woman's subordinate social position, and it was left to the men of science to discover the particular physiological determinants of female inadequacy. In earlier periods, woman's inferiority had been defined as a general "state" intimately related to the absence of qualities that would have rendered her a male and to the presence of reproductive equipment that destined her to be female. For centuries the mode of Eve's creation and her greater guilt for the fall from grace had been credited as the cause of woman's imperfect nature, but this was not an adequate explanation in a scientific age. Thus, science sought explanations for female inferiority that were more in keeping with contemporary scientific philosophy.

Although it had long been believed that the brain was the chief organ of the mind, the comparison of male and female mental powers traditionally included only allusions to vague "imperfections" of the female brain. More precise definition of the sites of these imperfections awaited the advancement of the concept of cortical localization of function. Then, as finer distinctions of functional areas were noted, there was a parallel recognition of the differences between those sites as they appeared in each sex.

At the beginning of the 19th century, the slowly increasing interest in the cerebral gyri rapidly gathered momentum with the popularization of phrenology. Introduced by Franz Joseph Gall, "cranioscopy," as he preferred to call it, postulated that the seat of various mental and moral faculties was located in specific areas of the brain's surface such that a surfeit or deficiency could be detected by an external examination of the cranium. Phrenology provided the first objective method for determining the neurological foundation of sex differences in intelligence and temperament that had long been promulgated. Once investigation of brain structure had begun, it was fully anticipated that visible sex differences would be found: Did not the difference between the sexes pervade every other aspect of physique and physiological function? Because physical differences were so obvious in every other organ of the body, it was unthinkable that the brain could have escaped the stamp of sex.

Gall was convinced that he could, from gross anatomical observation, discriminate between male and female brains, claiming that "if there had been presented to him in water, the fresh brains of two adult animals of any species, one male and the other female, he could have distinguished the two sexes" (Walker, 1850, p. 317). Gall's student and colleague, Johann Spurzheim, elaborated on this basic distinction by noting that the frontal lobes were less developed in females, "the organs of the perceptive faculties being commonly larger than those of the reflective powers." Gall also observed sex differences in the nervous tissue itself, "confirming" Malebranche's belief that the female "cerebral fibre" is softer than that of the male, and that it is also "slender and long rather than thick" (Walker, 1850, p. 318). Spurzheim also listed the cerebral "organs" whose appearance differed commonly in males and females: females tended to have the areas devoted to philoprogenetiveness and other "tender" traits most prominent, while in males, areas of aggressiveness and constructiveness dominated. Even though cranioscopy did not survive as a valid system of describing cortical function, the practice of comparing the appearance of all or part of the brain for anatomical evidence of quality of function remained one of the most popular means of providing proof of female mental inferiority. Most comparisons used adult human brains, but with the rise of evolutionary theory, increasing emphasis was placed on the value of developmental and cross-species comparisons. The argument for female mental inferiority took two forms: some argued that quality of intellect was proportional to absolute or relative brain size; others, more in the tradition of cortical localization, contended that the presence of certain mental qualities was dependent upon the development of corresponding brain centers.

The measurement of cranial capacity had long been in vogue as one method of determining intellectual ability. That women had smaller heads than men was taken by some as clear proof of a real disparity between male and female intelligence. The consistently smaller brain size of the female was cited as another anatomical indicator it is functional inferiority. More brain necessarily meant better brain; the exception only proved this rule. Alexander Bain (1875) was among those who believe that the smaller absolute brain size of females accounted for a lesser mental ability. George Romanes (1887) enumerated the "secondary sex characteristics" of mental abilities attributable to brain size. The smaller brain of women was directly responsible for their mental inferiority, which "displays itself most conspicuously in a comparative absence of originality, and this more especially in the higher levels of intellectual work" (p. 655). He, like many, allowed that women were to some degree compensated for intellectual inferiority by a superiority of instinct and perceptual ability. These advantages carried with them the germ of female failure, however, by making women more subject to emotionality.

Proof of the male's absolute brain-size superiority was not enough to secure his position of intellectual superiority, since greater height and weight tended to offset the brain-size advantage. Reams of paper were, therefore, dedicated to the search for the most "appropriate" relative measures, but results were equivocal: if the ratio of brain weight to body weight is considered, it is found that women possess a proportionately larger brain than men; if the ratio of brain surface to body surface is computed, it is found to favor men. That some of the ratios "favored" males while others "favored" females led some canny souls to conclude that there was no legitimate solution to the problem. That they had ever hoped for a solution seems remarkable; estimates of brain size from cranial capacity involved a large margin of error because brains differing as much as 15% have been found in heads of the same size (Elliott, 1969, p. 316).

Hughlings Jackson has been credited as the first to regard the frontal cortex as the repository of the highest mental capacities, but the notion must have held popular credence as early as the 1850s because that period saw sporadic references to the comparative development of the frontal lobes in men and women. Once the function of the frontal lobes had been established, many researchers reported finding that the male possessed noticeably larger and more well-developed frontal lobes than females. The neuroanatomist Hischke came to the conclusion in 1854 that woman is *homo parietalis* while man is *homo frontalis* (Ellis, 1934). Likewise, Rudinger in 1877 found the frontal lobes of man in every way more extensive than those of women, and reported that these sex differences were evident even in the unborn fetus (Mobius, 1901).

At the turn of the century, the parietal lobes (rather than the frontal lobes) came to be regarded by some as the seat of intellect, and the necessary sex difference in parietal development was duly corroborated by the neuroanatomists. The change in cerebral hierarchy involved a bit of revisionism:

> the frontal region is not, as has been supposed smaller in woman, but rather larger relatively. . . . But the parietal lobe is somewhat smaller, [furthermore,] a preponderance of the frontal region does not imply intellectual superiority . . . the parietal region is really the more important. (Patrick, 1895, p. 212)

Once beliefs regarding the relative importance of the frontal and parietal lobes had shifted, it became critical to reestablish congruence between neuroanatomical findings and accepted sex differences. Among those findings parietal predominance in men were Paul Broca,[1] Theodore Meynert, and the German Rudinger (see Ellis, 1934, p. 217).

Other neuroanatomical "deficiencies" of the female were found in (a) the area of the corpus callosum, (b) the complexity of the gyri and sulci, (c) the conformation of gyri and sulci, and (d) the rate of development of the cortex of the fetus (Woolley, 1910, p. 335). Franklin Mall (1909) objected to the use of faulty research methods that

---

1. Ellis (1934) claimed that Broca's opinion changed over time. Broca

> became inclined to think that it [the hypothesized male superiority of intellect] was merely a matter of education—of muscular . . . not merely mental, education—and he thought that if left to their spontaneous impulses men and women would tend to resemble each other, as happens in the savage condition. (p. 222)

gave spurious differences the appearance of being real. Among the most serious errors he noted was the practice of making observations with a knowledge of the sex of the brain under consideration.

The debate concerning the importance of brain size and anatomy as indicators of intelligence diminished somewhat with the development of mental tests; nevertheless, the brain-size difference was a phenomenon that many felt obligated to interpret. Max Meyer (1921) attempted to settle the matter by examining the various measures of relative difference that had been employed. After finding these methods far too equivocal, he concluded, in the best behavioristic terms, that sex differences in intelligence were simply "accidents of habits acquired."

Characteristics of the female brain were thought not simply to render women less intelligent but also to allow more "primitive" parts of human nature to be expressed in her personality. Instinct was thought to dominate woman, as did her emotions, and the resulting "affectability" was considered woman's greatest weakness, the reason for her inevitable failure. Affectability was typically defined as a general state, the manifestation of instinctive and emotional predispositions that in men were kept in check by a superior intellect.[2]

One of the most virulent critics of woman was the German physiologist Paul Mobius (1901), who argued that her mental incapacity was a necessary condition for the survival of the race. Instinct rendered her easily led and easily pleased, so much the better for her to give her all to bearing and rearing children. The dependence of woman also extracted a high price from man:

> All progress is due to man. Therefore the woman is like a dead weight on him, she prevents much restlessness and meddlesome inquisitiveness, but she also restrains him from noble actions, for she is unable to distinguish good from evil. (p. 629)

Mobius observed that woman was essentially unable to think independently, had strong inclinations to be mean and untrustworthy, and spent a good deal of her time in an emotionally unbalanced state. From this he was forced to conclude that "If woman was not physically and mentally weak, if she was not as a rule rendered harmless by circumstances, she would be extremely dangerous (Mobius, 1901, p. 630). Diatribes of this nature were relatively common German importations; woman's severest critics in this country seldom achieved a similar level of acerbity. Mobius and his ilk (e.g., Weininger, 1906) were highly publicized and widely read in the United States, and not a little of their vituperation crept into serious scientific discussions of woman's nature. For example, Porteus and Babcock (1926) resurrected the brain-size issue, discounting the importance of size to intelligence and instead associating it with the "maturing of other powers." Males, because of their larger brains would be more highly endowed with these "other powers," and so more competent and achiev-

---

2. Burt and Moore (1912, p. 385), inspired by contemporary theories of cortical localization of function, proposed a neurological theory of female affectability. On the basis of the popular belief that the thalamus was "the center for the natural expression of the emotions" while "control of movements and the association of ideas" was localized in the cortex and the common assumption that the male was more inclined to be intellectual and rational and the female more passionate and emotional, they concluded that in the adult male the cortex would tend to be "more completely organized," while in the adult female "the thalamus tends to appear more completely organized." They came to the general conclusion that "the mental life of man is predominantly cortical; that of woman predominantly thalamic."

ing. Proposals such as these which were less obviously biased than those of Mobius, Weininger, and others, fit more easily into the current social value system and so were more easily assimilated as "good science" (cf. Allen, 1927, p. 294).

The Variability Hypothesis

The first systematic treatment of individual differences in intelligence appeared in 1575. Juan Huarte attributed sex differences in intelligence to the different humoral qualities that characterized each sex, a notion that had been popular in Western thought since ancient Greece. Heat and dryness were characteristic of the male principle, while moisture and coolness were female attributes. Because dryness of spirit was necessary for intelligence, males naturally possessed greater "wit." The maintenance of dryness and heat was the function of the testicles, and Huarte (1959) noted that if a man were castrated the effects were the same "as if he had received some notable dammage in his very braine" (p. 279). Because the principles necessary for cleverness were only possessed by males, it behooved parents to conduct their lifestyle, diet, and sexual intercourse in such a manner as to insure the conception of male. The humoral theory of sex differences was widely accepted through the 17th century, but with the advent of more sophisticated notions of anatomy and physiology, it was replaced by other, more specific, theories of female mental defect: the lesser size and hypothesized simpleness of the female brain, affectability as the source of inferiority, and complementarity of abilities in male and female. It was the developing evolutionary theory that provided an overall explanation for why these sex differences existed and why they were necessary for the survival of the race.

The theory of evolution as proposed by Darwin had little to say regarding the intellectual capacity of either sex. It was in Francis Galton's (Charles Darwin's cousin) anthropometric laboratory that the investigation of intellectual differences took an empirical form (Galton, 1907). The major conclusion to come from Galton's research was that women tend in all their capacities to be inferior to men. He looked to common experience for confirmation, reasoning that:

> If the sensitivity of women were superior to that of men, the self interest of merchants would lead to their being always employed; but as the reverse is the case, the opposite supposition is likely to be the true one. (pp. 20–21).

This form of logic—women have not excelled, therefore they cannot excel—was often used to support arguments denigrating female intellectual ability. The fact of the comparative rarity of female social achievement was also used as "evidence" in what was later to become a widely debated issue concerning the range of female ability.

Prior to the formulation of evolutionary theory, there had been little concern with whether deviation from the average or "normal" occurred more frequently in either sex. One of the first serious discussions of the topic appeared in the early 19th century when the anatomist Meckel concluded on pathological grounds that the human female showed greater variability than the human male. He reasoned that because man is the superior animal and variability a sign of inferiority, this conclusion was justified (in Ellis, 1903, p. 237). The matter was left at that until 1871. At that time Darwin took up the question of variability in *The Descent of Man* while attempting to explain how it could be that in many species males had developed greatly modified secondary sexual characteristics while females of the same species had not. He determined that this was originally caused by the males' greater activity and "stronger passions" that were in turn more likely (he believed) to be transmitted to male offspring. Because the females would prefer to mate with the strong and passionate, sexual selection would insure the survival of those traits. A tendency toward greater variation per se was not thought to be responsible for the appearance of unusual characteristics, but "development of such characters would be much aided, if the males were more liable to vary than the females" (Darwin, 1922, p. 344). To support this hypothesis of greater male variability, he cited recent data obtained by anatomists and biologists that seemed to confirm the relatively more frequent occurrence of physical anomaly among males.

Because variation from the norm was already accepted as the mechanism of evolutionary progress (survival and transmission of adaptive variations) and because it seemed that the male was the more variable sex, it soon was universally concluded that the male is the progressive element in the species. Variation for its own sake took on a positive value because greatness, whether of an individual or a society, could not be achieved without variation. Once deviation from the norm became legitimized by evolutionary theory, the hypothesis of greater male variability became a convenient explanation for a number of observed sex differences, among them the greater frequency with which men achieved "eminence." By the 1890s it was popularly believed that greater male variability was a principle that held true, not only for physical traits but for mental abilities as well:

> That men should have greater cerebral variability and therefore more originality, while women have greater stability and therefore more "common sense," are facts both consistent with the general theory of sex and verifiable in common experience. (Geddes & Thomson, 1890, p. 271)

Havelock Ellis (1894), an influential sexologist and social philosopher, brought the variability hypothesis to the attention of psychologists in the first edition of *Man and Woman*. After examining anatomical and pathological data that indicated a greater male *variational tendency* (Ellis felt this term was less ambiguous than *variability*), he examined the evidence germane to a discussion of range of intellectual ability. After noting that there were more men than women in homes for the mentally deficient, which indicated a higher incidence of retardation among males, and that there were more men than women on the roles of the eminent, which indicated a higher incidence of genius among males, he concluded that greater male variability probably held for all qualities of character and ability. Ellis (1903) particularly emphasized the wide social and educational significance of the phenomenon, claiming that greater male variability was "a fact which has affected the whole of our human civilization" (p. 238), particularly through the production of men of genius. Ellis (1934) was also adamant that the female's tendency toward the average did not necessarily imply inferiority of talent; rather, it simply limited her expertise to "the sphere of concrete practical life" (p. 436).

The variability hypothesis was almost immediately challenged as a "pseudo-scientific superstition" by the statistician Karl Pearson (1897). Though not a feminist, Pearson firmly believed that the "woman question" deserved impartial, scientific study. He challenged the idea of greater male variability primarily because he thought it contrary to the fact and theory of evolution and natural selection. According to evolutionary theory (Pearson, 1897), "the more intense the struggle the less is the variability, the more nearly are individuals forced to approach the type fittest to their surroundings, if they are to survive" (p. 258). In a "civilized" community one would expect that because men have a "harder battle for life," and difference in variation should favor women. He took Ellis to task by arguing it was (a) meaningless to consider secondary sex characteristics (as Ellis had done) and, likewise, (b) foolish to contrast the sexes on the basis of abnormalities (as Ellis had done). By redefining the problem and the means for its solution, he was able to dismiss the entire corpus of data that had been amassed: "the whole trend of investigations concerning the relative variability of men and women up to the present seems to be erroneous" (Pearson, 1897, p. 261). Confining his measurements to "normal variations in organs or characteristics not of a secondary sexual character," he assembled anthropometric data on various races, from Neolithic skeletons to modern French peasants. He also challenged the adequacy of statistical comparison of only the extremes of the distribution, preferring to base his contrasts on the dispersion of measures around the mean. Finding a slight tendency toward greater female variability, he concluded that the variability hypothesis as stated remained a "quite unproven principle."

Ellis countered Pearson in a lengthy article, one more vicious than that ordinarily due an intellectual affront.[3] Pearson's greatest sins (according to Ellis) were his failure to define "variability" and his measurement of characteristics that were highly subject to environmental influence. Ellis, of course, overlooked his own failure to define variability and his inclusion of environmentally altered evidence.

In the United States the variability hypothesis naturally found expression in the new testing movement, its proponents borrowing liberally from the theory of Ellis and the statistical technique of Pearson. The favor that was typically afforded the hypoth-

esis did not stem from intellectual commitment to the scientific validity of the proposal as much as it did from personal commitment to the social desirability of its acceptance. The variability hypothesis was most often thought of in terms of its several corollaries: (a) genius (seldom, and then poorly, defined) is a peculiarly male trait; (b) men of genius naturally gravitate to positions of power and prestige (i.e., achieve eminence) by virtue of their talent; (c) an equally high ability level should not be expected of females: and (d) the education of women should, therefore, be

3. One of Ellis's biographers (Calder-Marshall, 1959, pp. 97–98) has suggested that Ellis was "wildly jealous" of Karl Pearson's influence on Olive Schreiner, the controversial South African writer. Schreiner first met Pearson in 1885, over a year after she had met Ellis, and according to Calder-Marshall "was vastly attracted to him [Pearson] in what she considered to be a selfless Hintonian sense. . . . She regarded him as a brilliant young man, dying of tuberculosis, whose few remaining years it was here selfless duty to solace" (Pearson died in 1936). Calder-Marshall summed up the triangle in few, but insinuating, phrases:

> Exactly what was happening between Karl Pearson and Olive Schreiner during these months [August 1885–December 1886] is a matter more for any future biographer of Olive Schreiner . . . it is enough to know that Olive did her best to remain loyal to both her friends without telling too many lies, and that while Olive remained the most important person in Havelock's life, the most important person in Olive's was Karl Pearson from the time she first met him to a considerable time after she left England. (p. 98)

Ellis's rivalry with Pearson could explain his bitter and supercilious treatment of Pearson's venture into "variational tendency," since Ellis was not one to easily accept an assault on his ego. For his part Pearson "despised the Hinton group, including Ellis. He thought they were flabby-minded, unhealthy and immoral" (p. 97). But these opinions, while possibly influencing him to write on variation originally, did not intrude upon a fair-minded scientific discussion of the matter.

consonant with their special talents and special place in society as wives and mothers.

Woman's Education

The "appropriate" education for women had been at issue since the Renaissance, and the implications of the variability hypothesis favored those who have been arguing for a separate female education. Late in the 18th century, Mary Wollstonecraft Godwin (1759–1797) questioned the "natural" roles of each sex, contending that for both the ultimate goal was the same: "the first object of laudable ambition is to obtain a character as a human being, regardless of the distinction of sex" (Wollstonecraft, 1955, p. 5). Without education, she felt, women could not contribute to social progress as mature individuals, and this would be a tragic loss to the community. Though not the first to recognize the social restrictions arbitrarily placed on women, she was the first to hold those restrictions as directly responsible for the purported "defective nature" of women. She emphasized that women had never truly been given an equal chance to prove or disprove their merits. Seventy years later, John Stuart Mill (1955) also took up the cause of women's education, seeing it as one positive action to be taken in the direction of correcting the unjust social subordination of women. He felt that what appeared as woman's intellectual inferiority was actually no more than the effort to maintain the passive-dependent role relationship with man, her means of support:

> When we put together three things— first, the natural attraction between the sexes; secondly, the wife's entire dependence on the husband . . . and lastly, that the principal object of human pursuit, consideration, and all objects of social ambition, can in general be sought or obtained by her only

through him, it would be a miracle if the object of being attractive to men had not become the polar star of feminine education and formation of character. (pp. 232–233)[4]

Although Mill objected to fostering passivity and dependency in girls, other educators felt that this was precisely their duty. One of the more influential of the 19th century, Hannah More, rejected outright the proposal that women should share the same type of education as men, because "the chief end to be proposed in cultivating the understanding of women" was "to qualify them for the practical purposes of life" (see Smith, 1970. p. 101). To set one's sights on other than harmonious domesticity was to defy the natural order. Her readers were advised to be excellent women rather than indifferent men; to follow the "plain path which Providence has obviously marked out to the sex . . . rather than . . . stray awkwardly, unbecomingly, and unsuccessfully, in a forbidden road" (Smith, 1970, pp. 100–101). Her values were consonant with those held by most of the middle class, and so her *Strictures on the Modern System of Female*

4. One of the severest critics of Mills' defense of women was Sigmund Freud. He felt Mill's propositions were in direct contradiction to woman's "true" nature:

> It is really a stillborn thought to send women into the struggle for existence exactly as men. . . . I believe that all reforming action in law and education would break down in front of the fact that, long before the age at which a man can earn a position in society, Nature has determined woman's destiny through beauty, charm, and sweetness. Law and custom have much to give women that has been withheld from them, but the position of women will surely be what it is: in youth an adored darling and in mature years a loved wife. (quoted in Reeves, 1971, pp. 163–164)

Education (More, 1800) enjoyed widespread popularity for some time.

By the latter part of the century, the question had turned from whether girls should be educated like boys to how much they should be educated like boys. With the shift in emphasis came the question of coeducation. One of the strongest objections to coeducation in adolescence was the threat it posed to the "normalization" of the menstrual period. G. Stanley Hall (1906) waxed poetic on the issue.

> At a time when her whole future life depends upon normalizing the lunar month, is there not something not only unnatural and unhygienic, but a little monstrous, in daily school associations with boys, where she must suppress and conceal her instincts and feelings, at those times when her own promptings suggest withdrawal or stepping a little aside to let Lord Nature do his magnificent work of efflorescence. (p. 590)

Edward Clarke (see Sinclair, 1965, p. 123) had earlier elucidated the physiological reason for the restraint of girls from exertion in their studies: by forcing their brains to do work at puberty, they would use up blood later needed for menstruation.

Hall proposed an educational system for girls that would not only take into consideration their delicate physical nature but would also be tailored to prepare them for their special role in society. He feared that women's competition with men "in the world" would cause them to neglect their instinctive maternal urges and so bring about "race suicide." Because the glory of the female lay in motherhood, Hall believed that all educational and social institutions should be structured with that end in mind. Domestic arts would therefore be emphasized in special schools for adolescent girls, and disciplines such as philosophy, chemistry, and mathematics would be treated only superficially. If a girl had a notion to stay in the "male" system, she should be able to but, Hall warned, such a woman selfishly interested in self-fulfillment would also be less likely to bear children and so be confined to an "agamic" life, thus failing to reproduce those very qualities that made her strong (Hall, 1918).

Throughout Hall's panegyric upon the beauties of female domestic education, there runs an undercurrent of the *real* threat that he perceived in coeducation, and that was the "feminization" of the American male. David Starr Jordan (1902) shared this objection but felt that coeducation would nevertheless make young men more "civilized" and young women less frivolous, tempering their natural pubescent inclinations. He was no champion of female ability though, stressing that women "on the whole, lack originality" (p. 100). The educated woman, he said, "is likely to master technic rather than art; method, rather than substance. She may know a good deal, but she can do nothing" (p. 101). In spite of this, he did assert that their training is just as serious and important as that of men. His position strongly favored the notion that the smaller range of female ability was the cause of lackluster female academic performance.

The issue of coeducation was not easily settled, and even as late as 1935, one finds debates over its relative merits (*Encyclopedia of the Social Sciences,* 1935, pp. 614–617).

The Biological Biases of Sex Differences

The variability hypothesis was compatible not only with prevailing attitudes concerning the appropriate form of female education but also with a highly popular theory of the biological complementarity of the sexes. The main tenet of Geddes and Thomson's (1890) theory was that males are primarily "catabolic," females "anabolic." From this difference in metabolism, all other sex differences in physical, intellectual, and emotional makeup were derived. The male was more agile, creative, and variable; the female was truer to the species type and therefore, in all respects, less variable. The conservatism of the female insured the continuity of the species. The authors stressed the metabolic antecedents of female conservatism and male differentiation rather than variational tendency per se, and also put emphasis on the complementarity of the two natures:

The feminine passivity is expressed in greater patience, more open-mindedness, greater appreciation of subtle details and consequently what we call more rapid intuition. The masculine activity lends a greater power of maximum effort, of scientific insight, or cerebral experiment with impressions, and is associated with an unobservant or impatient disregard of minute details, but with a more stronger grasp of generalities. (p. 271)

The presentation of evolutionary theory anchored in yin-yang concepts of function represents the most positive evaluation of the female sex offered by 19th-century science. Whatever woman's shortcomings, they were necessary to complete her nature, which itself was necessary to complete man's: "Man thinks more, woman feels more. He discovers more, but remembers less: she is more receptive, and less forgetful" (Geddes & Thomson, 1890, p. 271).

Variability and the Testing Movement

Helen Thompson (later Woolley) put Geddes and Thomson's and other theories of sex dif-

ferences in ability to what she felt was a crucial experimental test (see Thompson, 1903). Twenty-five men and 25 women participated in nearly 20 hours of individual testing of their intellectual, motor, and sensory abilities. Of more importance than her experimental results (whether men or women can tap a telegraph key more times per minute has lost its significance to psychology) was her discussion of the implications of the resulting negligible differences for current theories of sex differences. She was especially critical of the mass of inconsistencies inherent in contemporary biological theories:

Women are said to represent concentration, patience, and stability in emotional life. One might logically conclude that prolonged concentration of attention and unbiased generalization would be their intellectual characteristics, but these are the very characteristics assigned to men. (p. 173)

In the face of such contradictions, she was forced to conclude that "if the author's views as to the mental differences of sex had been different, they might as easily have derived a very different set of characteristics" (pp. 173–174). Thompson singled out the variability hypothesis for special criticism, objecting not only to the use of physical variation as evidence for intellectual variation but also to the tendency to minimize environmental influences. She held that training was responsible for sex differences in variation, and to those who countered that it is really a fundamental difference of instincts and characteristics that determines the differences in training, she replied that if this were true, "it would not be necessary to spend so much time and effort in making boys and girls follow the lines of conduct proper to their sex" (p. 181).

Thompson's recommendation to look at environmental factors went unheeded, as more and more evidence of woman's incapability of attaining eminence was amassed. In the surveys of eminent persons that were popular at the turn of the century, more credence was given to nature (à la Hall) than nurture (à la Thompson) for the near absence of eminent women (Cattell, 1903; Ellis, 1904). Cattell (1903) found a ready-made explanation in the variability hypothesis: "Women depart less from the normal than man," ergo "the distribution of women is represented by a narrower bell-shaped curve" (p. 375). Cora Castle's (1913) survey of eminent women was no less critical of woman's failure to achieve at the top levels of power and prestige.

One of the most influential individuals to take up the cause of the variability hypothesis was Edward Thorndike. Much of the early work in the testing movement was done at Columbia University, which provided the perfect milieu for Thorndike's forays into the variability problem as applied to mental testing and educational philosophy. Thorndike based his case for the acceptance of the variability hypothesis on the reevaluation of the results of two studies (Thompson, 1903; Wissler, 1901) that had not themselves been directed toward the issue. Thorndike insisted that greater male variability only became meaningful when one examined the distribution of ability at the highest levels of giftedness. Measurement of more general sex differences could only "prove that the sexes are closely alike and that sex can account for only a very small fraction of human mental differences in the abilities listed" (Thorndike, 1910, p. 185). Since the range of female ability was narrower, he reasoned, the talents of women should be channeled into fields in which they would be most needed and most successful because "this one fundamental difference in variability is more important than all the dif-

ferences between the average male and female capacities" (Thorndike, 1906):

> Not only the probability and the desirability of marriage and the training of children as an essential feature of woman's career, but also the restriction of women to the mediocre grades of ability and achievement should be reckoned with by our educational systems. The education of women for . . . professions . . . where a very few gifted individuals are what society requires, is far less needed than for such professions as nursing, teaching, medicine, or architecture, where the average level is the essential. (p. 213)

He felt perfectly justified in this recommendation because of "the patent fact that in the great achievements of the world in science, as, invention, and management, women have been far excelled by men" (Thorndike, 1910, p. 35). In Thorndike's view, environmental factors scarcely mattered.

Others, like Joseph Jastrow (1915), seemed to recognize the tremendous influence that societal pressures had upon achievement. He noted that even when women had been admitted to employment from which they had previously been excluded, new prejudices arose: "allowances and considerations for sex intrude, favorably or unfavorably; the avenues of preferment, though ostensibly open are really barred by invisible barriers of social prejudice" (pp. 567–568). This was little more than lip service because he was even more committed to the importance of variational tendency and its predominance over any possible extenuating factors: the effects of the variability of the male and the biological conservatism of the female "radiates to every distinctive aspect of their contrasted natures and expressions'' (p. 568).

A small but persistent minority challenged the validity of the variability hypothesis, and it is not surprising that this minority was composed mainly of women. Although the ''woman question'' was, to some degree, at issue, the larger dispute was between those who stressed ''nature'' as the major determinant of ability (and therefore success) and those who rejected nature and its corollary, instead emphasizing the importance of environmental factors. Helen Thompson Woolley, while remaining firmly committed to the investigation of the differential effects of social factors on each sex, did not directly involve herself in the variability controversy. Leta Stetter Hollingworth, first a student and then a colleague of Thorndike's at Teachers College of Columbia University, actively investigated the validity of the hypothesis and presented sound objections to it. She argued that there was no real basis for assuming that the distribution of ''mental traits'' in the population conforms without exception to the Gaussian distribution. The assumption of normality was extremely important to the validity of the variability hypothesis, because only in a normal distribution would a difference in variability indicate a difference in range. It was the greater range of male ability that was used to ''prove'' the ultimate superiority of male ability. Greater range of male ability was usually verified by citing lists of eminent persons (dominated by men) and the numbers and sex of those in institutions for the feebleminded (also dominated by men). Hollingworth (1914) saw no reason to resort to biological theory for an explanation of the phenomenon when a more parsimonious one was available in social fact. Statistics reporting a larger number of males among the feebleminded could be explained by the fact that the supporting data had been gathered in institutions, where men were more likely to be admitted than women of an equal degree of retardation. The better ability of feebleminded women to survive outside the institutional setting was simply a function of female social role:

> Women have been and are a dependent and non-competitive class, and when defective can more easily survive outside of institutions, since they do not have to compete *mentally* with normal individuals, as men do, to maintain themselves in the social *milieu*. (Hollingworth, 1914, p. 515)

Women would therefore be more likely to be institutionalized at an older age than men, after they had become too old to be ''useful'' or self-supporting. A survey of age and sex ratios in New York institutions supported her hypothesis: the ratio of females to males increased with the age of the inmates (Hollingworth, 1913). As for the rarity of eminence among women, Hollingworth (1914) argued that because the social role of women was defined in terms of housekeeping and child-rearing functions, ''a field where eminence is not possible,'' and because of concomitant constraints placed on the education and employment of women by law, custom, and the demands of the role, one could not possibly validly compare the achievements of women with those of men who ''have followed the greatest possible range of occupations, and have at the same time procreated unhindered'' (p. 528). She repeatedly emphasized (Hollingworth, 1914, 1916) that the true potential of woman could only be known when she began to receive social acceptance of her right to choose career, maternity, or both.

Hollingworth's argument that unrecognized differences in social training had misdirected the search for *inherent* sex differences had earlier been voiced by Mary Calkins (1896). Just as Hollingworth directed her response particularly at Thorndike's formulation of the variability hypothesis, Calkins objected to Jastrow's (1896) intimations that one finds "greater uniformity amongst women than amongst men" (p. 431).

Hollingworth's work was instrumental in bringing the variability issue to a crisis point, not only because she presented persuasive empirical data to support her contentions but also because this was simply the first major opposition that the variability hypothesis had encountered. Real resolution of this crisis had to await the development of more sophisticated testing and statistical techniques. With the United States' involvement in World War I, most testing efforts were redirected to wartime uses. This redirection effectively terminated the variability debate, and although it resumed during the postwar years, the renewed controversy never attained the force of conviction that had characterized the earlier period. "Variational tendency" became a statistical issue, and the pedagogic implications that had earlier colored the debate were either minimized or disguised in more egalitarian terms.

After its revival in the mid-1920s, investigation of the variability hypothesis was often undertaken as part of larger intelligence testing projects. Evidence in its favor began to look more convincing than it ever had. The use of larger samples, standardized tests, and newer methods of computing variation gave an appearance of increased accuracy, but conclusions were still based on insubstantial evidence of questionable character. Most discussions of the topic concluded that there were not enough valid data to resolve the issue and that even if that data were available, variation within each sex is so much greater than the difference in variation between sexes that the "meaning" of the variability hypothesis was trivial (Shields, Note 1).

Maternal Instinct

The concept of maternal instinct was firmly entrenched in American psychology before American psychology itself existed as an entity. The first book to appear in the United States with "psychology" in its title outlined the psychological sex differences arising from the physical differences between men and women. Differences in structure were assumed to imply differences in function, and therefore differences in abilities, temperament, and intelligence. In each sex a different set of physical systems was thought to predominate: "In man the arterial and cerebral systems prevail, and with them irritability; in woman the venous and ganglion systems and with them plasticity and sensibility" (Rausch, 1841, p. 81). The systems dominant in woman caused her greatest attributes to lie in the moral sphere in the form of love, patience, and chastity. In the intellectual sphere, she was not equally blessed, "and this is not accidental, not because no opportunity has offered itself to their productive genius . . . but because it is their highest happiness to be mothers" (Rausch, 1841, p. 88).[5]

Although there was popular acceptance of a maternal instinct in this country, the primary impetus for its incorporation into psychology came by way of British discussion of social evolution. While the variability hypothesis gained attention because of an argument, the concept of maternal instinct evolved without conflict. There was consistent agreement as to its existence, if not its precise nature or form. Typical of the evolutionary point of view was the notion that woman's emotional nature (including her tendency to nurturance) was a direct conse-

5. This sentiment was echoed by Bruno Bettelheim (1965) over 100 years later: "as much as women want to be good scientists to engineers, they want first and foremost to be womanly companions of men and to be mothers" (p. 15).

quence of her reproductive physiology. As Herbert Spencer (1891) explained it, the female's energies were directed toward preparation for pregnancy and lactation, reducing the energy available for the development of other qualities. This resulted in a "rather earlier cessation of individual evolution" in the female. Woman was, in essence, a stunted man. Her lower stage of development was evident not only in her inferior mental and emotional powers but also in the resulting expression of the parental instinct. Whereas the objectivity of the male caused his concern to be extended "to all the relatively weak who are dependent upon him" (p. 375), the female's propensity to "dwell on the concrete and proximate rather than on the abstract and remote" made her incapable of the generalized protective attitude assumed by the male. Instead, she was primarily responsive to "infantile helplessness."

Alexander Sutherland (1898) also described a parental instinct whose major characteristic (concern for the weak) was "the basis of all other sympathy," which is itself "the ultimate basis of all moral feeling" (p. 156). Like his contemporaries (e.g., McDougall, 1913, 1923; Shand, 1920; Spencer, 1891), Sutherland revered maternal sentiment but thought the expression of parental instinct in the male, that is, a protective attitude, was a much more significant factor in social evolution, an attitude of benevolent paternalism more in keeping with Victorian social ethic than biological reality. The expression of the parental instinct in men, Sutherland thought, must necessarily lead to deference toward women out of "sympathetic regard for women's weakness." He noted that male protectiveness had indeed wrought a change in the relations between the sexes, evident in a trend away from sexual motivations and toward a general improvement in moral tone, witness the "large number of men who lead perfectly chaste lives for ten or twenty years after puberty

before they marry," which demonstrated that the "sensuous side of man's nature is slowly passing under the control of sympathetic sentiments" (p. 288).[6]

Whatever facet of the activity that was emphasized, there was common agreement that the maternal (or parental) instinct was truly an instinct. A. F. Shand (1920) argued that the maternal instinct is actually composed of an ordered "system" of instincts and characterized by a number of emotions. Despite its complexity, "maternal love" was considered to be a hereditary trait "in respect not only of its instincts, but also of the bond connecting its primary emotions, and of the end which the whole system pursues, namely, the preservation of the offspring" (p. 42). The sociologist L. T. Hobhouse (1916) agreed that maternal instinct was a "true" instinct, "not only in the drive but in some of the detail." He doubted the existence of a corresponding paternal instinct, however, since he had observed that few men have a natural aptitude with babies.

The unquestioning acceptance of the maternal instinct concept was just as prevalent in this country as it was in Britain. William James (1950) listed parental love among the instincts of humans and emphasized the strength with which it was expressed in women. He was particularly impressed with the mother-infant relationship and quoted at length from a German psychologist concerning the changes wrought in a woman at the birth of her child: "She has, in one word,

6. Similar observations were made concerning women. Sutherland (1898) noted that because social morality had developed to such a high level, women "now largely enter upon marriage out of purely sympathetic attractions, in which sex counts for something, but with all its grosser aspects gone." He happily reported another's finding that "sexual desire enters not at all into the minds of a very large proportion of women when contemplating matrimony" (p. 288).

transferred her entire egoism to the child, and lives only in it'' (p. 439). Even among those who employed a much narrower definition of instinct than James, maternal behavior was thought to be mediated by inherent neural connections. R. P. Halleck (1895) argued that comparatively few instincts are fully developed in humans, because reason intervenes and modifies their expression to fit the circumstances. Maternal instinct qualified as a clear exception, and its expression seemed as primitive and unrefined as that of infants' reflexive behavior.

Others (e.g., Jastrow, 1915; Thorndike, 1914a, 1914b) treated instinct more as a quality of character than of biology. Edward Thorndike (1911) considered the instincts peculiar to each sex to be the primary source of sex differences: "it appears that if the primary sex characters—the instincts directly related to courtship, love, child-bearing, and nursing—are left out of account, the average man differs from the average woman far less than many men differ from one another" (p. 30). Thorndike taught that the tendency to display maternal concern was universal among women, although social pressures could "complicate or deform" it. He conceded that males share in an instinctive "good will toward children," but other instincts, such as the "hunting instinct," predominated (Thorndike, 1914b). He was so sure of the innate instinctual differences between men and women that it was his contention (Thorndike, 1914b) that even "if we should keep the environment of boys and girls absolutely similar these instincts would produce sure and important differences between the mental and moral activities of boys and girls" (p. 203). The expression of instincts therefore was thought to have far-reaching effects on seemingly unrelated areas of ability and conduct. For example, woman's "nursing instinct," which was most often exhibited in "unreasoning tendencies to pet, coddle, and 'do for' others," was

also "the chief source of woman's superiorities in the moral life" (Thorndike, 1914a, p. 203). Another of the females' instinctive tendencies was described as "submission to mastery":

> Women in general are thus by original nature submissive to men in general. Submissive behavior is apparently not annoying when assumed as the instinctive response to its natural stimulus. Indeed, it is perhaps a common satisfier. (Thorndike, 1914b, p. 34)

The existence of such an "instinct" would, of course, validate the social norm of female subservience and dependence. An assertive woman would be acting contrary to instinct and therefore contrary to *nature*. There is a striking similarity between Thorndike's description of female nature and that of the Freudians with their mutual emphasis on woman's passivity, dependency, and masochism. For Thorndike, however, the *cause* of such a female attitude was thought to be something quite different from mutilation fears and penis envy.

The most vocal proponent of instinct, first in England and later in this country, was William McDougall (1923). Unlike Shand, he regarded "parental sentiment" as a primary instinct and did not hesitate to be highly critical of those who disagreed with him. When his position was maligned by the behaviorists, his counterattack was especially strong:

> And, when we notice how in so many ways the behavior of the human mother most closely resembles that of the animal-mother, can we doubt that . . . if the animal-mother is moved by the impulse of a maternal instinct, so also is the woman? To repudiate this view as

baseless would seem to me the height of blindness and folly, yet it is the folly of a number of psychologists who pride themselves on being strictly "scientific." (p. 136)

In McDougall's system of instincts, each of the primary instincts in humans was accompanied by a particular emotional quality. The parental instinct had as its primary emotional quality the "tender emotion" vaguely defined as love, tenderness, and tender feeling. Another of the primary instincts was that of "pairing," its primary emotional quality that of sexual emotion or excitement, "sometimes called love—an unfortunate and confusing usage" (p. 234). Highly critical of what he called the "Freudian dogma that all love is sexual," McDougall proposed that it was the interaction of the parental and pairing instincts that was the basis of heterosexual "love." "Female coyness," which initiated the courtship ritual, was simply the reproductively oriented manifestation of the instincts of self-display and self-abasement. The appearance of a suitable male would elicit coyness from the female, and at that point the male's parental instinct would come into play:

A certain physical weakness and delicacy (probably moral also) about the normal young woman or girl constitute in her a resemblance to a child. This resemblance . . . throws the man habitually into the protective attitude, evokes the impulse and emotion of the parental instinct. He feels that he wants to protect and shield and help her in every way. (p. 425)

Once the "sexual impulse" had added its energy to the relationship, the young man was surely trapped, and the survival of the species was insured. McDougall, while firmly committed to the importance of instinct all the way up the evolutionary ladder, never lost his sense of Victorian delicacy: while pairing simply meant reproduction in lower animals, in humans it was accorded a tone of gallantry and concern.

The fate of instinct at the hands of the radical behaviorists is a well-known tale. Perhaps the most adamant, as well as notorious, critic of the instinct concept was J. B. Watson (1926). Like those before him who had relied upon observation to prove the existence of maternal instinct, he used observation to confirm its nonexistence:

We have observed the nursing, handling, bathing, etc. of the first baby of a good many mothers. Certainly there are no new ready-made activities appearing except nursing. The mother is usually as awkward about that as she can well be. The instinctive factors are practically nil. (p. 54)

Watson attributed the appearance of instinctive behavior to the mother's effort to conform to societal expectations of her successful role performance. He, like the 19th-century British associationist Alexander Bain, speculated that not a little of the mother's pleasure in nursing and caring for the infant was due to the sexually stimulating effect of those activities.[7]

---

7. Bain's (1875) position was similar except that he believed that there *was* an innate tendency to nurture that initiated the entire cycle of positive affect-positive action. The instinct was thought to be a natural "sentiment," which was fostered by the long period of gestation and the "special energies" required of the mother to sustain the infant. The positive affect arising from activity connected with the infant then brought about increased nurturance and increased pleasure. At least part of this pleasure was thought to be physical in nature.

Even the most dedicated behaviorists hedged a bit when it came to discarding the idea of instinct altogether. Although the teleology and redundancy of the concept of instinct were sharply criticized, some belief in "instinctive activity" was typically retained (cf. Dunlap, 1919–1920). W. B. Pillsbury (1926), for example, believed that the parental instinct was a "secondary" instinct. Physical attraction to the infant guided the mother's first positive movements toward the infant, but trial and error guided her subsequent care. Instinct was thought of as that quality which set the entire pattern of maternal behavior in motion.

In time instinct was translated into *drive* and *motivation,* refined concepts more in keeping with behavioristic theory. Concomitantly, interest in the maternal instinct of human females gave way to the study of mothering behavior in rodents. The concept of maternal instinct did find a place in psychoanalytic theory, but its definition bore little resemblance to that previously popular. Not only did maternal instinct lose the connotation of protectiveness and gentility that an earlier generation of psychologists had ascribed to it, but it was regarded as basically sexual, masochistic, and even destructive in nature (cf. Rheingold, 1964).

The Ascendancy of Psychoanalytic Theory

The functionalists, because of their emphasis on "nature," were predictably indifferent to the study of social sex roles and cultural concepts of masculine and feminine. The behaviorists, despite their emphasis on "nurture," were slow to recognize those same social forces. During the early 1930s, there was little meaningful ongoing research in female psychology: the point of view taken by the functionalists was no longer a viable one, and the behaviorists with their emphasis on nonsocial topics (i.e., learning and motivation) had no time for serious consideration of sex differences. While the functionalists had defined laws of behavior that mirrored the society of the times, behaviorists concentrated their efforts on defining universal laws that operated in any time, place, or organism. Individual differences in nature were expected during the functionalist era because they were the sine qua non of a Darwinian view of the world and of science. The same individual differences were anathema to early learning-centered psychology because, no longer necessary or expedient, they were a threat to the formulation of universal laws of behavior.

In the hiatus created by the capitulation of functionalism to behaviorism, the study of sex differences and female nature fell within the domain of psychoanalystic theory—the theory purported to have all the answers. Freudian theory (or some form of it) had for some years already served as the basis for a psychology of female physiological function (cf. Benedek & Rubenstein, 1939). The application of principles popular in psychiatry and medicine (and their inescapable identification with pathology) to academic psychology was easily accomplished. Psychoanalytic theory provided psychology with the first comprehensive theoretical explanation of sex differences. Its novelty in that respect aided its assimilation.

Psychology proper, as well as the general public, had been well-prepared for a biological, and frankly sexual, theory of male and female nature. Havelock Ellis, although himself ambivalent and even hostile toward Freudian teachings, had done much through his writing to encourage openness in the discussion of sexuality. He brought a number of hitherto unmentionable issues to open discussion, couching them in the commonly accepted notion of the complementarily of the

82

sexes, thus insuring their popular acceptance. Emphasis on masculinity and femininity as real dimensions of personality appeared in the mid-1930s in the form of the Terman Masculinity-Femininity Scale (Terman & Miles, 1968). Although Lewis Terman himself avoided discussion of whether masculinity and femininity were products of nature or nurture, social determinants of masculinity and femininity were commonly deemphasized in favor of the notion that they were a type of psychological secondary sexual characteristic. Acceptance of social sex role soon came to be perceived as an indicator of one's mental health.

The traps inherent in a purely psychoanalytic concept of female nature were seldom recognized. John Dewey's (1957) observation, made in 1922, merits attentions, not only for its accuracy but because its substance can be found in present-day refutations of the adequacy of psychoanalytic theory as an explanation of woman's behavior and "nature":

> The treatment of sex by psycho-analysts is most instructive, for it flagrantly exhibits both the consequences of artificial simplification and the transformation of social results into psychic causes. Writers, usually male, hold forth on the psychology of women, as if they were dealing with a Platonic universal entity, although they habitually treat men as individuals, varying with structure and environment. They treat phenomena which are peculiarly symptoms of civilization of the West at the present time as if they were the necessary effects of fixed nature impulses of human nature. (pp. 143–144)

The identification of the psychology of women with psychoanalytic theory was nearly complete by the mid-1930s and was so successful that many psychologists today, even those most deeply involved in the current movement for a psychology of women, are not aware that there was a psychology of women long before there was a Sigmund Freud. This article has dealt only with a brief period in that history, and then only with the most significant topics of that period. Lesser issues were often just a hotly debated, for example, whether there is an innate difference in the style of handwriting of men and women (cf. Allen, 1927; Downey, 1910).

And what has happened to the issues of brain size, variability, and maternal instinct since the 1930s? Where they are politically and socially useful, they have an uncanny knack of reappearing albeit in an altered form. For example, the search for central nervous system differences between males and females has continued. Perhaps the most popular form this search has taken is the theory of prenatal hormonal "organization" of the hypothalamus into exclusively male or female patterns of function (Harris & Levine, 1965). The proponents of this theory maintain an Aristotelian view of woman as an incomplete man:

> In the development of the embryo, nature's first choice or primal impulse is to differentiate a female. . . . The principle of differentiation is always that to obtain a male, something must be added. Subtract that something, and the result will be a female. (Money, 1970, p. 428)

The concept of maternal instinct, on the other hand, has recently been taken up and refashioned by a segment of the woman's movement. Pregnancy and childbirth are acclaimed as important expressions of womanliness whose satisfactions cannot be truly appreciated by males. The idea that women are burdened with "unreasoning tendencies to pet, coddle, and 'do for' others" has been disposed of by others and replaced by the semiserious proposal that if any "instinctive" component of parental concern exists, it is a peculiarly male attribute (Stannard, 1970). The variability hypothesis is all but absent from contemporary psychological work, but if it ever again promises a viable justification for existing social values, it will be back as strongly as ever. Conditions which would favor its revival include the renaissance of rugged individualism or the "need" to suppress some segment of society, for example, women's aspirations to positions of power. In the first case the hypothesis would serve to reaffirm that there are those "born to lead," and in the latter that there are those "destined to follow."

Of more importance than the issues themselves or their fate in contemporary psychology is the recognition of the role that they have played historically in the psychology of women: the role of social myth. Graves (1968, p. v) included among the functions of mythologizing that of justification of existing social systems. This function was clearly operative throughout the evolutionist-functionalist treatment of the psychology of women: the "discovery" of sex differences in brain structure to correspond to "appropriate" sex differences in brain function; the biological justification (via the variability hypothesis) for the enforcement of woman's subordinate social status; the Victorian weakness and gentility associated with maternity; and pervading each of these themes, the assumption of an innate emotional, sexless, unimaginative female character that played the perfect foil to the Darwinian male. That science played handmaiden to social values cannot be denied. Whether a parallel situation exists in today's study of sex differences is open to question.

Reference Note

1. Shields, S. A. *The variability hypothesis and sex differences in intelligence.* Unpublished manuscript, 1974. (Available from Department of Psychology, Pennsylvania State University.)

References

Allen C. N. Studies in sex differences. *Psychological Bulletin*, 1927, *24*, 294–304.

Bain, A. *Mental science.* New York: Appleton, 1875.

Benedek, T., and Rubenstein, B. B. The correlations between ovarian activity and psychodynamic processes. II. The menstrual phase. *Psychosomatic Medicine*, 1939, *1*, 461–485.

Bettelheim, B. The commitment required of a woman entering a scientific profession in present-day American society. In J. A. Mattfield & C. G. Van Aken (Eds.), *Women and the scientific professions.* Cambridge, Mass.: M.I.T. Press, 1965.

Burt, C., and Moore, R. C. The mental differences between the sexes. *Journal of Experimental Pedagogy*, 1912, *1*, 355–388.

Calder-Marshall, A. *The sage of sex.* New York: Putnam, 1959.

Calkins, M. W. Community of ideas of men and women. *Psychological Review*, 1896, *3*, 426–430.

Castle, C. A. A statistical study of eminent women. *Columbia Contributions to Philosophy and Psychology*, 1913, *22*(27).

Cattell, J. McK. A statistical study of eminent men. *Popular Science Monthly*, 1903, *62*, 359–377.

Darwin, C. *The descent of man* (2nd ed.). London: John Murray, 1922. (Originally published, 1871; 2nd edition originally published, 1874.)

Dewey, J. *Human nature and conduct.* New York: Random House, 1957.

Downey, J. E. Judgment on the sex of handwriting. *Psychological Review*, 1910, *17*, 205–216.

Dunlap, J. Are there any instincts? *Journal of Abnormal and Social Psychology*, 1919–1920, *14*, 307–311.

Elliott, H. C. *Textbook of neuroanatomy* (2nd ed.). Philadelphia: Lippincott, 1969.

Ellis, H. *Man and woman: A study of human secondary sexual characters*. London: Walter Scott; New York: Scribner's, 1894.

Ellis, H. Variation in man and woman. *Popular Science Monthly*, 1903, *62*, 237–253.

Ellis, H. *A study of British genius*. London: Hurst & Blackett, 1904.

Ellis, H. *Man and woman, a study of secondary and tertiary sexual characteristics* (8th rev. ed.). London: Heinemann, 1934.

Encyclopedia of the Social Sciences. New York: Macmillan, 1935.

Galton, F. *Inquiries into the human faculty and its development*. London: Dent, 1907.

Geddes, P., & Thomson, J. A. *The evolution of sex*. New York: Scribner & Welford, 1890.

Graves, R. Introduction. In *New Larousse encyclopedia of mythology* (Rev. ed.). London: Paul Hamlyn, 1968.

Hall, G. S. The question of coeducation. *Munsey's Magazine*, 1906, *34*, 588–592.

Hall, G. S. *Youth, its education, regimen and hygiene*. New York: Appleton, 1918.

Halleck, R. *Psychology and psychic culture*. New York: American Book, 1895.

Harris. G. W., and Levine, S. Sexual differentiation of the brain and its experimental control. *Journal of Physiology*, 1965, *181*, 379–400.

Hobhouse, L. *Morals in evolution*. New York: Holt, 1916.

Hollingworth, L. S. The frequency of amentia as related to sex. *Medical Record*, 1913, *84*, 753–756.

Hollingworth, L. S. Variability as related to sex differences in achievement. *American Journal of Sociology*, 1914, *19*, 510–530.

Hollingworth, L. S. Social devices for impelling women to bear and rear children. *American Journal of Sociology*, 1916, *22*, 19–29.

Huarte, J. *The examination of mens wits* (trans. from Spanish to Italian by M. Camilli; trans. from Italian to English by R. Carew). Gainesville, Fla.: Scholars' Facsimiles and Reprints, 1959.

James, W. *The principles of psychology*. New York: Dover, 1950.

Jastrow, J. Note on Calkins' "Community of ideas of men and women." *Psychological Review*, 1896, *3*, 430–431.

Jastrow, J. *Character and temperament*. New York: Appleton, 1915.

Jordan. D. S. The higher education of women. *Popular Science Monthly*, 1902, *62*, 97–107.

Mall, F. P. On several anatomical characters of the human brain, said to vary according to race and sex, with especial reference to the weight of the frontal lobe. *American Journal of Anatomy*, 1909, *9*, 1–32.

McDougall, W. *An introduction to social psychology* (7th ed.). London: Methuen, 1913.

McDougall, W. *Outline of psychology*. New York: Scribner's, 1923.

Meyer, M. *Psychology of the other-one*. Columbia: Missouri Book, 1921.

Mill, J. S. *The subjection of women*. London: Dent, 1955.

Mobius, P. J. The physiological mental weakness of woman (A. McCorn, Trans.). *Alienist and Neurologist*, 1901, *22*, 624–642.

Money, J. Sexual dimorphism and homosexual gender identity. *Psychological Bulletin*, 1970, *74*, 427–440.

More, H. *Strictures on the modern system of female education. With a view of the principles and conduct prevalent among women of rank and fortune*. Philadelphia, Pa.: Printed by Bud and Bertram for Thomas Dobson, 1800.

Patrick, G. T. W. The psychology of women. *Popular Science monthly*, 1895, *47*, 209–225.

Pearson, K. Variation in man and woman. In *The chances of death* (Vol. 1). London: Edward Arnold, 1897.

Pillsbury, W. B. *Education as the psychologist sees it*. New York: Macmillan, 1926.

Porteus, S., and Babcock, M. E. *Temperament and race*. Boston: Gorham Press, 1926.

Rausch, F. A. *Psychology; Or, a view of the human soul including anthropology* (2nd rev. ed.). New York: Dodd, 1841.

Reeves, N. *Womankind*. Chicago: Aldine-Atherton, 1971.

Rheingold, J. *The fear of being a woman.* New York: Grune & Stratton, 1964.

Romanes, G. J. Mental differences between men and women. *Nineteenth Century,* 1887, *21,* 654–672.

Shand, A. F. *The foundations of character.* London: Macmillan, 1920.

Sinclair, A. *The better half: The emancipation of the American woman.* New York: Harper & Row, 1965.

Smith, P. *Daughters of the promised land.* Boston: Little, Brown, 1970.

Spencer, H. *The study of sociology.* New York: Appleton, 1891.

Stannard, U. Adam's rib, or the woman within. *Trans-Action,* 1970, *8,* 24–35.

Sutherland, A. *The origin and growth of the moral instinct* (Vol. 1). London: Longmans, Green, 1898.

Terman, L., and Miles, C. C. *Sex and personality.* New York: Russell and Russell, 1968.

Thompson, H. B. *The mental traits of sex.* Chicago: University of Chicago Press, 1903.

Thorndike, E. L. Sex in education. *The Bookman,* 1906, *23,* 211–214.

Thorndike, E. L. *Educational psychology* (2nd ed.). New York: Teachers College, Columbia University, 1910.

Thorndike, E. L. *Individuality.* Boston: Houghton Mifflin, 1911.

Thorndike, E. L. *Educational psychology* (Vol. 3). New York: Teachers College, Columbia University, 1914. (a)

Thorndike, E. L. *Educational psychology briefer course.* New York: Teachers College, Columbia University, 1914. (b)

Walker, A. *Woman physiologically considered.* New York: J. & H. G. Langley, 1850.

Watson, J. B. Studies on the growth of the emotions. In *Psychologies of 1925.* Worcester, Mass.: Clark University Press, 1926.

Weininger, O. *Sex and character* (trans.). London: Heinemann, 1906.

Wissler, C. The correlation of mental and physical tests. *Psychological Review Monograph Supplements,* 1899–1901, *3*(6, Whole No. 16).

Wollstonecraft, M. *A vindication of the rights of woman.* New York: Dutton, 1955.

Woolley, H. T. Psychological literature: A review of the recent literature on the psychology of sex. *Psychological Bulletin,* 1910, *7,* 335–342.

Wundt, W. *Ethics.* Vol. 3: *The principles of morality, and the departments of the moral life* (M. F. Washburn, Trans.). London: Sonnenschein, 1901.

Laurel Furumoto
Elizabeth Scarborough

Placing Women in the History of Psychology: The First American Women Psychologists*

ABSTRACT: *This article presents an account of the first American women psychologists. The article provides data on the origins, education, marital status, and careers of the 22 women who identified themselves as psychologists in the first edition of* American Men of Science. *Further, it explores how gender shaped their experience in relation to educational and employment opportunities, responsibilities to family, and the marriage versus career dilemma. Illustrations are drawn from the lives of Mary Whiton Calkins, Christine Ladd-Franklin, Margaret Floy Washburn, and Ethel Puffer Howes. Sources used include archival materials (manuscripts, correspondence, and institutional records) as well as published literature. The article calls attention to the necessity of integrating women into the history of the discipline if it is to provide an adequate understanding of psychology's past.*

Laurel Furumoto and Elizabeth Scarborough, "Placing women in the history of psychology: The first American women psychologists." *American Psychologist*, 1986, *41*, pp. 35–42. Copyright (c) 1986 by the American Psychological Association. Reprinted by permission.

*The authors contributed equally; listing is in alphabetical order. We thank Michael M. Sokal especially for his extensive comments on a draft of the article.

This research was supported in part by grants from the Research Foundation of State University of New York and State College at Fredonia to Elizabeth Scarborough (Goodman) and from the Brachman-Hoffman Small Grant Program of Wellesley College to Laurel Furumoto.

Correspondence concerning this article should be addressed to Elizabeth Scarborough, Department of Psychology, State College at Fredonia, Fredonia, New York 14063.

1. A comprehensive study of the lives, contributions, and experience of early women psychologists will be published by Columbia University Press under the title *Untold Lives: The First Generation of American Women Psychologists*.

Women psychologists have been largely overlooked in histories of the discipline. This is so despite the early participation and contributions of women to American psychology from its beginnings as a science. Here we offer a preliminary account of the first American women psychologists, describing them and the manner in which gender shaped their experiences.[1]

As early as 1960, the history of psychology was identified as a "neglected area" (Watson, 1960). Watson's call for attention was followed by a dramatic surge of interest in historical scholarship (Watson, 1975). In subsequent years, history of psy-

Table 1
Characteristics of Women Psychologists Listed in American Men of Science, 1906

Name	Birth year	Subject of research[a]	Baccalaureate degree	Doctoral degree
Bagley, Mrs. W. C. (Florence Winger)	1874	Fechner's color rings	Nebraska 1895	Cornell 1901[c]
Calkins, Prof. Mary Whiton	1863	Association of ideas	Smith 1885	Harvard 1895[d]
Case, Prof. Mary S(ophia)	1854	None given	Michigan 1884	No graduate study
Franklin, Mrs. Christine Ladd	1847	Logic, color vision	Vassar 1869	Hopkins 1882[d]
Gamble, Prof. E(leanor) A(cheson) McC(ullough)	1868	Smell intensities	Wellesley 1889	Cornell 1898
Gordon, Dr. Kate	1878	Memory and attention	Chicago 1900	Chicago 1903
Gulliver, Pres. Julia H(enrietta)	1856	Dreams, subconscious self	Smith 1879	Smith 1888
Hinman, Dr. Alice H(amlin)	1869	Attention and distraction	Wellesley 1893	Cornell 1897
Martin, Prof. Lillien J(ane)	1851	Psychophysics	Vassar 1880	Gottingen 1898[c]
McKeag, Prof. Anna J(ane)	1864	Pain sensation	Wilson 1895	Pennsylvania 1900
Moore, Mrs. J. Percy (Kathleen Carter)	1866	Mental development	Pennsylvania 1890[e]	Pennsylvania 1896
Moore, Prof. Vida F(rank)	1867	Metaphysics	Wesleyan 1893	Cornell 1900
Norsworthy, Dr. Naomi	1877	Abilities of the child	Columbia 1901	Columbia 1904
Parrish, Miss C(elestia) S(usannah)	1853	Cutaneous sensation	Cornell 1896	No graduate study
Puffer, Dr. Ethel D(ench)	1872	Esthetics	Smith 1891	Radcliffe 1902
Shinn, Dr. M(ilicent) W(ashburn)	1858	Development of the child	California 1880	California 1898
Smith, Dr. Margaret K(eiver)	1856	Rhythm and work	Oswego Normal 1883[e]	Zurich 1900
Smith, Dr. Theodate (Louise)	1860	Muscular memory	Smith 1882	Yale 1896
Squire, Mrs. C(arrie) R(anson)	1869	Rhythm	Hamline 1889	Cornell 1901
Thompson, Dr. Helen B(radford)	1874	Mental traits of sex	Chicago 1897	Chicago 1900
Washburn, Prof. Margaret F(loy)	1871	Space perception of skin	Vassar 1891	Cornell 1894
Williams, Dr. Mabel Clare	1878	Visual illusions	Iowa 1899	Iowa 1903

Note. Names are given as they appeared in the directory.
[a]Major topics through 1906. [b]Positions listed in *American Men of Science,* first and third editions. [c]Doctoral study, no degree granted. [d]Doctoral program completed, no degree granted due to prohibition against women. [e]Program of study less than 4-year course.

chology has developed as a vigorous specialty field. However, new scholarship has paid scant attention to women in the discipline. To date, work that has been done on women, whether presented in published sources or in delivered papers, has been limited in scope and descriptive rather than interpretive. It consists generally of efforts to identify some prominent women in previous generations and to provide information about their achievements (see Bernstein and Russo, 1974; O'Connell, 1983; O'Connell & Russo, 1980; Russo, 1983; Stevens & Gardner, 1982). Furthermore, the number of women mentioned in even the most recently published history of psychology textbooks is astonishingly small (see Goodman, 1983).

Omission of women from history is not unique to psychology. As Gerda Lerner (1979), an American historian well known for her work in women's history, pointed out,

Date of Marriage	Husband	Children	Professional positions[b]	
			1906	1921
1901	William C. Bagley	2 sons, 2 daughters	Unemployed	Not listed
			Professor, Wellesley	Professor, Wellesley
			Associate Professor, Wellesley	Not listed
1882	Fabian Franklin	1 son, 1 daughter	Lecturer, Hopkins	Lecturer, Columbia
			Associate Professor, Wellesley	Professor, Wellesley
1943	Ernest C. Moore	0	Associate Professor, Mt. Holyoke	Associate Professor, Carnegie Tech.
			President, Rockford	Not listed.
1897	Edgar L. Hinman	1 daughter	Lecturer, Nebraska	Lecturer, Nebraska
			Assistant Professor, Stanford	Private practice
			Associate Professor, Wellesley	Professor, Wellesley
1892	J. Percy Moore	1 son, 2 daughters	Head, Bardwell School	(deceased 1920)
			Professor, Elmira	(deceased 1915)
			Instructor, Columbia Teachers College	(deceased 1916)
			Teacher, Georgia Normal	(deceased 1918)
1908	Benjamin A. Howes	1 daughter, 1 son	Instructor, Radcliffe, Wellesley, Simmons	Unemployed
			Unemployed	Unemployed
			Director, New Paltz Normal	New Paltz Normal
			Research Assistant, Clark	(deceased 1914)
1891	William N. Squire	Unknown	Professor, Montana Normal	Not listed
1905	Paul G. Woolley	2 daughters	Professor, Mt. Holyoke	Director Cincinnati Schools
			Associate Professor, Vassar	Professor, Vassar
1924	T. W. Kemmerer	0	Unemployed	Assistant Professor, Iowa

Traditional history has been written and interpreted by men in an androcentric frame of reference; it might quite properly be described as the history of men. The very term "Women's History" calls attention to the fact that something is missing from historical scholarship. (p. xiv)

Beyond calling attention to what is missing from the history of psychology, this article begins to fill the gap by sketching an overview of the lives and experiences of those women who participated in the development of the discipline in the United States around the turn of the century. First, we identify early women psychologists. Second, we describe the women and note some comparisons between them and men psychologists. And last, we discuss women's experiences, focusing on how gender influenced their careers.

Identifying Early Psychologists

In 1906 James McKeen Cattell published the first edition of *American Men of Science* (Cattell, 1906), a biographical directory containing more than 4,000 entries. This ambitious project provided for the first time a comprehensive listing of all individuals in North America who had "carried on research work in the natural and exact sciences" (p. v). Inclusion in the directory required that a person must have done "work that has contributed to the advancement of pure science" or be "found in the membership lists of certain national societies" (p. v). Cattell himself was a highly visible and influential member of the psychological establishment, centrally involved in founding and controlling the early direction of the American Psychological Association (APA). Not surprisingly then, among the national societies he surveyed was the APA, which in 1906 was 14 years old and had about 175 members.

Although neither the title nor Cattell's preface suggests it, his directory of "men of science" did, in fact, include some women (see Rossiter, 1974). Among these women scientists, a group of 22 identified themselves as psychologists either by field or by subject of research (see Table 1). Our analysis is based on biographical information on these women, who constituted 12% of the 186 psychologists listed in the directory. It should be noted that omitted from the directory were five women who held APA membership in 1906: Elizabeth Kemper Adams, Margaret S. Prichard, Frances H. Rousmaniere, Eleanor Harris Rowland, and Ellen Bliss Talbot. Conversely, nine women were listed who did *not* belong to the APA: Bagley, Case, Gulliver, V. F. Moore, Parrish, Shinn, and Squire, plus McKeag and Williams (who joined after 1906). Presumably those who did not belong to the APA were included because they had made research contributions to the field. The group we are considering therefore omits a few women who clearly qualified for inclusion in *American Men of Science* (*AMS*) and includes some who never identified themselves with professional psychology. By focusing on the 22, however, we have designated a fairly complete group of early American women psychologists for whom basic biographical information is available. This makes it possible to analyze certain aspects of their lives and compare them with their male cohort.

These women shared with men psychologists the experience of being pioneers in what Cattell called "the newest of the sciences" (Cattell, 1903a, p. 562). Women participated from the beginning in the evolution of the new discipline. They began joining the national professional association soon after it was formed in 1892 and presented papers at annual meetings. They published regularly in the fledgling journals, contributing original research, reviews, and commentaries. The group included several who were prominent and influential (e.g., Mary Calkins, Christine Ladd-Franklin,[2] Lillien Martin, and Margaret Washburn) and others who were recognized by their peers as notable contributors (e.g., Kate Gordon, Milicent Shinn, and Helen Thompson). Included also, however, were women whose careers were short lived, ending with publication of their graduate research, as was true for Florence Winger Bagley and Alice Hamlin Hinman.

Besides being among the first psychologists, these women were also poineers in another sense. They were in the vanguard of women seeking collegiate and even graduate education in the decades following the Civil War (see Solomon, 1985). The skepticism about women's mental fitness to under-

---

2. At some point after her marriage, Christine Ladd began identifying herself as Ladd-Franklin. In Table 1 in this article she is listed as Franklin.

take a rigorous course of studies at the college level had been quickly challenged by their academic successes. However, there were still those who argued against advanced education for women on the grounds that scholarly work would ruin their health or atrophy their reproductive organs, or both (see Walsh, 1977). Women who undertook higher education in the 19th century did so despite the widespread belief that it would make them unfit to fulfill the obligations prescribed by the widely accepted notion of women's sphere: piety, purity, submissiveness, and domesticity (see Welter, 1966).

The phrase "women's sphere," with its connotation of boundaries that limited a woman's activity, could result in personal anguish for those who challenged it. Kate Gordon (1905), one of the first psychologists, spoke of this in discussing women's education:

> The question of woman's education is seductively close to the question of woman's "sphere." I hold it to be almost a transgression even to mention woman's sphere—the word recalls so many painful and impertinent deliveries, so much of futile discussion about it—and yet the willingness to dogmatize about woman in general is so common an infirmity that I am emboldened to err. (p. 789)

To pursue higher education was, for a woman, to risk serious social sanctions; to attempt this in a coeducational situation, which implied competition with men, was commonly considered to be personally disastrous (Thomas, 1908). And yet just this was necessary to gain the graduate training required for entry into the field of psychology.

Description of Early Psychologists

Each scientist listed in *AMS* had filled out and returned to Cattell a form that requested the following: name, title, and address; field; place and date of birth; education and degrees; current and previous positions held; honorary degrees and other scientific honors; memberships in scientific and learned societies; and chief subjects of research. Thus, working from the entries alone, it is possible to examine comparative data on pertinent variables.

Women psychologists in 1906 can be described generally as Anglo-Saxon Protestants of privileged middle-class backgrounds. They were similar to men psychologists on most of the variables reported in *AMS*. Most were born in the Northeastern or Middle-Western United States, though some were Canadians and a few of the men were European born; several were born abroad as children of missionaries. The range of birth years was 1847 to 1878 for women (see Table 1) and 1830 to 1878 for men. The median age of the women in 1906 was 39.5, and the median age for men was 39. The median age at completion of the undergraduate degree for the women was 22.5, for the men 22. In their undergraduate study, the women followed a pattern similar to what Cattell identified for the entire group of psychologists he surveyed in 1903: dispersion across a wide variety of types and locations of undergraduate institutions (Cattell, 1903b). Ten of them had earned their degrees in four women's colleges (Smith, Vassar, Wellesley, and Wilson); the remaining 12 had studied at 11 coeducational institutions, both public and private (see Table 1).

All but two of the women (Case and Parrish) reported graduate work. Approximately one third had traveled to Europe to study at some time, and 18 had completed the requirements for the PhD by 1906 (see Table 1). Cornell University, unusual in that it was founded as a coeducational *private* institution in 1865, was the most hospitable and accessible graduate site for early women psychologists. Six of the group undertook their advanced study there. Cornell was a noted exception to the norm during this period because it not only admitted women as fully recognized students but also considered them eligible for fellowship support. Indeed, four of the women in this sample held the prestigious Susan Linn Sage Fellowship in Philosophy and Ethics: Washburn in 1893–1894, Hinman in 1895–1896, Gamble in 1896–1897, and Bagley in 1900–1901. The other two women who studied at Cornell received graduate scholarships: V. F. Moore in 1897–1898 and Squire in 1900–1901. (Three other women, omitted from the 1906 *AMS*, had also received PhDs in psychology from Cornell during this period: Ellen Bliss Talbot and Margaret Everitt Schallenberger were Sage Fellows in 1897–1898 and 1899–1900, respectively, and Stella Sharp held a graduate scholarship in 1897–1898.) For the men psychologists, however, Cornell placed a poor fifth as an institution for advanced study, running behind Clark, Columbia, Leipzig, and Harvard—each of which, however, denied women access to graduate degrees in psychology in the 1890s. The remaining 14 women who reported advanced work were spread across 11 different institutions.

The women were somewhat older than the men by the time they completed their graduate studies, with a median age for the women of 31 compared to 29 for the men. The difference is not great, but given the close similarity to men on the other variables, it merits some attention. The two-year gap was not due to the women's prolonging their advanced degree programs. Once they began graduate study, they generally completed their course in good time. A notable exception is Julia Gulliver, who stated that in the time between her 1879 baccalaureate and

1888 doctorate (both from Smith College) she was "at home studying for my degree, in addition to many other occupations." She explained her reason for undertaking study at home: "It was the best I could do, as I could not afford to go elsewhere" (Gulliver, 1938). Gulliver was exceptional also in that she was the only woman in the group to hold a long-term appointment as a college president.

Seven women (Bagley, Gordon, Hinman, Norsworthy, Thompson, Washburn, and Williams) went directly to graduate study after college. Thirteen, however, reported delays ranging from 5 to 18 years between receiving the baccalaureate and the doctorate. During the hiatus, which averaged 11 years, all but three of the women (Gulliver, Shinn, and Squire) were engaged in teaching—primarily in women's colleges and public schools. Squire, who was married a year after her college graduation and widowed the following year, reported no occupational positions before her doctoral study.

The seven women who progressed without interruption from college to graduate study were a later-born cohort, with birth dates ranging from 1869 to 1878. Several factors may have been important in guiding their academic course and delaying the progress of the older women. Prior to the early 1890s, very few graduate programs in any field were open to women, and none of the institutions granting doctoral degrees in psychology admitted women as degree candidates. Thus, the older women had to wait for access, whereas the younger ones were able to move directly into a few available graduate study programs. Furthermore, the older women were not exposed to psychology as a scientific discipline during their college days. As the "new" psychology gained attention in the 1890s, however, it is possible that they learned of it through their teaching activities and saw advanced study as a way of satisfying their continuing intellectual interests or as a means of career enhancement. For some of the women, financial difficulties delayed their academic pursuits. Several taught before attending college as well as afterward to finance their education.

Despite the similarities they shared in several areas, the professional attainments of the women were diverse. Three patterns may be identified. Two of the 22 (Bagley and Shinn) reported no employment following advanced study. Twelve found a permanent place in higher education—seven held teaching or administrative positions at women's colleges, four at coeducational universities, and one at a normal school—and their careers show advancement through the academic ranks. The remaining eight found employment in a variety of positions, academic and applied, full and part-time. Their career paths were marked by frequent job changes, discontinuities in type of work, gaps in employment records, and little or no evidence of professional advancement. This pattern is associated, not coincidentally we believe, with marital status. Six of the eight women whose careers are characterized by discontinuity and lack of advancement were married. (Nine of the 22 did marry; all of those produced children, except the one who was widowed early and the two who married late in life. See Table 1.)

In considering the relation of gender to professional advancement, a comparison of the women with their male counterparts is relevant. Rates of employment within academia were tabulated for both groups. (Comparison is limited to academic institutions, because employment opportunities for psychologists during this period were restricted almost exclusively to that setting.) Counting each psychologist who was a college or university president or a full, associate, or assistant professor in the 1906 AMS, it was found that whereas 65% of the men occupied one of these ranks, this was true for only 50% of the women. A comparison of the two groups 15 years later, when most of the individuals were in their mid-50s, based on the third edition of AMS (Cattell & Brimhall, 1921), revealed a continuing gap. At that time 68% of the men and 46% of the women held a presidency or professorial rank. (See Table 1 for positions held by women in 1906 and 1921.)

All of the women who attained an academic rank of assistant professor or higher were unmarried. (Squire was a widow, and Thompson, listed in AMS 1906 as professor at Mt. Holyoke, had actually left that position when she married in 1905.) Furthermore, the institutions in which they found employment were predominantly women's colleges; and, finally, all but one of the women who held the position of college president or full professor did so within institutions for women. (Lillien J. Martin, who was listed as professor emeritus in the 1921 AMS, had held the rank of full professor at a coeducational university, Stanford, from 1911 until her retirement at age 65 in 1916.)

Concerning employment, then, there was a definite "women's place" for women psychologists: teaching at undergraduate institutions for women. However, there is no indication that these women were restricted to what has been labeled "women's work," as was the case for women in other sciences (see Rossiter, 1982, Ch. 3). An article assessing the status of American psychology in 1904 noted that the field had become differentiated into a host of subfields including—besides experimental psychology—educational, comparative, and a wide variety of other specialty areas (Miner, 1904). The women were active in virtually all areas. Furthermore, the women's research interests spread across the breadth of the discipline in a pattern not discernibly different from that of the men. (See Table 1 for major research interests of the women through 1906.)

To summarize, the first women psychologists were similar in age and training to their more numerous male colleagues. However, when we evaluate the professional development of these women over a 15-year span, it is clear that they were less likely to achieve professional status equivalent to that of the men. When high professional status was attained, it was held exclusively by unmarried women who were employed for the most part in colleges for women.

Women's Experience

Although the women psychologists as a group fared less well professionally than the men, three did receive stars in the first edition of *AMS,* placing them among the 1,000 scientists whom Cattell had identified in 1903 as the most meritorious in the country (Cattell, 1903a). They were Mary Whiton Calkins (1863–1930), Christine Ladd-Franklin (1847–1930), and Margaret Floy Washburn (1871–1939), who ranked 12th, 19th, and 42nd among 50 starred psychologists. Three other women among the un-starred psychologists in 1906 received stars in subsequent editions of *AMS:* Ethel Dench Puffer (Howes), Lillien Jane Martin, and Helen Bradford Thompson (Woolley). Here we focus primarily on the three who were most prominent, showing how gender influenced their lives. As they are the best known women of the period, there are a few secondary sources that provide additional biographical information for them (e.g., Boring, 1971; Furumoto, 1979, 1980; Goodman, 1980; Hurvich, 1971; Onderdonk, 1971).

The first three of psychology's eminent women shared several common experiences and in these ways may be considered prototypes for those who, by entering a male-dominated profession, challenged the cultural stereotype that defined women's sphere. Each encountered institutional discrimination in pursuing the PhD. Each experienced limited employment opportunities. Each had to confront the marriage-versus-career dilemma.

And each wrestled with family obligations that conflicted strongly with career advancement.

Ladd-Franklin, Calkins, and Washburn began their graduate studies as "special students" at Johns Hopkins, Harvard, and Columbia, respectively. Their "special" status reflected the female-exclusionary policies of these institutions, policies that were waived only partially for them. Ladd-Franklin was admitted because a prominent Johns Hopkins mathematics professor, having been impressed by professional work she had already published, interceded for her. Calkins secured the privilege of attending seminars at Harvard on a petition from her father, accompanied by a letter from the president of Wellesley College (where she was a faculty member). Though both Ladd-Franklin and Calkins completed all requirements, each was denied the doctorate. Washburn would probably have met the same fate had she remained at Columbia. She was advised, however, to transfer to Cornell, where she was eligible for both a degree and a fellowship. There she studied under E. B. Titchener and in 1894 became the first woman to receive a PhD in psychology. Ladd-Franklin was granted the degree in 1926 (44 years after earning it), when Hopkins celebrated its 50th anniversary. Calkins was offered the PhD under the auspices of Radcliffe College in 1902 for work she completed in 1895, but she declined the dubious honor of that arrangement worked out for women who had studied at Harvard.

Employment for women in psychology was almost totally limited to the women's colleges and normal schools. Thus, Calkins spent her entire career at Wellesley College, and Washburn taught first at Wells College and then at Vassar for 34 years. Exclusion from the research universities, then the centers of professional activity, necessarily limited the women's research activities as well as their interaction with the leading figures in the emerging field of psychology. There were, however, personal advantages for faculty at the women's colleges. Recently completed research on the Wellesley College professorate provides a richly illustrated portrayal of faculty life that concurs with material we have collected on the women psychologists.

Patricia Palmieri's (1983) study is a collective portrait of the women at Wellesley College who had been on the faculty there for more than five years and held the rank of associate or full professor by 1910. These women came mainly from closeknit New England families notable for the love and support given to their bright daughters. Among that group, described as "strikingly homogeneous in terms of social and geographic origins, upbringing, and socio-cultural worldview" (p. 197), were five of the 22 psychologists, including Mary Calkins.

Palmieri emphasized *community* as a central theme that "illuminates the history of academe as it was writ by women scholars, outside the research universities so commonly thought to be the only citadels of genuine intellectual creativity" (1983, p. 196). She drew a sharp contrast between the experience of the academic women at Wellesley and that of men at the research universities. She characterized the male academic of the period as an isolated specialist, whereas the female academic lived within a network of relationships:

> These academic women did not shift their life-courses away from the communal mentality as did many male professionals; nor did they singlemindley adhere to scientific rationalism, specialization, social science objectivity, or hierarchical association in which vertical mobility took precedence over sisterhood. (Palmieri, 1983, pp. 209–210)

There were, as Palmieri noted, costs as well as benefits associated with the creation and maintenance of a community such as the one she described. For example, there were tensions surrounding the question of commitment to social activism versus institutional loyalty. In one instance, when a prominent faculty member was terminated by Wellesley College because of her pacifist views during World War I, Mary Calkins felt compelled to offer the trustees her resignation because she herself held the same views; her request, however, was refused (Trustees Minutes, 1919). Finally, to remain a member of the Wellesley community, a woman had to forego marriage and motherhood, for Wellesley, like other institutions of higher education in that era, did not consider it acceptable to include married women on its faculty.

Personal relationships were particularly important for each of psychology's first three eminent women; gender and marital status were crucial in determining how these relationships interacted with career. For Ladd-Franklin, marriage and motherhood precluded professional employment. The accepted view in the late 19th and early 20th century was that, for a man, the potential for professional accomplishment was enhanced by marriage. For a woman, however, marriage and career were incompatible. Thus, an educated woman was faced with what was then termed the "cruel choice." A friend of Ladd-Franklin, with whom she had discussed the marriage-versus-career dilemma plaguing women, expressed the sentiment of the time:

> As human nature stands and with woman's physical organization to consider, . . . she ought to be taught that she cannot serve two masters, that if she chooses the higher path of learning and wants to do herself and her sex justice, she must forego matrimony. (Ridgely, 1897)

95

Whether or not Ladd-Franklin herself agreed with this verdict, she nevertheless was subject to the strong social sanctions against women's combining of marriage and career. She never held a regular faculty appointment.

For Calkins and Washburn, the "family claim"—an unmarried daughter's obligations to her parents—was paramount. Calkins maintained very close ties with her family, living with her mother and father in the family home near Wellesley College for her entire adult life. In 1905 she was offered a unique career opportunity, which she confided to her brother Raymond:

> We go on a walk and she tells me of her brilliant offer from Barnard and Columbia, to be Professor of Psychology with graduate classes from both colleges. A very perplexing decision, involving as it would, the breaking up of her Newton home, hard for mother and father. (R. Calkins, 1905)

As Calkins later explained in a letter to her graduate school mentor, Hugo Munsterberg, her reason for refusing to consider the offer hinged on what she perceived to be her family's best interests. She wrote:

> The deciding consideration was a practical one. I was unwilling to leave my home, both because I find in it my deepest happiness and because I feel that I add to the happiness of my mother's and father's lives. They would have considered transferring the home to New York, but I became convinced that it would be distinctly hurtful to them to do so. (M. W. Calkins, 1905)

Like Calkins, Washburn was particularly close to her parents and felt a strong sense of responsibility for them. Her situation is another example of how the obligations of a daughter might impede professional advancement. As an only child, Washburn clearly acknowledged the demands that the family claim held for her. In 1913 she wrote to Robert Yerkes, to resign responsibility as review editor for the *Journal of Animal Behavior:*

> I doubt if anyone else on the board is teaching eighteen hours a week, as I am. I simply must cut down my work somewhere. If I am ever to accomplish anything in psychology, it must be done in the next five years, for as my parents get older, I shall have less and less command of my time. (Washburn, 1913)

Significantly, the work that she considered her most important contribution was published not long after, as *Movement and Mental Imagery* (Washburn, 1916).

The early women psychologists who remained unmarried and both developed their scholarly careers and lived their lives within the context of the women's colleges shared a common set of experiences. Those who chose to marry, however, as did Ladd-Franklin, constituted another group, whose experiences were similar to each other but different from the unmarried women. None of the married women had regular or permanent academic affiliations. Their career patterns tended to be erratic and without signs of advancement. Even if an individual was able to reconcile the duties and obligations of the domestic and professional roles, her status as a married woman rendered her ineligible for consideration as a candidate for an academic position. Christine Ladd-Franklin, married and without a regular academic appointment, nevertheless managed to continue some scientific work and to earn a star in *AMS;* most who chose to marry were not as fortunate.

Another one of those who married was Ethel Puffer. We use her experience to illustrate the keenly felt conflict between marriage and career that bedeviled this group. It is worth noting that Puffer and Calkins had several things in common. Besides their Protestant New England heritage, their first-born status in their families, and their undergraduate education at Smith College, they both did their doctoral work in the Harvard Philosophy Department with Hugo Munsterberg as thesis advisor. We suggest that the choice for marriage by Puffer and for career by Calkins contributed to their quite different professional attainments.

After completing her doctoral study in 1898, Puffer held concurrent positions in psychology at Radcliffe and Simmons College in Boston and also taught at Wellesley. Her book *The Psychology of Beauty* was published in 1905. In August 1908 she married an engineer, Benjamin Howes, at which point her career in psychology halted. A letter dated April 29, 1908, from the president of Smith College highlights the negative impact that choosing to marry had on a woman's academic career:

> Dear Miss Puffer: If you really are disposed to think seriously of the position at Barnard I am sure it would be well for your friends in Cambridge to recommend you to President Butler, although I fear the rumor which reached me concerning your engagement may have also affected the recommendation which I myself sent, and that a candidate has already been selected to present to the trustees of Columbia at their next commencement. (Seelye, 1908)

A few years after their marriage, Ethel and Benjamin Howes settled in Scarsdale, New York, where in 1915 and 1917 (when Ethel was in her 40s) two children were born: Ellen and Benjamin, Jr. During this decade, she also found time to do organizational work for the suffrage movement and the war effort.

In 1922, Ethel Howes turned 50. World War I was over, the vote was won, and her two children were of school age. In that year, she publicly addressed the inherent contradiction facing women who attempted to combine a career and marriage. Her typed notes for two articles that appeared in the *Atlantic Monthly* (Howes, 1922a, 1922b) highlight her own struggle and conflict. In the excerpt presented here, we retain the capital letters Howes used for emphasis. The notes begin: "The basic inhibition still operating to suppress the powers of women is the persistent vicious alternative—MARRIAGE *OR* CAREER—full personal life vs. the way of achievement" (Howes, undated). Howes reasoned that even if every woman were granted the right to marry and go on with her job, a major problem remained. It was how to reconcile the demands of a career with those of being a mother, for most women who married would have children. Success in a career demanded concentration, and this meant "long sustained intensive application . . . [and] freedom from irrelevant cares and interruptions" (Howes, undated). Such concentration, she maintained, was precisely what was unavailable to a woman who was a mother.

The incompatibility between having a successful career and being a successful mother led Howes to advise married women "EXPLICITLY *TO FOREGO THE CAREER*." She regarded aspirations to a full-fledged career as unrealistic and advised married women to "TRANSCEND THE WHOLE NOTION OF A CAREER, WITH ITS CONNOTATIONS OF COMPETITION, SUCCESS, REWARDS, HONORS, TITLES" (Howes, undated). In her view, this could be done by contracting the scope or modifying the type of professional work: finding opportunities in "borderline subjects," in a "fringe of special research," or in consulting, criticizing, and reviewing. The accommodation to marriage and parenthood that Howes envisioned as necessary for educated women, then, called for an adjustment of professional activity and goals that men have not, until very recently, even had to consider—much less adopt.

Conclusions

What do we conclude concerning the first American women psychologist and how gender shaped their personal and professional experiences? First, they were similar to American men psychologists on basic demographic variables such as family and geographic origins, age, and social class membership. They were similar to the men in some aspects of their educational experience. They held equivalent degrees but were restricted in the number and types of institutions where both baccalaureate and graduate studies might be undertaken. The women diverged from the men most obviously in the area of career advancement.

Second, these women demonstrated three career patterns: no career beyond the doctorate, continuous careers restricted mainly to teaching in women's colleges and normal schools, and interrupted or disjointed careers with lapses in employment or shifts in employment setting and type of work. Of those women who pursued careers, the unmarried group followed the continuous pattern, whereas the married women displayed the interrupted pattern.

Third, certain gender-specific factors profoundly affected the women's experience: exclusion from important educational and employment opportunities, the responsibility of daughters to their families, and the marriage-versus-career dilemma. These factors are illustrated in the lives of the women dis-

cussed here—Calkins, Washburn, Ladd-Franklin, and Puffer.

Acknowledging the early women's presence and their experience is a first step toward placing women in the history of psychology. Integrating women into that history is necessary if we are to achieve a more complete understanding of psychology's past.

References

Bernstein, M. D., and Russo, N. F. (1974). The history of psychology revisited: Or, up with our foremothers. *American Psychologist, 29,* 130–134.

Boring, E. G. (1971). Washburn, Margaret Floy. In E. T. James (Ed.), *Notable American women, 1607–1950: A biographical dictionary* (Vol. 3, pp. 546–548). Cambridge, MA: Belknap Press.

Calkins, M. W. (1905, June 18). Letter to H. Munsterberg. (From the Hugo Munsterberg Papers, Boston Public Library, Boston, MA)

Calkins, R. (1905, May 28). Entry in log. (From papers held by the Calkins family)

Cattell, J. M. (1903a). *Homo scientificus Americanus:* Address of the president of the American Society of Naturalists. *Science, 17,* 561–570.

Cattell, J. M. (1903b). Statistics of American psychologists. *American Journal of Psychology, 14,* 310–328.

Cattell, J. M. (Ed.). (1906). *American men of science: A biographical directory.* New York: Science Press.

Cattell, J. M., and Brimhall, D. R. (Eds.). (1921). *American men of science: A biographical directory* (3rd ed.). Garrison, NY: Science Press.

Furumoto, L. (1979). Mary Whiton Calkins (1863–1930): Fourteenth president of the American Psychological Association. *Journal of the History of the Behavioral Sciences, 15,* 346–356.

Furumoto, L. (1980). Mary Whiton Calkins (1863–1930). *Psychology of Women Quarterly, 5,* 55–67.

Goodman, E. S. (1980). Margaret F. Washburn (1871–1939): First woman Ph.D. in psychology. *Psychology of Women Quarterly, 5,* 69–80.

Goodman, E. S. (1983). History's choices [Review of *History and systems of psychology* and *A history of western psychology*]. *Contemporary Psychology, 28*, 667–669.

Gordon, K. (1905). Wherein should the education of a woman differ from that of a man. *School Review, 13*, 789–794.

Gulliver, J. H. (1938, March 1). Letter to E. N. Hill. (From the Smith College Archives, Northampton, MA)

Howes, E. P. (undated). Notes for "Accepting the universe" and "Continuity for women." (From the Faculty Papers, Smith College Archives, Northampton, MA)

Howes, E. P. (1922a). Accepting the universe. *Atlantic Monthly, 129*, 444–453.

Howes, E. P. (1922b). Continuity for women. *Atlantic Monthly, 130*, 731–739.

Hurvich, D. J. (1971). Ladd-Franklin, Christine. In E. T. James, J. W. James, & P. S. Boyer (Eds.), *Notable American women, 1607–1950: A biographical dictionary* (Vol. 2, pp. 354–356). Cambridge, MA: Belknap Press.

Lerner, G. (1979). *The majority finds its past: Placing women in history*. New York: Oxford University Press.

Miner, B. G. (1904). The changing attitude of American universities toward psychology. *Science, 20*, 299–307.

O'Connell, A. N. (1983). Synthesis: Profiles and patterns of achievement. In A. N. O'Connell & N. F. Russo (Eds.), *Models of achievement: Reflections of eminent women in psychology* (pp. 297–326). New York: Columbia University Press.

O'Connell, A. N., & Russo, N. F. (Eds.). (1980). Eminent women in psychology: Models of achievement [special issue]. *Psychology of Women Quarterly, 5*(1).

Onderdonk, V. (1971). Calkins, Mary Whiton. In E. T. James, J. W. James, & P. W. Boyer (Eds.), *Notable American women, 1607–1950: A biographical dictionary* (Vol. 1, pp. 278–290). Cambridge, MA: Belknap Press.

Palmieri, P. A. (1983). Here was fellowship: A social portrait of academic women at Wellesley College, 1895–1920. *History of Education Quarterly, 23*, 195–214.

Puffer, E. D. (1905). *The psychology of beauty*. Boston: Houghton Mifflin.

Ridgely, H. W. (1897, February 15). Letter to Mrs. Franklin. (From the Franklin Papers, Columbia University Library, New York, NY)

Rossiter, M. W. (1974). Women scientists in American before 1920. *American Scientist, 62*, 312–323.

Rossiter, M. W. (1982). *Women scientists in American: Struggles and strategies to 1940*. Baltimore, MD: Johns Hopkins University Press.

Russo, N. F. (1983). Psychology's foremothers: Their achievements in context. In A. N. O'Connell & N. F. Russo (Eds.), *Models of achievement: Reflections of eminent women in psychology* (pp. 9–24). New York: Columbia University Press.

Seelye, L. C. (1908, April 29). Letter to Ethel D. Puffer. (From the Morgan-Howes Papers, Schlesinger Library, Cambridge, MA)

Solomon, B. M. (1985). *In the company of educated women*. New Haven, CT: Yale University Press.

Stevens, G., and Gardner, S. (1982). *The women of psychology*. (Vols. 1–2). Cambridge, MA: Schenkman.

Thomas, M. C. (1908). Present tendencies in women's college and university education. *Educational Review, 35*, 64–85.

Trustees minutes. (1919, May 9). Minutes of the Trustees meeting. (From the Wellesley College Archives, Wellesley, MA)

Walsh, M. R. (1977). *Doctors wanted: No women need apply:* New Haven, CT: Yale University Press.

Washburn, M. F. (1913, October 24). Letter to R. M. Yerkes. (From R. M. Yerkes papers, Manuscripts and Archives, Yale University Library, Hartford, CT)

Washburn, M. F. (1916). *Movement and mental imagery: Outlines of a motor theory of the complexer mental processes*. Boston: Houghton Mifflin.

Watson, R. I., Sr. (1960). The history of psychology: A neglected area. *American Psychologist, 15*, 251–255.

Watson, R. I., Sr. (1975). The history of psychology as a specialty: A personal view of its first fifteen years. *Journal of the History of the Behavioral Sciences, 11*, 5–14.

Welter, B. (1966). The cult of true womanhood, 1820–1860. *American Quarterly, 18*, 151–174.

Nancy Felipe Russo
Florence L. Denmark

Contributions of Women to Psychology

Until recently, the history of psychology has been virtually equivalent to the history of male psychology. The contributions of women psychologists have been largely unrecognized, undervalued, and invisible in historical accounts. New generations of psychologists have been denied the opportunity to acquire a full picture of their intellectual roots. By understanding how the view of psychology's history has been distorted, we can develop a new, broader vision of what psychology has been, is, and can be.

In a 1976 review of biographies and autobiographies of persons contributing to psychology, only 9 out of 255 books identified (3.5%) dealt with the lives of women (Benjamin & Heider 1976). In an expanded listing of 700 short biographical and autobiographical references, only 33 references to female psychologists were uncovered (Benjamin 1974). In 1980, an extensive search of the literature identified approximately 100 sources of biographical and autobiographical material on female contributors to the discipline (Benjamin 1980). The number of women mentioned in recently published texts in the history of psychology remains small (Goodman 1983).

In response to the historical neglect of women's roles and contributions, a subfield

of "women's history in psychology" has begun to evolve—a subfield that in many respects mirrors the development of the field of women's history in general (cf Lerner 1979, 1981). The first step—compensating for the omission of women in historical accounts—is well under way. Women neglected in psychology's history books have begun to be identified, and their contributions are beginning to receive long overdue recognition.

Women's history in psychology has gone beyond the level of identifying "missing women," and has begun to preserve history as defined and interpreted by women in psychology. The impact of the social context and societal institutions on the evolution of psychology and the contributions of women psychologists has begun to be analyzed, and the contributions of psychologists who have challenged sex bias in psychological research and theory have begun to receive attention. Psychology's institutions are changing as a result of these contributions.

In this chapter we summarized the literature of women's contributions to psychology, provide an overview of women's participation and status in the discipline, and focus on some major female contributors. We also discuss how the social context has affected the contributions of women psychologists and examine the current status and prospects of contemporary women in the field.

Reproduced, with permission, from the Annual Review of Psychology, Volume 38, (c) 1987 by Annual Reviews Inc.

Women's Participation
in Psychology

An overview of studies of women's participation in psychology provides a picture of
inequities in education and training, career
development, employment, compensation,
achievements, and professional recognition
(Over 1983). Nonetheless, women have been
involved in psychology form the field's
beginnings, have made critical contributions
to the discipline, and have risen to positions
of unquestioned leadership and distinction.

Some of the work on women's participation in and contributions to psychology
has focused on countries outside of the U.S.
(cf Canziani 1975, Gold Fein 1973, Harper
et al 1985), particularly in the countries of
Australia, Canada, Great Britain, and New
Zealand (Over 1983). Most of the literature,
however, deals with psychology and psychologists in the U.S., a partial reflection of
where the majority of psychologists, male
and female, have trained and/or spent a considerable proportion of their careers.

At least 20 women obtained U.S. doctorates in psychology prior to 1901 (Eells
1957). Of the 186 individuals identified as
psychologists in the first edition of the mis-
named *American Men of Science* (Cattell
1906), 22 (12%) were women. Not included
in that volume were five women who held
membership in the newly formed American
Psychological Association (APA) (Furumoto
& Scarborough 1986).

Despite widespread barriers to education and employment, the numbers of women
in psychology have steadily climbed. In
1920, 62 women in America held PhDs in
psychology (Rossiter 1974). From 1920–
1974, as psychology grew, so did the numbers of women in the field. Of the 32,855
American doctorates awarded in psychology
during this period, 7464 went to women.

Women were pursuing degrees in psychology in Europe as well. For example,
Bluma Zeigarnik, whose dissertation reported
the "Zeigarnik effect," received her PhD
from the University of Berlin in 1927. Maria
Rickers-Ovsiankina and Tamara Dembo, two
of the women who later became associated
with Kurt Lewin, earned their degrees from
the University of Giessen in 1928 and from
the University of Berlin in 1930, respectively. Marie Jahoda was awarded her degree
from the University of Vienna in 1932 (Stevens & Gardner 1982a).

At the end of the nineteenth century,
women could be found in all subfields of
psychology (Furumoto & Scarborough
1986). Over time, however, they became
concentrated in applied subfields that reflected societal stereotypes of the "women's
sphere." Women's history in psychology
has identified some of the complex forces
that created and maintained sex segregation
in American psychology. Historical opportunities for women's employment in women's
colleges, state colleges, schools, and guidance clinics are important factors. In the
United States, the progressive education and
child welfare movements at the turn of the
century interacted with stereotypes about
women at that time, creating employment
settings hospitable to women. In addition,
concern about the quality of draftees in
World War I stimulated interest in child development and mental testing (Russo 1983).

From 1920 to 1974, 48% of U.S. PhDs
in developmental and gerontological psychology and 32% of PhDs in school psychology
went to women. In contrast, 6% of PhDs in
industrial, 14% in psychometrics, 15% in
comparative, 18% in experimental, 20% in
physiological, and 23% in social psychology
went to women. During this same period, the
proportions of women in the field of clinical,
counseling and guidance, and general psychology were similar: 24%. For educational
psychology the figure was 25%. The year

1974 is used as an end point to include graduates who began their doctoral training in 1970. This assumes a four-year period for graduate study (Russo 1984).

During the 1970s, along with the changes in American society that evolved with the growth of the women's movement, dramatic changes occurred in psychology 's enrollment picture. In 1974, women were 31% of the 2598 U.S. doctoral recipients in psychology. In 1983, ten years later, that figure was nearly 48%. In 1985–1986, women were 56% of the 17,562 full-time doctoral students in U.S. departments of psychology: 12% of these 9854 women were identified as members of minority groups (Pion et al 1985).

Sex segregation in psychology's subfields has been reduced. Increases in the proportion of women enrolled in doctoral programs are found in both research and practice specialties, although the proportions of women students are still slightly higher in the applied fields: 58% of full-time doctoral enrollments in clinical, counseling, and school psychology are female, compared to 55% of such enrollments in research specialties. Although an increasing number of developmental psychologists work in applied settings, developmental psychology is still a research specialty. That field continues to have the highest proportion of women receiving doctorates—75% in 1983 (Russo 1984).

Although the numbers are small, the largest *rate* of increase over the decade 1973–1983 is found in the male-dominated field of industrial/organizational (I/O) psychology. In 1973, 6 women comprised 8% of the doctorates awarded in I/O psychology. In 1984, 40 women comprised 38% of the doctorates awarded in that field (CEHR 1985).

While the proportions of women in all subfields of psychology have increased, the concentration of women psychologists in traditionally "female" fields has also increased, partially because these fields were also expanding during the 1970s. However, men are entering these expanding fields as well. In 1973, 46% of psychology doctorates granted to men were in the fields of clinical, counseling, school, or developmental psychology, compared to 53% of doctorates granted to women (National Science Foundation 1983)—a ratio of .87. In 1983 the figures were 57% vs 62% (National Research Council 1983)—a ratio of .92. The more rapid increase of men compared to women over this period is bringing a more equal balance of numbers of women and men in these fields. (Note that NSF figures only consider research doctorates and do not include Doctors of Education or Doctors of Psychology).

While the educational barriers in graduate school have lessened, the legacy of sex discrimination in academic employment has been more difficult to overcome, even with expanding opportunities in the decade of the 1970s. In 1944, 26% of psychologists employed in departments of psychology were women (Bryan & Boring 1946). In 1984, 25% of psychologists employed in U.S. departments of psychology (full- and part-time) were women. Higher proportions of women were still found in part-time positions (41%) compared to full-time positions (22%). Considering only doctoral departments, 21% of the full-time faculty and 39% of the part-time faculty were female (Pion et al 1985). Women are concentrated in lower ranks, and salary differentials favoring men persist, even when years of experience are controlled (Russo et al 1981).

The membership of the American Psychological Association is divided into divisions that can be considered professional networks for psychology's subfields. Membership in these networks continues to be largely male dominated. In 1985, only one of APA's 42 divisions had a membership that was less than 50% male (Division 35, the Psychology of Women, had a membership that was 5.3% male). Thirteen divisions had a membership that was more than 80% male, including Experimental (84.4%), Physiological and Comparative (84.6%), I/O (84.8%), Military (90.5%), and Applied Experimental and Engineering (91.8%). The divisions with between 50–60% male membership were: Developmental Psychology (54.2%), Counseling Psychology (57%), Child, Youth, and Family Services (59.4%), Psychoanalysis (57.1%), and the Society for the Psychological Study of Gay and Lesbian Issues (50.9%) (APA 1985). The first three of these clearly fall into areas that can be considered traditionally female.

Minority Women

Unfortunately, historical information about minority women in psychology continues to be scarce. It was not until 1933, 71 years after the first blacks received college degrees (Mary Jane Patterson and John Brown Russworm, Oberlin; Edward Jones, Amherst), that a black woman, Inez Prosser, received an EdD in educational psychology from the University of Cincinnati (Guthrie 1976). Guthrie (1976) has described the context of the time and how the need for teachers, preachers, and trade workers profoundly affected the development of curricula in the black colleges. Psychology in these schools was limited to its applied aspects and associated with departments of education. As late as 1940 an undergraduate major in the field was only offered in four black colleges. Thirty-two doctorates in psychology (PhD) and education (EdD) went to blacks in the years between 1920–1950, eight of them earned by black women.

The participation of Hispanic, Asian, and Native American women in psychology has received even less attention than that of blacks. Statistical reports rarely present breakdowns by race/ethnicity and sex so that monitoring the changing status of women in the various ethnic minority groups is difficult. In 1984, the National Science Foundation reported that of the total population of approximately 11,900 employed female psychologists holding research doctorates in 1982, 400 (3.4%) were black, 200 (1.7%) were Asian, and 100 (.8%) were Native American. Similarly, 100 (.8%) were Hispanic. Since the National Science Foundation rounds its figures to the nearest 100, these figures are only approximations (National Science Foundation 1984).

Women in Psychology: Some Major Contributors

A critical element for studying the history of women in psychology is to identify the contributions of women psychologists that have been historically neglected. Considerable work has been expended toward that end (Bernstein & Russo 1974, Benjamin 1980, Denmark 1980, 1983, Furumoto & Scarborough 1986, Gavin 1983, Gold Fein 1973, 1985, Kimmel 1976, O'Connell & Russo 1980, 1983, Over 1983, Sexton 1969, Stevens & Gardner 1982a,b).

Women contributors to psychology are also identified by historians interested in women's history in general (Crovitz & Buford 1978, James et al 1971, Sicherman & Green 1980, Tinker 1983) and women's history in science in particular (Rossiter 1982).

The work has varied in quality and depth, some authors relying on second- and third-hand sources whose accuracy may be suspect (Ross 1985). As a body of literature, however, it irrefutably documents the extensive involvement and invaluable contributions of female psychologists. The autobiographies of the female pioneers, told in their own words, matter-of-factly, with surprisingly little bitterness or recrimination, provide a human complement to the participation statistics. It is impossible in the brief space allotted here to describe or even mention all of the women identified in these publications. Only a few major contributors can be highlighted.

As early as 1903, three women—Mary Whiton Calkins, Christine Ladd-Franklin, and Margaret Floy Washburn—were cited among the 50 most famous U.S. psychologists by James McKeen Cattell, founder of *American Men of Science* (Sexton 1969). In the fifth edition of that volume, 22% of the 539 psychologists recognized were women. Looking at the first seven editions of that work, of the 127 names starred for distinction, eight (6.3%) were women: Mary Whiton Calkins, Christine Ladd-Franklin, Margaret Floy Washburn, Ethel Puffer Howes, Lillien Jane Martin, Helen Thompson Woolley, June Etta Downey, and Florence Goodenough (Bryan & Boring 1944).

These early women exhibited a variety of interests. Mary Whiton Calkins, who founded the psychological laboratory at Wellesley College in 1981 and invented the paired associate technique, created a theoretical system of self psychology that brought her recognition in both psychology and philosophy (Furumoto 1980). Christine Ladd-Franklin developed a widely influential theory of color vision besides making contributions to logic that resulted in her being compared to Aristotle (Stevens & Gardner 1982a). Margaret Floy Washburn became the first woman to earn a PhD in psychology. Her landmark work, *The Animal Mind,* was a precursor and impetus to behaviorism (Goodman 1980). Ethel Puffer Howes focused on esthetics and published her book, *The Psychology of Beauty,* in 1905 (Furumoto & Scarborough 1986).

Lillien Jane Martin, a major contributor to work in psychophysics, esthetics, and imagery, was the first woman to become a department head at Stanford University. After retiring from that post in 1916, she founded the first mental hygiene clinic for "normal"

preschoolers. In 1929, at age 78, she started the Old Age Center, the first counseling center for senior citizens (Stevens & Gardner 1982a). Helen Thompson Woolley was a leader in rebutting myths about women's alleged inferiority in mental abilities. A major figure in child development, she, along with Helen Cleveland, developed the Merrill-Palmer Scales which became a widely used tool for testing the mental abilities of children (Rosenberg 1982).

June Etta Downey, a pioneer in the study of traits and developer of the Downey Will-Temperament Test, in 1915 became the first woman to head a department of psychology in a state university, the University of Wyoming (Stevens & Gardner 1982a). Florence Goodenough developed the Draw-a-Man Test. She was also an innovator in the development of observational methods of child development and designed a method of episode-sampling used in research on children's social behavior (Sicherman & Green 1980). Her work, *Anger in Young Children,* continues to be cited frequently in developmental textbooks (Thompson 1983).

Thus, although concentrated in applied fields, women nonetheless have been major contributors to basic research in psychology. Some of these achievements have received recognition. Table 1 contains the names of women receiving awards given by the American Psychological Association and the American Psychological Foundation, along with the reference to the biographical descriptions that accompanied the award announcements appearing in the *American Psychologist.*

As seen in Table 1, from 1956–1985 the American Psychological Association has presented Distinguished Scientific Contribution Awards to five women. In 1966, Nancy Bayley, who pioneered in studies of the measurement and meaning of intelligence, and whose longitudinal studies of infant development evolved into landmark studies of

Table 1

Women receiving awards from the American Psychological Association and American Psychological Foundation by award area, to 1985.

Year of award	Name of winner	Reference to award citation in *American Psychologist*	

AMERICAN PSYCHOLOGICAL ASSOCIATION

Distinguished Scientific Contributions

1976	Beatrice C. Lacey (with John Lacey)	*32* (1) Jan. 11, 1977	54–61
1973	Brenda Milner	*29* (1) Jan. 19, 1974	36–38
1972	Dorothea Jameson (with Leo Hurvich)	*28* (1) Jan. 19, 1973	55–74
1968	Eleanor J. Gibson	*23* (12) Dec. 19, 1968	857–867
1966	Nancy Bayley	*21* (12) Dec. 19, 1966	1190–1200

Distinguished Applications in Psychology

1981	Anne Anastasi	*37*(1) Jan. 1982	52–29

Distinguished Professional Contributions

1982	Carolyn R. Payton	*38* (1) Jan. 1983	32–33
1981	Jane W. Kessler	*37* (1) Jan. 1982	65

Distinguished Contributions to Psychology in the Public Interest

1979	Marie Jahoda	*35* (1) Jan. 1980	74–81

Distinguished Scientific Awards for an Early Career Contribution to Psychology

1984	Marta Kutas	*40* (3) Mar. 1985	309–312
1983	Carol L. Krumhansl	*39* (3) Mar. 1984	284–286
1982	Martha McClintock	*38* (1) Jan. 1983	57–60
1981	Lyn Abramson	*37* (1) Jan. 1982	79–83
1980	Lynn Cooper	*36* (1) Jan. 1981	78–81
	Shelley Taylor	"	81–84
	Camille Wortman	"	84–87
1977	Judith Rodin	*33* (1) Jan. 1978	75–83
1976	Sandra Bem	*32* (1) Jan. 1977	88–97
	Rochel S. Gelman	"	

AMERICAN PSYCHOLOGICAL FOUNDATION

Gold Medal Award

1984	Anne Anastasi	*40* (3) Mar. 1985	340–341
1982	Nancy Bayley	*38* (1) Jan. 1983	61–63
1980	Pauline Snedden Sears (with Robert Sears)	*36* (1) Jan. 1981	88–91

Distinguished Teaching in Psychology

1982	Carolyn Wood Sheriff	*38* (1) Jan. 1983	64–65
1975	Bernice L. Neugarten	*31* (1) Jan. 1976	83–86
1970	Freda Rebelsky	*26* (1) Jan. 1971	91–95

aging, became the first woman to receive this prestigious award. Eleanor J. Gibson, the second woman to receive the award [1968], made major contributions to the understanding of perceptual learning and development and experimental research on reading. Dorothea Jameson [1972, shared with Leo Hurvich], advanced scientific knowledge in the area of color vision. Brenda Milner [1973] contributed to understanding of relationships of brain structure to functioning, particularly with regard to localization of speech, pattern perception, and memory. Beatrice C. Lacey (shared with John I. Lacey) made outstanding contributions to understanding the relationship between the autonomic nervous system and behavior.

Using an international panel of psychologists, Watson (1974) developed a listing of persons living between 1600 and 1967 who were recognized as eminent contributors to psychology. Of the 538 contributors, 228 were identified as psychologists while the others reflected psychology's links to other sciences, philosophy, and medicine.

Eight of the psychologists identified were women: Augusta Bronner, Mary Whiton Calkins, June Etta Downey, Else Frenkel-Brunswick, Florence Goodenough, Leta Stetter Hollingworth, Christine Ladd-Franklin, and Margaret Floy Washburn. There were also three psychoanalysts (Frieda Fromm-Reichmann, Karen Horney, Melanie Klein), one anthropologist (Ruth Benedict), the first Italian woman to earn an M.D. (Maria Montessori), and one layperson (Dorothea Dix) (Russo & O'Connell 1980).

Prior to 1970, only one woman who can be "claimed" as a contributor to psychology was elected to membership in the National Academy of Sciences: Margaret Floy Washburn [1931]. Since 1970, psychologists Eleanor J. Gibson [1971] and Dorothea Jameson [1975] have joined the membership of that prestigious body. Women in related fields who have contributed to the

psychological literature include anthropologists Frederica DeLaguna and Margaret Mead [1975] and Elizabeth Colson [1977], and linguist Mary K. Haas [1978].

Two women, Mary Whiton Calkins [1905] and Margaret Floy Washburn [1921], served as President of APA between 1982 and 1970. Since that time, five women have achieved the distinction of that office: Anne Anastasi [1972], Leona Tyler [1973], Florence L. Denmark [1980], Janet Taylor Spence [1984], and Bonnie R. Strickland [1987].

In 1984, 22.9% of the individuals elected to Fellow status in the American Psychological Association were women, up from 8.0% of those elected in 1970. It will take time for such increases to change the overall statistics. Thus in 1985, women were 33.8% of the membership of the American Psychological Association, but only 16.3% of APA members holding Fellow status (APA 1985).

Although women have been underrepresented in I/O psychology, they have been involved in the field form its inception and have made significant contributions both in Europe and the U.S. For example, Franziska Baumgarten-Tramer, who received her PhD from the university of Berlin in 1917, was one of the first industrial psychologists, and made major contributions to the understanding of job satisfaction and personnel selection. In the U.S., Lillian Moller Gilbreth, who received her PhD in Industrial Psychology from Brown University in 1915, became an internationally recognized efficiency expert for time and motion studies. She also made pioneering contributions to kitchen design, including the foot-pedal trash can and storage shelves on refrigerator doors. As a consultant to the Institute of Rehabilitation Medicine at New York University Medical Center, she designed a kitchen to serve the needs of handicapped persons that became an internationally known training center (Sicherman & Green 1980). On February 24, 1985, she became the first psychologist to be featured on a U.S. postage stamp.

Minority Women

The emphasis on women's history in psychology came in time to preserve the autobiographies of some of the minority women who were pioneers in the discipline, including Ruth Howard (Bechham), the first black woman to receive a PhD in psychology (Howard 1983), and Mamie Phipps Clark, whose coauthored research (with her husband Kenneth Clark) cited in *Brown v. the Board of Education,* was instrumental in the United State's Supreme Court ruling to desegregate the Nation's schools (Clark 1983). Such stories offer sources of information as well as inspiration to future generations of psychologists.

The contributions of Hispanic, Asian, and Native American women to psychology have yet to receive adequate attention. However, the autobiography of Martha Bernal (1984), the first Chicana to earn a PhD in psychology, who went on to become a highly cited contributor to the behavior therapy and parenting literatures, has been recorded.

The Societal Context: Its Impact on Women's Contributions

Women's history in psychology has begun to analyze the relationship of the societal context to women psychologists' careers and contributions (Lewin 1984, Rossiter 1982, Rosenberg 1982, Russo & O'Connell 1980, Russo 1983, Shields 1975a,b).

Psychology in the United States began its growth at the end of the 19th century, at a time of great economic and social change in America. It was a time when belief in women's innate moral superiority had become a truism of American life, and women were called upon to use their "superior" qualities to reform society (Hymowitz & Weissman 1978). Attending to the needs of the "young, helpless and distressed" (Terman & Miles 1936) was considered an extension of "true womanhood" (Welter 1966), a reflection of women's "biological destiny."

It was also a time in America when women demanded equal political rights and better conditions of employment. These goals became justified as a means to enable women to reform society. Women's rights were particularly linked with child welfare (Sears 1975). Motherhood was reified, and the "mother's heart" was even used to justify women's fight for suffrage (Ehenreich & English 1978).

The aspirations and interests of women in psychology were shaped and limited by the societal context. Psychology itself was used to justify the exclusion of women from higher education—helping to perpetuate the belief that developing one's intellectual capabilities was incompatible with the female qualities needed to fulfil the obligations of the "women's sphere" and attain "true womanhood" (Lewin 1984, Rosenberg 1982, Welter 1966). Thus, in order to gain the education needed to become a psychologist, women had to face myths perpetuated by psychology itself.

Past Luminaries of psychology such as G. Stanley Hall, the founder of the American Psychological Association, proclaimed that the educated woman who selfishly aspired to work rather than to marriage violated her biological ethic—to the detriment of her mammary function, among other evils (Ehrenreich & English 1978). Stephanie Shields (1975a) has developed a classic summary of the stereotypes and prejudices pervading psychology at the turn of the century that should be required reading for all persons who aspire to work in the discipline.

Hall warned that coeducation in adolescence would disrupt the "normalization" of the menstrual period, and that educating women to compete with men "in the world" would cause "race suicide" as maternal

107

urges would become neglected (Shields 1975a,b). The warnings of Hall and other "experts" against the dangers of education of women were not without effect. For example, Martha Carey Thomas, President of Bryn Mawr College, reported that as a young woman, after reading Hall's pronouncements on the female sex, that she had been "terror struck lest she and every other woman . . . were doomed to live as pathological invalids . . . as a result of their education" (Ehrenreich & English 1978, p. 117).

The first women in psychology had to face barriers justified by these stereotypes, and many used their professional knowledge and skills to refute them. The first psychologist (male or female) to receive a PhD from the University of Chicago was Helen Thompson (Woolley), who obtained it in 1903 through the department of philosophy (Heidbreder 1933). Helen Thompson Woolley deserves special mention here because she was the first of these early "greats" of psychology to successfully integrate her interest in science with her commitment to social reform and use her scientific skill to rebut myths about sex differences (Rosenburg 1982).

Influenced by the work of Woolley, Leta Stetter Hollingworth also stands out as a role model *par excellence* for individuals who wish to combine a commitment to scientific excellence with work in the public interest. Leta Hollingworth, who received her PhD in education from Columbia in 1916, came to eminence in psychology primarily because of her contributions to child psychology and education, particularly for her innovative work on exceptional children. She was the first to use the term "gifted," and her book on adolescence became a classic (Benjamin 1975). However, it was her pioneering work on the psychology of women that gives her a special place in any discussion of women's history in psychology.

Leta Hollingworth demanded that psychology apply scientific rigor in research on women. She proceeded to refute the myths of the time through empirical research on mental and physical performance during the menstrual cycle, on the variability hypothesis (which erroneously explained men's higher status due to greater male variability), and women's sex roles (Shields 1975b).

Since psychology has been an academic enterprise (Rossiter 1974), the status of women in academia has affected women's ability to fulfil their scientific potential in psychology. It took independence and a strong will to overcome the social, educational, and employment barriers facing women. By 1900, less than one-fifth of all educational degrees, and only 6% of the doctorates (or equivalent) went to women (Mandel 1981). Even the most talented women were not exempt from the institutional discrimination of our educational systems. Mary Whiton Calkins was denied a degree for her work at Harvard (Furumoto 1980). The fact that the distinguished William James judged her his brightest student was not persuasive to the Harvard trustees (Sexton 1973/1974). Margaret Floy Washburn left Columbia University for Cornell because there were no fellowships even for the brightest women. Cornell was unusual because it both admitted women and considered them eligible for fellowships (Furumoto & Scarborough 1986).

Once women psychologists overcame educational hurdles and obtained their degrees, they faced barriers to employment in the major universities. Employment was to be found in women's colleges and normal schools, where women could pursue interests that spanned all areas of psychology (Furumoto & Scarborough 1986).

Antinepotism rules were particularly hard on the large number of married couples in psychology. Again, even the most distinguished women were not exempt. For example, National Academy of Sciences member Eleanor Gibson and her psychologist husband James J. Gibson were both able to participate fully in Koffka's faculty at Smith; but when Koffka died and they moved to Cornell in 1949, Eleanor Gibson found that she was no longer allowed to teach (Gibson 1966).

In 1976, a study by the American Association of University Women found that one out of every four institutions still had antinepotism policies. Such policies were more likely to be found in large coeducational and public institutions where larger numbers of psychologists were likely to be employed (Howard 1978).

The Emergence of Sex Segregation in Psychology

With the turn of the century came a change in attitudes toward children and a "professional approach to child care." Never before had children's welfare played such a significant role in the nation's political agenda. The role of "mother" became viewed as "a scientific vocation that required intelligence and training" (Filene 1975). This view of motherhood provided a "legitimate" sphere for women in the world of work and a rationale for their higher education.

Society's interest in child welfare stimulated psychological research on child development, mental retardation, and mental testing. The use of mental tests exploded, and many women became pioneers in the testing movement (Denmark 1980, Russo & O'Connell 1980, Sexton 1969, 1973/1974).

The first psychological clinic, established by Lightner Witmer at the University of Pennsylvania in 1896, was founded "for the study and treatment of children who were mentally or morally retarded and of those who had physical defects that slowed development or progress" (French 1984, p. 976). In 1900, Witmer graduated his first PhD student, Anna Jane McKeag. Of Witmer's first 25 students to receive the PhD, 8 were women (French 1984).

In 1909, the Juvenile Psychopathic Institute, considered to be the first mental health clinic, was established in Chicago by psychiatrist William Healy and psychologists Augusta F. Bronner and Grace Fernald. Child guidance clinics spread in the 1920s, and in 1924, child guidance clinicians founded the American Orthopsychiatric Association. In 1931, Augusta Bronner was elected to its presidency (Reisman 1976). Concern with child welfare also led to an expansion of the juvenile court system, where the work of women psychologists can be seen as precursor to what later emerged as the subfield of law and psychology (Russo & O'Connell 1980).

Thus, during the first three decades of the 20th Century the child guidance and progressive education movements provided a place for women psychologists to apply their talents in a way congruent with society's conceptions of women's interests and abilities. Milton Senn (1975) has provided an excellent account of the child development movement in the United States. Although there are other historical treatments of the field (e.g. Anderson 1956, Sears 1975), his is the only one that gives visibility to women.

In the 1930s, as the child guidance movement declined, interest in psychoanalysis increased. Numerous women were involved in the early psychoanalytic circle that had an impact on the development of clinical and child psychology. Early greats such as Frieda Fromm-Reichmann, Karen Horney, Melanie Klein, and Clara Thompson challenged the givens of the Freudian psychoanalytic scheme that so contributed to the myths held about women at the time (Russo & O'Connell 1980).

Other eminent figures include Susan Isaacs, who was a cofounder of the British Psychoanalytic Society. Studies of children based on psychoanalytic perceptions of Anna Freud, Melanie Klein, and Susan Isaacs are considered to have been particularly important in stimulating child development researchers to go beyond the question of *how* to the question of *why* (Senn 1975). Then there was Charlotte Buhler, who was one of the first to begin to look at age and class variables in her research on children, and who is regarded as the first "humanistic psychologist" (Krippner 1977).

In the 1920s, the Laura Spelman Rockefeller Memorial funded institutes for child study that provided supportive employment settings for women to work in the area of child development in the U.S. We might argue that the institutes contributed to the separation of the worlds of work for men and women, a trend fostered by the rapidly growing "female" science of home economics. At that time, there was some tension between the women who chose to pursue careers in male-dominated "scientific" fields and those who pursued the more "feminine" applied fields of child development and education. Nonetheless, the institutes created a source of employment for women that provided access to stimulating colleagues and research facilities. The list of women associated with them reads like a *Who's Who* of women psychologists (Russo & O'Connell 1980).

During the 1930s the depression had an impact on all psychologists. Employment opportunities were limited and salaries small, but women continued to enter psychology: 1 out of 4 psychology doctorates granted from 1933–1937 went to women. Little has been written about women psychologists in the decade of the 1930s, which included the beginning of the immigration of European Jewish contributors to psychology , such as Therese Benedek, Hedda Bolgar, Else Frenkel-Brunswick, Eugenia Hanfmann, Marie Jahoda, and Margaret Mahler, who came to the U.S. to escape Nazism. In her autobiography, Mary Henle talks about the anti-Semitism in the United States that has affected the careers of Jewish psychologists (Henle 1983).

In 1940, although women comprised 30% of psychologists, they held 51% of psychology positions in schools, educational systems, clinics, guidance centers, hospitals, and custodial institutions (Bryan & Boring 1946). A small 1941 study of employment opportunities for black psychologists found a similar pattern of concentration in women's fields. Eleven out of the 76 black psychologists identified were women. One was unemployed and 3 were in applied fields (school, consulting, and social work). The 7 employed in colleges or normal schools were described as concerned "for the most part with the teaching of Educational Psychology, Child Psychology, and the Psychology of Adolescence, with nursery school supervision and work as Dean of Women" (Brunschwig 1941, p. 676).

World War II contributed to sex segregation in psychology. It created opportunities for men by employing them in the war effort directly and by stimulating the growth of male-oriented subfields, particularly in industrial and personnel psychology. Of 1006 psychologists entering the armed forces, only 33 were women (Marquis 1944b).

The military provided intensive training and research experiences for civilian psychologists as well as enlisted personnel. In 1943, the army established a course in Advanced Personnel Psychology in the Army Specialized Training Program. According to Marquis (1944a), "approximately 1,300 enlisted *men* completed the intensive six-month course at 11 selected universities" (p. 472, italics ours). Psychologists became involved in devising personnel selection and training methods, human factors research, and civilian morale studies. This wartime experience stimulated male-dominated subfields of industrial and personnel psychology and created predominantly male social networks among researchers that shaped the postwar development of psychology.

The American Psychological Association (APA) played an active role in organizing psychologists during the war, but its initial efforts reflected the interests of male psychologists. During the 1939 convention, the APA authorized the creation of an Emergency Committee in Psychology, without representation of women psychologists. In response, a New York group of women psychologists organized what became the National Council of Women Psychologists (NCWP) "to promote and develop emergency services that women psychologists could render their communities as larger numbers of their male colleagues were drawn into military services" (Portenier, n.d., p. 15). Florence Goodenough served as its first President, with Helen Peak as Vice President, Gladys C. Schwesinger as Secretary, and Theodora M. Abel as Treasurer.

There have been a number of summaries of the research and service of women psychologists during the war years (Finison & Furumoto 1978, Murphy 1943, Portenier, n.d.). These activities reflected the sex segregation of psychology's subfields and focused on problems of civilian morale, relocation, refugees, children, and families in wartime.

This is not to say that women were not involved in every facet of psychology's wartime effort. Barbara Burks worked with Gordon Allport and Gardner Murphy to help settle refugee psychologists, who included Egon Brunswick and Else Frenkel. In the Office of Strategic Services (OSS), Edward Tolman, Donald MacKinnon, James G. Miller, Urie Bronfenbrenner, Donald Fiske, Eugenia Hanfmann, and Ruth Tolman, among others, assessed secret service candidates for assignment overseas. Rensis Likert headed the Morale Division of the U.S. strategic Bombing Survey, where such persons as Daonel Katz, Eugene Harley, Helen Peak, David Krech, and Richard Crutchfield worked on various aspects of civilian morale. In England, Heinz Ansbacher, Jerome Bruner, and Hazel Gaudet worked as part of a survey team (Russo & O'Connell 1980). In her autobiography, Eugenia Hanfmann (1983) communicates the excitement as well as the frustration of working as a psychologist for the OSS when it was necessary to burn all records and notes at the end of the war.

After World War II, the nation prepared for the return of its men. The war had created new and highly desirable positions in business and industry for male psychologists. Given the military's stimulation of training and personnel psychology and the expectation that opportunities in business and industry were open to "men" (Marquis 1944b, p. 661), it is not surprising that I/O psychology remained the subfield of psychology with the highest proportion of men through the decade of the 1970s (Russo 1984).

The needs of male-oriented employment settings shaped the knowledge base of psychology, even in those cases where women psychologists have traditionally participated. There were 16 million veterans of World War II and 4 million veterans of previous wars. The Veterans Administration (VA) cooperated with the United States Public Health Service to create funds for clinical training to serve the predominately male population of patients in need of mental health services. Experience in working with outpatients and women and children was neglected (Resiman 1976). In 1944, women psychologists had a higher _un_employment rate than they had at the beginning of the war (Walsh 1986).

The women psychologists were operating at a time when there was little societal support for such activities. After the war, in the hopes of raising the status of women in psychology by becoming affiliated with the American Psychological Association, the NCWP voted to change its name and purpose. In 1947, the International Council of

111

Women Psychologists was born, with Gertrude Hildreth as President, and the purpose of the group was now to "further international understanding by promoting intercultural relations to practical applications of psychology" (Portenier n.d.). When subsequently told that APA would not admit a single sex organization, males were admitted to membership and the group was renamed the International Council of Psychologists (Portenier n.d.). Nonetheless, efforts to affiliate with APA were rejected. They were told it was inappropriate to have an international group affiliate with a national organization (Walsh 1986).

The repressive climate for American women in the 1950s eventually gave way to social reform. In 1961, President John F. Kennedy established the first President's Commission on the Status of Women which called attention to sex bias in education, including vocational and guidance counseling, and identified the need to rebut myths and stereotypes about women (Peterson 1983). Concern about women's rights received an expected boost from the civil rights movement when legal prohibition against sex discrimination in employment was included in the 1965 Civil Rights Act in an attempt to kill that legislation. During this period careers of women in psychology once again began to receive attention and were the subject of workshops organized at APA's annual meetings (Sexton 1973/1974).

The 1970s brought new opportunities for women in all areas of American society, and psychology was no exception. Although recognition of the accomplishments of female psychologists has continued to lag behind their performance, substantial changes began to occur.

In 1970, psychologist Bernice Sandler, who had experienced sex discrimination in her search for an academic position, began to file class-action suits under the aegis of the Women's Equity Action League. Complaints were filed at over 250 colleges and universities and helped lead to the passage of Title IX of the Education Amendments of 1972, which prohibited sex discrimination in educational institutions receiving federal financial assistance. Sandler continued her leadership in the area of sex equity in education, helping to draft the Women's Educational Equity Act of 1972 and heading the Project on the Status and Education of Women of the Association of American Colleges (Millsap 1983).

In the late 1960s, women again organized in psychology, this time in a more supportive climate. In 1969 the Association for Women in Psychology dramatically communicated their concern with inequities in the field at the annual convention of the APA. In response, in October of 1970, APA established a task force charged with preparing a paper on the status of women in psychology, with Helen Astin as Chair (Task Force 1973). When the Task Force was discharged in 1972, an ad hoc Committee on the Status of Women was formed, chaired by Martha Mednick, which became a continuing Committee on Women in Psychology (CWP) under Mednick's leadership in 1973. The mission of the committee was to "function as a catalyst, by means of interacting with and making recommendations to the various parts of the Association's governing structure. . . ." (Russo 1984).

CWP recommended the establishment of the Division of the Psychology of Women (Division 35), which was formed in 1973 "to promote the research and study of women . . . to encourage the integration of this information about women with current psychological knowledge and beliefs in order to apply the gained knowledge to the society and its institutions" (Russo 1984). For a description of the history of the Division and the evolution of the field, see Mednick (1978) and Denmark (1977). In addition to having an impact on increasing women's participation in nearly all areas of APA's complex governance structure (Russo 1984), both Division 35 and CWP have played major roles in encouraging attention to the history of women in psychology (O'Connell et al 1978, O'Connell & Russo 1980, 1983).

Current Status and Prospects

Women's history in psychology has focused attention on how the social context affects the evolution of psychology and shapes women's contributions to the discipline. This historical perspective can help to build broader understanding of the societal factors that underlie the changing demographic trends in the discipline. From this historical perspective, the increasing proportion of women in psychology reflects an expansion of traditionally female applied fields as much as it does a change in women's career patterns.

The more we study women's history, the more we appreciate the power of society's norms and institutions to affect the development of psychology as well as the career paths of individual psychologists. This knowledge is having an effect on the discipline. Led by women, both women and men are working to eliminate sex bias in psychology and to legitimize the study of women's experiences.

Women psychologists can gain inspiration from the lessons of women's history and recognize that disappointments and setbacks are not necessarily defeat. All psychologists can take pride in the excellence and perseverance of women psychologists revealed by women's history in psychology. We look forward to a synthesis of the new scholarship on women and a reconstruction of psychology's history so that we have an enriched understanding of the works of all psychologists—past, present, and future.

Acknowledgments

The authors would like to thank Allen Meyer, Bonnie Strickland, and Robert Wesner for their comments on the manuscript, and acknowledge the assistance of Michelle Marquand in assembling materials and tracking down references. This work was supported by the Minigrant Program of the College of Liberal Arts, Arizona State University.

Literature Cited

American Psychological Association. 1985. *Membership Directory*. Washington, DC: Am. Psychol. Assoc.

Anderson, J. E. 1956. Child development: An historical perspective. *Child Dev.* 27: 181–96.

Benjamin, L. T. Jr. 1974. Prominent psychologists: A selected bibliography of biographical sources. *JSAS Cat. Sel. Doc. Psychol.* 4:1. MS. 535. 33 pp.

Benjamin, L. T. Jr. 1975. The pioneering work of Leta Hollingworth in the psychology of women. *Nebr. Hist.* 56: 493–505

Benjamin. L. T. Jr. 1980. Women in psychology: Biography and autobiography. *Psychol. Women Q.* 5: 140–44

Benjamin. L. T. Jr., Heider, K. L. 1976. History of psychology in biography: A bibliography. *JSAS Cat. Sel. Doc. Psychol.* 6: 61. MS. 1276. 21 pp.

Bernal, M. 1984. *The life of a Chicana psychologist*. Presented at Ann. Meet. Am. Psychol. Assoc., Anaheim, CA

Berstein, M., Russo, N. F. 1974. The history of psychology revisited: Or. up with our foremothers. *Am. Psychol.* 29: 130–34

Brunschwig, L. 1941. Opportunities for Negroes in the field of psychology. *J. Negro Educ.* 10: 664–76

Bryan, A. I., Boring, E. G. 1944. Women in American psychology: Prolegomenon. *Psychol. Bull.* 41: 447–54

Bryan, A. I., Boring, E. G. 1946. Women in American psychology: Statistics from the OPP Questionnaire. *Am. Psychol.* 1: 71–79

Canziani, W. 1975. Contributions to the history of psychology: XXIII. I. Franziska Baumgarten-Tramer. *Percept. Mot. Skills 41: 479–86.*

Cattell, J. M., ed 1906. *American Men of Science: A Biographical Directory.* New York: Science.

Clark, M. 1983 Mamie Phipps Clark. See O'Connell and Russo 1983, pp. 267–78

Committee on Employment and Human Resources. 1985. *The Changing Face of American Psychology.* Washington, DC: Am. Psychol. Assoc.

Crovitz, E., Buford, E. 1978. *Courage Knows No Sex.* North Quincy, MA: Christopher. 186 pp.

Denmark, F. L. 1977. The psychology of women: An overview of an emerging field. *Pers. Soc. Psychol. Bull.* 3: 356–67

Denmark, F. L. 1980. Psyche: From rocking the cradle to rocking the boat. *Am. Psychol. 35: 1057–65*

Denmark, F. L. 1983. Integrating the psychology of women into introductory psychology. *The G. Stanley Hall Lecture Series,* ed. C. J. Scheier, A. Rogers, 3: 33–75. Washington, DC: Am. Psychol. Assoc.

Eells, W. c. 1957. Doctoral dissertations by women in the nineteenth century. *Am. Psychol.* 12: 230–31

Ehrenreich, B., English, D. 1978. *For Her Own Good.* NU: Anchor. 325 pp.

Filene, P. G. 1975 *Him/Her/Self: Sex Roles in Modern America.* New York: Harcourt, Brace Jovanovich

Finison, L., Furumoto, L. 1978. *An historical perspective on psychology, social action, and women's rights.* Presented at Ann. Meet. Am. Psychol. Assoc., Toronto

French, J. L. 1984. On the conception, birth, and early development of school psychology. *Am. Psychol.* 39 976–87

Furumoto, L. 1980. Mary Whiton Calkins (1863–1930). *Psychol. Women Q.* 5: 55–68

Furumoto, L., Scarborough, E. 1986. Placing women in the history of psychology: The first American women psychologists. *Am. Psychol.* 41: 35–42

Gavin, E. 1983. *Prominent women in psychology as determined by ratings of distinguished peers.* Presented at Ann. Meet. Am. Psychol. Assoc.

Gibson, J. J. 1966. James J. Gibson. In *History of Psychology in Autobiography,* ed. E. G. Boring, G. Lindzey, 5 124–44. New York: Appleton-Century-Crofts

Gold Fein, L., ed. 1973. Women in national and international psychology. *Int. Understanding* 10: 63–114

Gold Fein, L. 1985. *Changing status of women in psychology over past half century.* Invited address, Ann. Meet. Am. Psychol. Assoc.

Goodman, E. 1980. Margaret Floy Washburn (1871–1939): First woman Ph.D. in psychology. *Psychol. Women. Q.* 5: 69–80

Goodman, E. 1983. History's choices. *Contemp. Psychoanal.* 28: 667–69

Guthrie, R. V. 1976. *Even the Rat Was White.* New York: Harper & Row

Hanfmann, E. 1983. Eugenia Hanfmann. See O'Connell & Russo, pp. 141–54.

Harper, R. S., Newman, E. B., Schab, F. R. 1985. Gabriele Gräfin von Wartensleben and the birth of *Gestaltpsychologie. J. Hist. Behav. Sci.* 21: 118–23

Heidbreder, E. 1933. *Seven Psychologies.* New York: Appleton-Century

Henle, M. 1983. Mary Henle. See O'Connell & Russo, pp. 220–32

Howard, R. W. 1983. Ruth W. Howard. See O'Connell & Russo, pp. 55–68

Howard, S. 1978. *But We Will Persist. A Comparative Research Report on the Status of Women in Academe.* Washington, DC: Am. Assoc. Univ. Women

Hymowitz, C., Weissman, M. 1978. *A History of Women in America.* New York: Bantam. 400 pp.

James, E. T., James, J. W., Boyer, P. W., eds. 1971. *Notable American Women, 1607–1950: A Biographical Dictionary,* Vols. 1–3. Cambridge, MA/London, Engl: Belknap Press of Harvard Univ. Press

Kimmel, E. 1976. Contributions to the history of psychology: XXIV. Role of women psychologists in the history of psychology in the South. *Psychol. Rep.* 38: 611–18

Krippner, S. 1977. Humanistic psychology: Its history and contributions. *J. Am. Soc. Psychosom. Med.* 24: 15–20

114

Lerner, G. 1979. *The Majority Finds Its Past.* New York: Oxford. 217 pp.

Lerner, G. 1981. *Teaching Women's History.* Washington, DC: Am. Historical Assoc. 88 pp.

Lewin, M., ed. 1984. *In the Shadow of the Past: Psychology Portrays the Sexes.* New York: Columbia Univ. 337 pp.

Mandel, J. D. 1981. *Women and Social Change in America.* Princeton, NJ: Princeton Univ. Press

Marquis, D. G. 1944a. The mobilization of psychologists for war service. *Psychol. Bull.* 41: 469–73

Marquis, D. G. 1944b. Post-war reemployment prospects in psychology. *Psychol. Bull.* 41 653–63

Mednick, M. T. S. 1978. Now we are four: What should we be when we grow up? *Psychol. Women Q.* 3: 123–38

Millsap, M. 1983. Sex equity in education. See Tinker 1983, pp. 91–119

Murphy, G. 1943. Service of women psychologists to the war: Foreward. *J. Consult. Psychol.* 4: 249–51

National Research Council. 1983. *Summary Report: 1983 Doctorate Recipients from United States Universities.* Washington DC: Natl. Acad. Press

National Science Foundation. 1978. *Increasing the Participation of Women in Scientific Research.* Washington DC: Natl. Sci. Found.

National Science Foundation. 1983. *Science and Engineering Doctorats: 1960–1983.* Washington, DC: Natl. Sci. Found.

National Science Foundation. 1984. *Women and Minorities in Science and Engineering.* Washington, DC: Natl. Sci. Found.

O'Connell, A. N., Alpert, J., Richardson, M. S., Rotter, N., Ruble, D. N., et all. 1978. Gender-specific barriers to research in psychology: Report of the Task Force on Women Doing Research—APA Division 35. *JSAS Cat. Sel. Doc. Psychol.* MS. 1753, 8: 1–10

O'Connell, A. N., Russo, N. F., eds. 1980. *Eminent Women in Psychology: Models of Achievement.* New York: Human Sci. Press. 144 pp.

O'Connell, A. N., Russo, N. F., eds. 1983. *Models of Achievement: Reflections of Eminent Women in Psychology.* New York: Columbia Univ. 338 pp.

Over, R. 1983. Representation, status, and contributions of women in psychology: A bibliography. *Psychol. Doc.* 13: 1–25

Peterson, E. 1983. The Kennedy Commission. See Tinker 1983, pp. 21–34

Pion, G., Bramblett, P., Wicherski, M., Stapp. J. 1985. *Summary Report of the 1984–85 Survey of Graduate Departments of Psychology.* Washington, DC: Am. Psychol. Assoc. 36 pp.

Potenier, L. G., ed. (n.d.) *International Council of Psychologists, Inc.: The First Quarter-Century, 1942–1967.* Int. Counc. Psychol. 48 pp.

Reisman, J. 1976. *A History of Clinical Psychology.* New York: Irvington

Rosenberg, R. 1982. *Beyond Separate Spheres: Intellectual Roots of Modern Feminism.* New Haven: Yale Univ., 228 pp.

Ross, B. 1985. Scholars, status and social context. *Contemp. Psychoanal.* 30: 853–60

Rossiter, M. W. 1974. Women scientists in America before 1920. *Am. Sci.* 62: 312–23

Rossiter, M. W. 1982 *Women Scientists in America: Struggles and Strategies to 1940.* Baltimore: Johns Hopkins. 439 pp.

Russo, N. F. 1983. Psychology's foremothers: Their achievement in context. See O'Connell & Russo 1983, pp. 9–24

Russo, N. F. 1984. *Women in the American Psychological Association.* Washington, DC: Women's Programs Off., Am. Psychol. Assoc.

Russo, N. F., O'Connell, A. N. 1980. Models from our past: Psychology's foremothers. *Psychol. Women Q.* 5: 11–54

Russo, N. F., Olmedo, S., Stapp, J., Fulcher, R. 1981. Women and minorities in psychology. *Am. Psychol.* 36: 1315–63

Scarborough, E., Furumoto, L. 1986. *Untold Lives: The First Generation of Women Psychologists.* New York: Columbia Univ. In press

Sears, R. R. 1975. *Your Ancients Revisited: A History of Child Development.* Chicago: Univer. Chicago Press

Senn, M. 1975. Insights on the child development movement in the United States. *Monogr.*

Soc. Res. Child Dev. 40(3–4, Ser. 16): 1–106

Sexton, V. S. 1969. Women's accomplishments in American psychology: A brief survey. *Pak. J. Psychol.* 2: 29–35

Sexton, V. S. 1973/1974. Women in American psychology: An overview. *Int. Understanding* 10: 66–77

Shields, S. A. 1975a. Functionalism, Darwinism, and the psychology of women: A study of social myth. *Am. Psychol.* 30: 739–54

Shields, S. A. 1975b. Ms. Pilgrim's progress: The contributions of Leta Stetter Hollingworth to the psychology of women. *Am. Psychol.* 30: 852–57

Sicherman, B., Green, C. H., with Kantrov, I., Walker, H., eds. 1980. *Notable American Women: The Modern Period.* Cambridge. MA: Belknap. 773 pp.

Stevens, G., Gardner, S. 1982a. *The Women of Psychology: Pioneers and Innovators.* Vol. I. Cambridge, MA: Schenkman. 240 pp.

Stevens, G., Gardner, S. 1982b. *The Women of Psychology: Expansion and Refinement,* Vol. II. Cambridge, MA: Schenkman. 273 pp.

Task Force on the Status of Women in Psychology. 1973. Report of the Task Force on the Status of Women in Psychology. *Am. Psychol.* 28: 611–16

Terman, L. M., Miles, C. C. 1936. *Sex and Personality.* New Haven: Yale Univ. Press

Thompson, D. 1983. Psychological classics: Older works in developmental psychology frequently cited today. *J. Genet. Psychol. 143: 169–74*

Tinker, I. 1983. *Women in Washington: Advocates for Public Policy.* Beverly Hills, CA: Sage. 327 pp.

Walsh, M. R. 1986. Academic professional women organizing for change: The struggle in psychology . *J. Soc. Issues* 41: 17–27

Watson, R. I. 1974 *Eminent Contributors to Psychology: A Bibliography of Primary References,* Vol. I. New York: Springer. 470 pp.

Welter, B. 1966. The cult of True Womanhood: 1820–1860. *Am. Q.* 18: 151–74

As with the evaluation of the previous section, these questions are designed to allow you the opportunity to evaluate the readings in *Section II* and their impact on your overall learning experience. Your replies to these questions will provide your instructor with information about the usefulness of the articles and an idea of students' reaction to and understanding of the readings. Your responses will serve as feedback for your instructor in using this book effectively, and will also serve future students by guiding revisions of the book. As before, your thoughtful replies will be appreciated.

1. **Please rate each of the readings from 1 to 5 on the following dimensions:**
   (1 = poor; 3 = average; 5 = exceptional)

	Shields	Furumoto & Scarborough	Russo & Denmark
a. Clearly written, readable	___	___	___
b. Presents new information I'd not found elsewhere	___	___	___
c. Stimulated my interest in topics it raised	___	___	___
d. Caused me to re-think ideas I'd held previously	___	___	___

2. **To what extent do these readings fulfill the following aims:** (1 = not helpful; 3 = moderately helpful; 5 = extremely helpful)

	Shields	Furumoto & Scarborough	Russo & Denmark
a. Helps to clarify how histories are shaped by context	___	___	___
b. Helps to explain women's invisibility in histories of psychology	___	___	___
c. Is useful as a basis for re-placing women in psychology	___	___	___

3. **Briefly explain what you believe is the strongest point of each reading:**

Shields:

Furumoto and Scarborough:

Russo and Denmark:

4. **Briefly explain what you believe is the greatest shortcoming of each reading:**
Shields:

Furumoto and Scarborough:

Russo and Denmark:

5. **Are there any areas where you see conflicts or disagreements between these readings and material presented in your text or in lectures?**

6. **Do you have any other comments about these readings?**

Review Questions

These questions are designed to fulfill two purposes: 1) to review and integrate the readings in *Section II* and to relate them to earlier parts of this book, and 2) to encourage connections between this material and that found in standard texts. The questions are conceptual in format, and encourage you to consider the issues raised by the readings rather than to focus on the details presented in the articles.

I. Shields comments that "science played handmaiden to social values." Address the implications of this statement by answering the following:
   a. Shields focuses on three expressions of this dynamic: (sex differences in brain structure, the variability hypothesis, and maternal instinct). Briefly explain how her "handmaiden" assertion applies to each of these.
   b. How can the "science as handmaiden" comment be explained in terms of paradigms? In terms of the social construction of gender? What role did Darwinian theory play in this process?
   c. Find an illustration of a similar dynamic among ideas from your text: where can you identify a concept or theory which clearly reflects then-dominant social (or disciplinary) beliefs?

II. Furumoto and Scarborough discuss the contexts which shaped the lives and work of America's first women psychologists.
   a. Discuss the information they present in terms of the social construction of gender. That is, how did society's understanding about what gender "really is" determine the lives and work of these women?
   b. Psychologists are contributors to as well as products of the social construction of truth. How might the work of the women discussed by Furumoto and Scarborough have acted to influence psychology or social beliefs? Select another person from your text and discuss how her/his work might have influenced social or psychological thought.

III. Russo and Denmark outline a broad range of social and historical forces that have shaped women's place in psychology.
   a. How is the analysis done by Russo and Denmark compatible with Furumoto's "new history?" With Lerner's "transitional" history?
   b. As Russo and Denmark discuss the forces which have influenced women's place in psychology, what role was played by the construction of gender? By psychology's own self-definition (the selection of topics, of methods, the role of applied psychology, etc)?

IV. Both the article by Furumoto and Scarborough and that by Russo and Denmark depict the social context surrounding early American psychology.
   a. As you read about this period in your text, relate the contextual forces mentioned by these authors to other events in the discipline's history. How was other work framed by these same historical forces?
   b. Were women affected by different forces than were men?
   c. Explain your discoveries in terms of the interaction between the construction of psychology (the field's understanding or definition of itself) and the construction of gender.

Psychology Including Women: New Answers, New Questions

Viewed through a constructionist prism, knowledge and history are fluid, living phenomena which can be grasped only be considering the complex web of contexts in which they are created and transmitted. As those contexts change, so does our grasp. It is not possible to alter context without also altering our understanding of reality. Consequently, when significant changes occur in the experience of an individual, a discipline, or a society, the "reality" of that person or group is altered.

Within this shifting reality of constructed truth, it is evident that re-placing women in psychology is both a product of changing contexts and a stimulant to further changes. Our current attention to women and their work is inarguably a response to sweeping historical and cultural changes which have brought issues of gender equity to the forefront of social consciousness. Yet attending to women not only reflects but also alters context. Re-placing women changes psychology.

From this conclusion derives the question addressed by readings in this final section: what will be the consequences of integrating women and their work into our histories? Will psychology look different when seen through a lens shaped more significantly than before by women? Will different questions be asked or different answers deemed legitimate? Will new methods emerge, more appropriate to a transformed conception of the discipline and its purpose? Or will adding women simply add new names to the roster of psychology's noteworthy practitioners? These readings approach this question from quite diverse perspectives.

Bernice Lott's article suggests that the impact of women's greater visibility and participation in psychology can have mutually beneficial consequences. Her assertion that women (especially feminist) psychologists are indeed approaching the discipline differently is joined by a conviction that psychology as traditionally conceived has much to contribute to feminist psychology, as well. This argument reflects the essentially dialectic undergirding of constructionism: elements influence and shape each other in a continuing and reciprocal interaction.

In a different vein, the article by Mary Crawford and Jeanne Marecek presents a constructionist analysis of a brief, recent historical period in psychology's attempts to explain gender. This article combines a constructionist historical explication with a discussion of the reciprocal impact of women in/on psychology. The article demonstrates that in recent years, in particular, the impact of feminist thought (a re-construction of gender) on psychology has been tremendous, as changes in research and theory dealing with gender illustrate. Psychological research and theory, in turn, have contributed to society's re-construction of gender. Psychology has thus been shaped by social change even as it has helped to create that change.

Finally, Martha Mednick takes a disquieting look at the dialectic interchange between psychology and society. The role of social forces in shaping the acceptance of certain psychological constructs is striking here, reminiscent of Shield's "science as handmaiden" in early American psychology. But here the challenge is reversed: Are feminist psychologists too quick, Mednick asks, to accept ideas which lack empirical support simply because they seem compatible with a particular agenda? She traces the widespread acceptance of certain currently popular ideas about gender to political realities of 1980's USA. The clear message is that we are no more immune to the distortions of context than were our predecessors. And women are no more immune to distortions about their own nature than were Social Darwinist thinkers of early America.

Summary

The readings in this section highlight the interactive nature of knowledge construction. Women's place in psychology has not only been framed by the social construction of gender and psychology's self-construction. In addition, women's presence in psychology has contributed to changing social understandings and has altered the face of the discipline. This dialectic process, in turn, raises new questions for society and psychology. From these articles one conclusion is clear: we are in process; the end is not yet visible. Women's integration into this discipline is re-shaping it and will undoubtedly continue to do so. The only question is how.

Bernice Lott

The Potential Enrichment of Social/Personality Psychology Through Feminist Research and Vice Versa*

ABSTRACT: Feminist scholarship is defined and its influence on mainstream social/personality psychology is examined in terms of its potential for enrichment of the field. Such enrichment is viewed as a consequence of: (a) critical analysis to uncover androcentric bias in both content and method, (b) the asking of new questions and formulation of new hypotheses and theories that stem from a focus on women's experiences, and (c) the challenge to some of the traditional assumptions about objectivity in science. In addition, it is argued that social/personality psychology has the potential to enrich feminist theory by contributing to an issue central to it, namely, the nature of gender differences and similarities. It is suggested that within-gender differences must also be examined to uncover the relationships between behavior and its antecedents. Because psychologists are best prepared to probe the connections between what people do, feel, and believe and the conditions that make particular behaviors, feelings, and ideas more probable, our research is essential to understanding how culture constructs gender.

Bernice Lott, "The potential enrichment of social/personality psychology through feminist research, and vice versa." *American Psychologist*, 1985, *40*, pp. 155–164. Copyright © 1985 by the American Psychological Association. Reprinted by permission.

*This is an expanded version of a paper read at the meeting of American Psychological Association in Anaheim, California, August 1983, as part of a Division 35 Special Symposium Series entitled "Educating for the Psychology of Women." I am grateful to an anonymous reader whose thoughtful and constructive suggestions have contributed to the presentation of these ideas.

Requests for reprints should be sent to Bernice Lott, Department of Psychology, University of Rhode Island, Kingston, Rhode Island 02881.

When I first began this article, my intent was to sketch how social/personality psychology has been challenged by the new women's movement—challenged to critically examine its hidden assumptions about women and men (i.e., its beliefs about gender), to raise new questions, and to formulate and test hypotheses derived from a new theoretical orientation. I speculated that those among us who are committed to the Lewinian proposition that behavior is a function of the interaction between person and environment could not fail to be attracted to feminist research, because it is precisely such an interaction that can explain gender and the vast number of its correlates. I had certainly been moved to reexamine old concepts and was caught up in the rich literature, energy, and insights of feminist scholarship. This, then, was a good time to step back and do some assessment in my own field. The results of that very limited first look, because I have just begun and can see the forests yet to be explored, led me to a somewhat different place from that which I had hoped to reach. My two general conclusions are reflected in the article's title. First, thus far, feminist influence on mainstream social/personality psychology seems to be modest although its potential remains enormous, and second, there are some fundamental issues in feminist theory for which psychological research and analysis are essential.

Supporting the first conclusion are the results of a simple frequency count of selected article titles in the *Journal of Personality and Social Psychology (JPSP)*. Although some may question how representative this journal is of research in our field, few will doubt its prestige and its reflection of issues supported by our academic leadership and funding agencies. It has been said by some in social science (e.g., Westkott, 1979) that "women have become the latest academic fad . . . [or] marketable commodities" (p. 427). It has been suggested that, like the case for blacks in an earlier period, social scientists are currently exploiting women as a prolific source of data and amassing facts without a complementary concern with improving the social conditions of women's lives. But this focus on women as objects of knowledge does not seem to be an accurate characterization of the present status of social/personality psychology. I checked all of the titles in five complete volumes of *JPSP* from 1962, 1967, 1972, 1977, and 1982, looking for subjects specifically relevant to women's lives. I read some abstracts where titles were ambiguous but relied primarily on the titles themselves. Omitting editorials and monographs, the percentage of such articles in *JPSP* is as follows: 2% (3 out of 135) in

1962, 6% (12 out of 205) in 1967, 4% (9 out of 210) in 1972, 11% (10 out of 92) in 1977, and 14% (32 out of 224) in 1982. We can be pleased by the steady increase in 20 years from 2% to 14%, or we can be dismayed by the current paucity of research focusing directly on women.[1] Contributing most heavily in 1982 to this research (23 of the 32 articles) were gender comparisons of various behaviors and studies of masculine, feminine, and androgynous personality types. Again, depending on your perspective, this can be a source of gratification or pain!

An earlier review by Denmark (cf. Grady, 1981) of *JPSP* and six other journals yielded similar findings to mine: In 1965 5% and in 1975 11% of the published articles were judged relevant to the psychology of women. One might keep in mind, in evaluating these figures, that the Association for Women in Psychology (AWP) was established in 1969, and APA's own Division 35 was formed in 1973. In addition, about 20,000 women's studies courses are taught at schools around the country, about 450 colleges offer women's studies programs, and 40 schools now have women's studies research centers (Azzi, 1983). Prominent within these programs and courses are topics on the psychology of women. More specifically, Russo (1982) has reported from a national survey of graduate departments of psychology that 670 faculty members in 219 programs identified themselves as having an interest in research or in clinical activities particularly relevant to women. There is also

1. I do not mean to imply that research on general issues such as altruistic behavior, aggression, impression formation, and so forth, are not relevant as much to women as to men. The concern here, however, was with investigations of topics particularly salient in women's lives (e.g., pregnancy, sexual assault) or in which women were identified and especially studied as actors, observers, or stimuli.

a formal effort underway in a number of colleges to mainstream the results of feminist research, that is, to incorporate into already existing courses and programs material on women, new insights, and feminist challenges to traditional scholarship.

It seems clear, nevertheless, that social/personality psychologists concerned with such issues cannot rely on our standard journals. Unger (1982) recently addressed this program of low visibility of women as a research area in our field and asked, "Is work in the psychology of women ignored or undercited because it is done by women, because it is about women, or because it stems from a new and revisionist theoretical perspective?" (p. 12). She suggested the latter, and I would concur.

Feminist Research

What is feminist scholarship? Definitions have been proposed in most of the disciplines in which such work is being done. In our field, Division 35's Task Force on Issues in Research in the Psychology of Women (1977) listed as objectives of feminist research the clarification of "psychological, biological, and social-cultural determinants of behavior," along with "the integration of this information about women (and men) into current psychological knowledge and theories," and the promotion "of a benevolent society in which individual self-actualization is possible" (p. 3). What Unger (1982) has called the "socially activist component of the psychology of women" (p. 5) is a distinguishing feature. Feminist research in psychology, according to the Task Force (1977), tends to be "cooperative, participative. . . , interdisciplinary, [and] nonhierarchical . . . [beginning] with personal experience" and recognizing that "truth is not separate from the person who 'speaks' it" (p. 3). A more recent Division 35 Task Force (1981) suggested that a vital function performed by feminist research is to present the alternative perspective of the "outsider." A number of feminist writers from a variety of disciplines have noted that feminists can provide particularly insightful criticism of their own fields because as women scientists, scholars, and academicians we both belong and do not belong to the primarily male establishment and are thus both insiders and outsiders (e.g., Keller, 1982; Westkott, 1979).

The feminist enrichment or potential enrichment of scholarship in any field takes two general and interrelated forms: (a) self-conscious and critical analyses of the discipline to uncover its androcentric bias in both content and method, thus revealing the "invisibility or distortion of women as objects of knowledge" (Westkott, 1979, p. 423), and (b) the indirect influence that arises from the asking of new questions, and the presentation of new hypotheses and theoretical formulations that follow from a focus on the experiences and conditions of women's lives. From both these sources can be abstracted specific influences on the content, methods, and theories in social/personality psychology. It is difficult to keep these categories separate because they are interdependent and each has an obvious or subtle effect on the other, but I will try to move in an orderly fashion from one to the other in answering the question: How can feminist research enrich our discipline?

Enrichment of
Social/Personality Psychology

1. There is ample evidence that gender is often a significant characteristic of participants in a situation and that it is a variable with predictable consequences (American Sociological Association, 1980; Grady, 1981; Wallston, 1981). For example, women and men have been found to respond differently to achievement situations (Horner, 1972), to

moral dilemmas (Gilligan, 1977, 1982a), and to conformity pressures (Eagly, 1978). Gilligan's work is particularly persuasive in pointing out that it is not the case that women do not attain the "highest" stages of morality, as had been concluded, but rather that Kohlberg's moral stages mirror the socialization of boys or men in our culture more than the experiences of women. Gilligan found evidence that many women tend to consider moral questions in the context of issues of responsibility and concern for others, not isolated from interpersonal consequences.

2. We must use both women and men in our search for general principles and note both differences and similarities. We cannot derive conclusions about behavior by using only male or only female samples as representative of the human population (Division 35 Task Force, 1981). If we are studying aggression, or interpersonal attraction, or empathy, or prosocial behavior, or any other behavior, we must observe women as well as men in similar situations and utilize the same dependent measures. Frodi, Macauley, and Thome (1977) have noted that most studies of aggression have utilized male participants, and that when women are used they are more likely to be asked to respond to paper-and-pencil measures than to the behavioral measures used with men. Similarly, but conversely, McKenna and Kessler (1977) found that interpersonal attraction studies tended to make use of female participants and that in both interpersonal attraction and aggression research "when females, rather than males, are subjects . . . the independent variable is less likely to involve . . . active treatment or arousal . . . and dependent variable measurement is less likely to involve . . . active behavior" (p. 124). This phenomenon illustrates well the connection between the implicit assumptions of researchers and both the content and methodology of our work.

3. It is not correct to assume that good functioning or mental health for women (or men) is necessarily related to fulfilling the "dictates of the gender stereotype" (Kahn & Jean, 1983, p. 660). There is, in fact, strong evidence to the contrary for women. Independent assessments must be made of satisfaction with self, effective functioning, and their correlates.

4. There are subjects pertaining exclusively or almost exclusively to women's lives about which we would know little were it not for the stimulus and volume of feminist scholarship (Division 35 Task Force, 1981): for example, housework, sexual harassment and assault, pregnancy, childbirth, and motherhood. These are areas, issues, or conditions to which women in our culture must learn responses, overt and attitudinal. They are anchored to our culture's definition of women and to our physiology as mediated by society. Similarly, there are women in special populations, such as prison inmates, victims of violence, single parents, widows, pink-collar workers, minority women, professionals, community activists, and poor women, who have been insufficiently studied.

Feminists are not surprised that the topics on which a discipline tends to focus reflect the background and interests of those who do the work in that discipline. In the natural sciences, as well as in the social sciences, women, as well as nonwhite and working-class persons, have been largely outsiders. It is cause for concern, but not surprising, that research problems in mainstream science reflect sexist assumptions and expectations. Thus, for example, Sherif (cf. Unger, 1982) pointed out that when early studies of the menstrual cycle failed to show any reliable impairment of behavior, the mostly male researchers turned to studies of self-reported mood. Now, feminist researchers are once again looking at performance and finding no consistent menstrual-related effects.

Whether the relative paucity of research on some issues can be attributed to an androcentric bias in our field is an intuitively compelling hypothesis, but one that remains to be decisively tested. It may well be (as one reviewer of this article suggested) that certain subjects, such as aspects of sexual functioning, are generally avoided, regardless of which sex they relate to. A careful count of research directly relevant to the lives of men would be instructive and should be done. We may find that increased concern about women's lives, spearheaded by feminist research, has been paralleled by increases in the study of issues specifically pertaining to men. It is the feminist recognition of gender (in general) as a cultural construction, with its enormous social, political, and personal consequences, that may impact on our discipline most profoundly.

5. New research questions present themselves when we cease thinking about women primarily in terms of relationships to others and when we cease thinking about women and men in terms of stereotyped roles and attributes. For example, when we study the workplace, we must not utilize only male participants, and when we study parents and children, we must not focus our attention only on mothers (American Sociological Association, 1980). We must not assume that employed men and unemployed women are representative of their respective groups (Division 35 Task Force, 1981). Baruch, Barnett, and Rivers (1983) have found that paid employment is a significant predictor of feelings of self-esteem and competence among women, which should not be surprising in view of the fact that half of the adult women in our country are salary or wage earners. Parlee (1981) has noted that choice of appropriate control groups reveals the investigator's assumptions and "implicit theoretical framework" as much as the choice of problem to study, hypothesis to test, procedures, participants, and measures.

6. We can no longer study the behavior of women without acknowledging and making explicit the greater status and power of men. Thus, the suggestion by Chesler in 1972 (cf. Alpert, 1978) that "men, including male therapists, drive women crazy in order that men may maintain their favorable position" (p. 966) is a hypothesis that must be taken seriously. Similarities in the behavior of oppressed persons, such as American blacks and women, are new subjects of inquiry, as is the behavior (verbal and nonverbal) of high-status persons, such as white men, directed toward the less powerful (e.g., Henley, 1977).

7. The study of women has guided feminist scholars and researchers to new sources of information—to journals, letters, and other historical and contemporary records of women's lives. Such records reflect attitudes, beliefs, and perceptions that are often at variance with observed social behavior, which is subject to more rigid sanctions (Westkott, 1979). More methods must be explored and accepted because "the narrowness of our methods may also shape the way we ask questions" (Wallston, 1981, p. 602) and the very nature of those questions. For example, whereas agentic methods tend to separate observer from the observed, communal methods recognize their interrelatedness and highlight the connection. Both modes of inquiry should yield information of value.

Social psychology has long been concerned with the study of human relationships. What we learn about social interaction and influence in general are lessons we have recently applied to our own methods of investigation. Detailed studies have focused on illuminating how the data generated in our laboratories by so-called objective methods are influenced by characteristics of the arranged conditions, by expectations and attitudes of the research participants, and by investigator-participant interaction. A generally accepted position now within mainstream social psychology is that the use of multiple methods increases the validity of our research findings. Yet, it is the feminist researcher who is more apt to practice what is preached. Lykes and Stewart (1983) compared articles published in *JPSP* with those in the *Psychology of Women Quarterly (PWQ)* for the years 1978 and 1983. Research reported in the latter journal was more likely to have sampled populations beyond the typical college group (83% in *PWQ* vs. 33% in *JPSP*) and to have utilized a wider range of methods; "fewer than 20% of the *PWQ* studies used traditional experimental methods while 68% of the *JPSP* studies did" (p. 13).

Feminist scholarship rejects no careful, rigorous, intersubjective, repeatable method of inquiry. Laboratory experiments are appropriate for some questions; other methods are better for others. The new research questions posed by feminist psychologists demand expansion in our field of inquiry, in acceptable sources of data, and in research techniques. Thus, issues of content become issues of method.

8. Among the most wide-ranging and significant lessons to be learned from feminist research is that which is the sine qua non of social psychology, namely, that behavior is a function of both the person and the context, and that the same person may behave differently in different situations. To understand gender, multiple contexts must be employed (Division 35 Task Force, 1981). For example, by examining aggression, influenceability, and self-confidence of women in different situations, Frodi et al. (1977), Eagly (1978), and Lenny (1977), respectively, have successfully refuted the stereotypic, widely held assumptions and conclusions that women are less aggressive than men, more influenceable, and less self-confident. This is true only in some situations, but not in others, we discover as we ask questions that have not been asked before. As Deaux has

reported (cf. Division 35 Task Force, 1981), gender by situation interactions are more the rule than the exception and have been found more frequently than main effects for gender. Related to this is a recognition that ordinarily in our society, women and men "are differentially distributed across situations" (Division 35 Task Force, 1981, p. 22), a fact of enormous significance.

Recognition of situational influences on behavior necessitates that we pay attention to the demand characteristics of the conditions present in laboratory or field studies. Are cues provided for differential responses according to gender, that is, for participants to conform to sex-typed expectations as for example when under public scrutiny (Unger, 1981)? It has been suggested that exploratory and qualitative methodologies may minimize researcher-imposed definitions of a situation (Division 35 Task Force, 1981).

9. In reporting gender differences on any measure, we should note, along with its statistical significance, the magnitude of the effect, because some reliable differences are found to be relatively trivial, as for example the much publicized average differences in mathematical/spatial skill (Hyde, 1981; Rossi, 1983). In addition, we should report within-gender variability so as to "accurately reflect the degree of overlap between the sexes and avoid translating small average differences into dichotomies" (Division 35 Task Force, 1981, p. 25).

10. Finally, feminist researchers have joined with other voices within philosophy and science (cf. Manicas & Secord, 1983) to challenge some of the traditional tenets of "objectivity" in science. There appear to be two major thrusts to the feminist challenge. The first is the recognition that values are an integral part of science, that they influence all phases of the process, and that they should be acknowledged and made explicit in the same way that we recognize that scientific truths are not independent of time and

place. Some social psychologists, such as Gergen and Morawski (1980), share this position. Sampson (1978), for example, has presented a number of illustrations from research and theory in our field that demonstrate "the affectivity (not affective neutrality) with which normal science is practiced" (p. 1340). The second challenge to traditional scientific thinking goes further and argues more explicitly that the language, objectives, and methods of individual disciplines, and of science itself, particularly as defined by the experimental method, have been shaped by "masculine" concerns, interests, and personality.

It is argued, relative to the first point, that the investigator and the object of the research, as well as those who serve as subjects/participants, are interrelated, separable for analytical purposes but tied together by expectations, assumptions, and hidden or overt values. Facts are always "construed" by an active investigator/interpreter (Morawski, 1982), and values (or biases) are present throughout the research process (Wallston, 1981; Wittig, 1982). Bleier (1984) has presented evidence from physiology, anthropology, and other life sciences to illustrate "that science is *not* the neutral, dispassionate, value-free pursuit of truth; that scientists are not . . . culturally disengaged from the questions they ask of nature or the methods they use to frame their answers" (p. 193). For example, she noted the argument present by Osler that "the question of sex differences in intellectual abilities and in our biological *natures* would not arise in a society in which gender were not an important social problem" (p. 195).

It is to be expected that research in social/personality psychology will reflect the values of our patriarchical culture. For example, when Eagly and Carli (1981) performed a meta-analysis of social influence studies they found that the sex of the investigator was related to the data reported. Men, who authored 79% of the influenceability studies, tended to find evidence of gender differences indicating greater persuasibility among women, whereas women investigators tended to find no reliable gender differences. Grady (1981) has suggested that "some of these biases can be corrected through an even-handed application of the principles of scientific method, and others require a raised consciousness, an awareness of the sexist society in which we live" (p. 634). Bleier (1984), too, has insisted that the feminist imperative to scientists is really that of "doing science well" and "examining and questioning all of our assumptions" (p. 206).

The second challenge is regarded by the biologist mathematician Keller (1982, 1983), one of its foremost proponents, as the "radical critique." Keller argued that because it is primarily men who have been doing science in Western society, women have been kept out (through lack of encouragement, training, or discrimination), the choice and definition of research problems have been affected, and men have been taken to be representative of the species. In addition, "masculinity" has intruded upon and distorted the goals and rationality of the entire scientific enterprise. Science, it is said, has stressed separation, compartmentalization, and the search for prime causes in contrast to an equally plausible focus on interaction, interdependence, and process; in this way science has reflected masculinity. According to the biologist Hubbard (cf. Fiske, 1981), the approach of men, and science, is "to reduce things to their component parts, not to envision them as a functioning whole" (p. B6).

The vocabulary of science manifests a preoccupation with power, dominance, and an adversarial stance vis-à-vis nature (Kahn & Jean, 1983; Keller, 1983). Thus, science "attacks" problems with the aim of "mastering" or "controlling," variables are "dependent" or "independent," and experimenters "manipulate'' the latter. Although cognizant of the fact that the traditional scientific mode has been criticized by male scientists and philosophers, Keller (1982) has insisted that this criticism must also follow from a vigorous feminist analysis. She has proposed that ''the emphasis on power and control so prevalent in the rhetoric of Western science [is a] projection of a specifically male consciousness'' (Keller, 1982, p. 598). What is required, she suggested, is not abandonment of objectivity, rationality, and empiricism but the addition of concern with complex interactions and with the dynamics of process, as well as a ''critical self-reflection'' on the part of scientists.

Although I agree with Keller's conclusion and recommendation, I find the argument that traditional science is a product of masculine personality problematic and not persuasive. First of all, such a proposed relationship rests upon the questionable assumption that masculinity is something other than a construct that summarizes certain cultural prescriptions. (This issue will be addressed in the final section of this article.) Second, although Keller has objected to the search for top-down theories and explanations in terms of governing causes, she unfortunately has embraced just such an explanation. She has utilized psychoanalytic theory in its modern guise as object-relations theory (acknowledging the influence of Chodorow, 1978, and Dinnerstein, 1977) to trace links among masculinity, a concern with objectivity/autonomy, and the focus of science on power and domination. Keller (1982) has argued that from the male infant's earliest experiences with his mother (his primary care-giver) are formed his conceptions of the world and his ''characteristic orientation to it'' and that the major attribute of this experience is separation. For females, on the other hand, the early experience is said to be connectedness and identification with the mother. Similar

arguments have been presented by other prominent feminist theorists. The philosopher Harding (1981), for example, has attempted to explain the connection between patriarchy and capitalism by ''focusing on the natures of the humans'' who designed both, that is, ''the stereotypically masculine personality, developed through the experience of separating [at infancy] from a devalued woman [the mother]'' (p. 153). Harding has extended Chodorow's explanation of the reproduction of mothering (nurturance) in girls to the reproduction of motivation for control in boys and has asserted that ''in both cases, the infant becomes the invisible perpetrator of much of human history'' (p. 153). Infantile experience is presented as the root of gender-based personality differences, which reproduce and maintain both sexism and classism. Thus, capitalism and patriarchy are seen as ''siblings sharing the genes of [masculine] psychological interests in maintaining the domination of others'' (p. 156).

Such infant experience explanations of male concern with power and dominance clearly rest on untested and naive assumptions: first, that the experience described for the prototypical Freudian nuclear family is universal or widespread, and second, that it has predictable consequences for the formation of stable personality traits such as motivation for power. In addition, such explanations (although acknowledging that learning does continue past the age of three years) basically ignore all the further years of continuing exposure to social conditions and the powerful positive and negative sanctions for adult behavior. It is here that the ''vice versa'' in the title of this article becomes relevant. Social/personality psychology has the potential to enrich feminist theory and to contribute to the vital debate on the nature of gender differences and similarities—a debate that is central to the feminist perspective.

Contribution to Feminist Theory

In the 19th century, the so-called Victorian era, women and men occupied largely separate spheres (at least within middle-class Western society) because it was believed that "there were such profound distinctions between what biological and psychological evolution had mandated for masculine and feminine thought and action that women could never enter the public sphere without contravening laws of nature and thus endangering their own health" (Cravens, 1983). This view was vigorously challenged by early 20th century scholars, particularly women in psychology, sociology, and anthropology, such as Helen Thompson Woolley, Jessie Taft, Elsie Clews Parson, Mary Roberts Smith Coolidge, Celia Duel Mosher, and Margaret Mead. There were also challenges from some influential men: John Dewey, George Mead, W. I. Thomas, and Franz Boas. What followed was a virtual disappearance of the subject of sex differences from the social science literature beginning in the 1920s. Women simply disappeared as a subject of concern and Man became the species representative and the fitting object for study about personality and culture (Cravens, 1983). Not until the 1970s was there a rediscovery of women in mainstream psychology, but as might have been predicted, the focus was on the differences from men, not the similarities.

The contemporary feminist response to the question of gender differences, a response still in its infancy in terms of its generation of mainstream research, has taken two major forms. The first is an emphasis on the role played by social factors in separating the lives and therefore the expectations, attitudes, and behaviors of women and men. This argument views socialization as an ongoing, lifelong process and looks for explanations of gender beyond the influence of early experience on individual personality.

Segregation by sex and sexism, that is, a commitment to the inferiority of women as expressed in negative attitudes, stereotyped beliefs, and discriminatory behavior, is found to be imbedded in all of our social institutions—in the media, family, economy, and political sphere (Lott, 1981a). These institutions maintain women's low status and low power throughout the life span and across divisions of class and ethnicity, thus reinforcing gender differences, in the same way as differential status and power contribute to observed differences among racial, ethnic, and socioeconomic class groups. Thus, Grady (1981) has urged that "awareness of the different social and economic conditions for men and women cannot be left to sociologists if psychology is to maintain its integrity as a science" (p. 635), and Parlee (1981) has noted that "sex, race, age, class—all are . . . variables that point to clusters of life experiences that are systematically different for different groups of people" (p. 642). In this view the more likely explanation of fear of success, for example, which is observed in some (but not all) women, is less a stable personality trait in the form of an acquired motive and more the result of the objective consequences that success is known to have for some women. Persons (women or men, black or white) will not avoid success if the outcomes are primarily positive, nor will they avoid aggression, competition, leadership, and so on, if the situation is appropriate and the consequences nonpunitive or satisfying.

A related but essentially divergent position in terms of its emphasis is represented by the work of Gilligan (1977, 1979, 1982a, 1982b) and Miller (1976). This position highlights and focuses on the positive effects of women's life experiences, in contrast to men's, and asserts that these experiences and the imposed separateness from men have created a women's culture with both historical and contemporary significance. We are urged to examine this culture carefully, to give recognition to its distinctiveness, and to study the situations that define women's lives, responsibilities, and roles. What we will find according to this view are expressive, sensitive, communal persons concerned with relationships, the needs of others, interpersonal responsibility, and harmony. Women are different from men in these ways, this approach goes on to note, and not only should these characteristics be valued, respected, and applauded in women but they should be strived for and learned by men. Thus, Gilligan (1977, 1979) has traced moral development in girls and women and found it to be different than for boys and men. She has rightly objected to the presentation of male-based data as the foundation for general theory, pointing out that men have shaped the constructs through which we are all supposed to see life. Examination of the experiences of girls and women, she has argued, suggests that different moral lessons are learned. For men, justice may be equated with abstract forms; for women, however, "the moral problem is seen to arise from conflicting responsibilities rather than from competing rights" (Gilligan, 1979, p. 442). Women, whose social experiences are rooted in attachment, are therefore concerned with expressiveness, caring, and contexts, whereas men, who have experienced separation, are more concerned with instrumentality and the balancing of individual rights. Women, Gilligan (1979) has asserted, judge themselves in terms of their ability to care. The value of intimacy, which contemporary men are now discovering in midlife, is something women acquire early.

In explaining such value differences between women and men, Gilligan has relied heavily although not exclusively on Chodorow's analysis of early mother-child interaction. Although cognizant of the later differences in experience between girls and boys, Gilligan appeared to give Chodorow's position centrality. Because, wrote Chodorow, "they are parented by a person of the same gender . . . girls come to experience themselves as less differentiated than boys, as more continuous with and related to the external object-world" (1978, p. 167). The end result is differing values, and Gilligan has concluded that "women bring to the life cycle a different point of view and . . . order human experiences in terms of different priorities" (1979, p. 445). The work of Miller (1976) complements such a conclusion, and both have emphasized that from the woman's point of view, the concern with harmony, caring, responsibility, and relationships emanates strength, not weakness.

Although such clear expositions of women's strengths are vital additions to our data and theory, one problem with this position is that in focusing on the differences between women and men observed in contemporary society, what tends to be deemphasized is that these differences are only a function of differing experience, reflecting historical, social class, ethnic, and racial factors. Note Gilligan's words: "Women's deference is rooted not only in their social circumstances, but also in the substance of their moral concern" (1979, p. 440). Does this suggest that women's moral concerns are not rooted in their social circumstances? If not, then from what other source?

The current focus on gender differences loses sight of their source in particular circumstances, history, expectations, and social sanctions, and in so doing overgeneralizes from some women (and some men) to all, a trap leading us back inevitably to gender stereotypes. The focus on differences ignores significant within-gender variability. "Ain't I a woman?" asked Sojourner Truth in countering the female stereotype of her day. Yes, Southern white upper-class women were supposed to be slender, weak, and too fragile to open carriage doors for themselves, but not the slave women who heaved sacks of potatoes or cotton and worked the fields along with their men, or did the cooking, the laundry, and the child care for the master's family as well as their own. There are similar and additional differences among groups of contemporary women; this has been argued with particular conviction by black women scholars (e.g., Hull, Scott, & Smith, 1982).

Basic principles of social/personality psychology should lead us to expect that women and men will differ to the extent that the behaviors they are able to practice and the reinforcements they receive continue to differ. This is also the case for within-gender differences and psychological disparities between the highly and less well educated, the poor and the affluent, black and white, urban and rural, and so on. To the extent that persons share life conditions, they will behave similarly. Thus, we must look for similarities as well as differences because both are explainable by the same principles of learning. We acquire responses to, and in, situations. When a society segregates individuals on the basis of sex (or race, etc.) and systematically exposes the segregated groups to different conditions, expectations, rewards, and access to society's resources, the result will be differences in interests, motives, and overt behavior. In our society such segregation by sex is complicated by other status factors. Thus, to know, for example, that Phyllis Schlafly, Margaret Thatcher, Shirley Chisholm, and Kate Millett are all women will permit reliable prediction of only some behavior. They all have been daughters and wives, probably menstruated regularly, and function in a society that oppresses and devalues women, but not evenly or homogeneously. Can we predict that each of these women is similar in her concern for relationships, caring, harmony, and responsibility? My guess is that we could more easily match Thatcher and Chisholm, for example, to two different men than to each other on values, interests, beliefs, and moral position. What we need to search out and understand are the antecedents and correlates of behavior. It is not sex that matters but those life conditions that are systematically related to it by cultural prescription, regulation, or arrangement. Where such experiential/situational correlates are weak or overridden by others, sex ceases to be a discriminating variable.

We need to understand that the culture-prescribed experiential/situational correlates of sex are only partially related to early childhood socialization and to past personal history. Sex typing is maintained in a society by contemporary cues for adult behavior and appropriate rewards and punishments. For example, Zanna and Pack (1975) found that under-graduate women who had an opportunity to work on a task with a "desirable" male senior from Princeton portrayed themselves as more or less conventional in terms of sex role depending on whether the Princeton man's views were traditional or nontraditional. In addition, the women working with a desirable but traditional man did less competent work on the joint task than those working with a nontraditional man. These findings illustrate the "now you see them, now you don't" quality of sex-related effects discussed by Unger (1981). She has attributed the inconsistencies to the use of different methodologies, but the Zanna and Pack (1975) data suggest a more parsimonious and fundamental explanation: Gender differences appear or do not appear depending on the social conditions or context of the behavior. This principle, well supported by empirical data, is emphasized by feminist research and is also the essence of the social psychological approach. Locksley and Colten (1979) articulated a similar position in a critical review of the androgyny literature, noting that:

Many situations continue to be structured with respect to sex, such that sex-appropriate behaviors generally procure psychological and material rewards, whereas sex-inappropriate behaviors may be costly. . . . [Thus] men and women will act differently because they have different ongoing tasks, responsibilities, and access to resources. (p. 1025)

In a previous article (Lott, 1981b), I argued that although the concept of androgyny was an advance over the earlier idea of masculine and feminine as either—or bipolar opposites, it continues to link behavior to gender and to label certain attributes as characteristic of women, and others as characteristic of men, with little regard for the abundant evidence of within-gender variability (often uncovered by the same research). Recently I have read other similar critiques. Morawski (1982), for example, has suggested that the androgyny model renovated rather than replaced "the assumptions of human nature that initially received criticism" (p. 395), and Wallston (1981) has now urged discontinuing the use of masculine/feminine labels that "imply false dichotomies." Bem (1981) has also come to recognize that the androgyny concept "is insufficiently radical from a feminist perspective because it continues to presuppose that . . . masculinity and feminity have an independent and palpable reality rather than being themselves cognitive constructs" (p. 363). The same general criticism is applicable to the approach that focuses on opposing feminine and masculine attitudes, values, perceptions, and behaviors. Although such a focus increases the visibility of women and the realities of their lives and exposes the androcentric bias in social science, it also tends to blur our vision of the variations in the behavior of women and reduces our attention to the behavior's antecedents. As Bleier (1984) has argued, the feminist contribution to science is its insistence that:

Hierarchies, relations of domination, subordination, power and control are not necessarily inherent in nature but are an integral part of the conceptual framework of persons bred in a civilization constructed on principles of stratification. (p. 200)

Like hierarchies, our cherished dualisms (e.g., subject-object, masculine-feminine) are also cultural constructions. Therefore, Bleier continued, "Science need not be permitted to define objectivity and creativity as that which the male mind does and subjectivity and emotionality as that which the female mind is" (p. 201). Such assertions and others that tie human characteristics to gender deny the abundance of contrary evidence and what we know about situational variation in behavior.

In conclusion, what social/personality psychology can profitably take from feminist research and theory is (a) recognition of the role played by sexist assumptions and biases in the development of hypotheses, procedures, and the exploration of problems; (b) expansion of areas of research concern and of methodologies; and (c) the consideration of new questions, theoretical formulations, and concepts. Reconstruction is required, as recently proposed by Wittig (1982), and for the reconstruction to be truly revolutionary, our scholarship must be "directed toward change."

Feminist theory can profit from psychology because it is psychologists who are best able to probe the connections between what people do, feel, and believe and the conditions that make particular behaviors, feelings, and beliefs more probable. To understand the learning or acquisition of behavior is to understand how culture constructs gender. Thus, we can consider seriously a question asked by Alpert (1978): When women and men share equally in the worlds of home and work, what will they be like then? We can anticipate that the range of experiences then available to individuals will increase and that individual differences will flourish whereas gender differences will cluster about those few biological imperatives that now distinguish the human sexes.

References

Alpert, J. L. (1978). The psychology of women: What should the field be called? *American Psychologist, 33,* 965–969.

American Sociological Association, Committee on the Status of Women in Sociology. (1980, spring). Sexist biases in sociological research: Problems and issues. [Newsletter]. *Project on the Status and Education of Women.* (Available from Association of American Colleges, 1818 R Street, N.W., Washington DC 20009).

Azzi, A. (1983, July 26). Colleges uncover women in history. *The Providence Evening Bulletin.*

Baruch, G. K., Barnett, R. C., & Rivers, C. (1983). *Lifeprints: New patterns of love and work for today's women.* New York: McGraw-Hill.

Bem, S. L. (1981). Gender schema theory: A cognitive account of sex typing. *Psychological Review, 88,* 354–364.

Bleier, R. (1984). *Science and gender: A critique of biology and its theories on women.* New York: Pergamon.

Chodorow, N. (1978). *The reproduction of mothering.* Berkeley: University of California Press.

Cravens, H. (1983). Underpinnings for sexual equality. *Science, 219,* 957–958.

Dinnerstein, D. (1977). *The mermaid and the minotaur.* New York: Harper & Row.

Division 35 Task Force. (1981, August). *Guidelines for nonsexist research* [Draft]. (Available from Irene Frieze, Department of Psychology, University of Pittsburgh, Pittsburgh, PA 15260)

Eagly, A. H. (1978). Sex differences in influenceability. *Psychological Bulletin, 85,* 86–116.

Eagly, A. H., & Carli, L. L. (1981). Sex of researchers and sex-typed communications as determinants of sex differences in influenceability: A meta-analysis of social influence studies. *Psychological Bulletin, 90,* 1–20.

Fiske, E. B. (1981, November 23). Scholars face a challenge by feminists. *New York Times,* pp. B1, B6.

Frodi, A., Macauley, J., & Thome, P. R. (1977). Are women always less aggressive than men? A review of the experimental literature. *Psychological Bulletin, 84,* 634–660.

Gergen, K. J., & Morawski, J. (1980). An alternative meta-theory for social psychology. In L. Wheeler (Ed.), *Review of personality and social psychology* (Vol. 1, pp. 326–352). Beverly Hills, CA: Sage.

Gilligan, C. (1977). In a different voice: Women's conceptions of the self and of morality. *Harvard Educational Review, 47,* 481–517.

Gilligan, C. (1979). Woman's place in man's life cycle. *Harvard Educational Review, 49,* 431–446.

Gilligan, C. (1982a). *In a different voice: Psychological theory and women's development.* Cambridge, MA: Harvard University Press.

Gilligan, C. (1982b, June). Why should a woman be more like a man? *Psychology Today,* pp. 68, 70–71, 73–74, 77.

Grady, K. E. (1981). Sex bias in research design. *Psychology of Women Quarterly, 5,* 628–636.

Harding, S. (1981). What is the real material base of patriarchy and capital? In L. Sargent (Ed.), *Women and revolution* (pp. 135–163). Boston: South End Press.

Henley, N. M. (1977). *Body politics: Power, sex, and nonverbal communication.* Englewood Cliffs, NJ: Prentice-Hall.

Horner, M. (1972). Toward an understanding of achievement-related conflicts in women. *Journal of Social Issues, 28,* 157–175.

Hull, G. T., Scott, P. B., & Smith, B. (1982). *But some of us are brave: Black women's studies.* Old Westbury, NY: Feminist Press.

Hyde, J. S. (1981). How large are cognitive gender differences? *American Psychologist, 36,* 892–901.

Kahn, A. S., & Jean, P. J. (1983). Integration and elimination or separation and redefinition:

The future of the psychology of women as a discipline. *Signs, 8*, 659–671.

Keller, E. F. (1982). Feminism and science. *Signs, 7*, 589–602.

Keller, E. F. (1983). Feminism as an analytical tool for the study of science. *Academe, 69*(5), 15–21.

Lenny, E. (1977). Women's self-confidence in achievement settings. *Psychological Bulletin, 84*, 1–13.

Locksley, A., & Colten, M. E. (1979). Psychological androgyny: A case of mistaken identity? *Journal of Personality and Social Psychology, 37*, 1017-1031.

Lott, B. (1981a). *Becoming a woman: The socialization of gender*. Springfield, IL: Charles C Thomas.

Lott, B. (1981b). A feminist critique of androgyny: Toward the elimination of gender attributions for learned behavior. In C. Mayo & N. M. Henley (Eds.), *Gender and nonverbal behavior* (pp. 171–180). New York: Springer.

Lykes, M. B., & Stewart, A. J. (1983, August). *Evaluating the feminist challenge in psychology: 1963–1983*. Paper presented at the meeting of the American Psychological Association, Anaheim, CA.

Manicas, P. T., & Secord, P. F. (1983). Implications for psychology of the new philosophy of science. *American Psychologist, 38*, 399–413.

McKenna, W., & Kessler, S. J. (1977). Experimental design as a source of sex bias in social psychology. *Sex Roles, 3*, 117–128.

Miller, J. B. (1976). *Toward an understanding of the psychology of women*. Boston: Beacon Press.

Morawski, J. G. (1982). On thinking about history as social psychology. *Personality and Social Psychology Bulletin, 8*, 393–401.

Parlee, M. B. (1981). Appropriate control groups in feminist research. *Psychology of Women Quarterly, 5*, 637–644.

Rossi, J. S. (1983). Ratios exaggerate gender differences in mathematical ability. *American Psychologist, 38*, 348.

Russo, N. F. (1982). Psychology of women: Analysis of the faculty and courses of an emerging field. *Psychology of Women Quarterly, 7*, 18–31.

Sampson, E. E. (1978). Scientific paradigms and social values: Wanted—a scientific revolution. *Journal of Personality and Social Psychology, 36*, 1332–1343.

Task Force on Issues in Research in the Psychology of Women. (1977, October). Task Force on Issues in Research in the Psychology of Women—Final Report. *Division 35 Newsletter, 4*(4), 3–6.

Unger, R. K. (1981). Sex as a social reality: Field and laboratory research. *Psychology of Women Quarterly, 5*, 645–653.

Unger, R. K. (1982). Advocacy versus scholarship revisited: Issues in the psychology of women. *Psychology of Women Quarterly, 7*, 5–17.

Wallston, B. S. (1981). What are the questions in psychology of women? A feminist approach to research. *Psychology of Women Quarterly, 5*, 597–617.

Westkott, M. (1979). Feminist criticism of the social sciences. *Harvard Educational Review, 49*, 422–430.

Wittig, M. A. (1982, August). *Value-fact-intervention dilemmas in the psychology of women*. Paper presented at the meeting of the American Psychological Association, Washington, DC.

Zanna, M. P., & Pack, S. J. (1975). On the self-fulfilling nature of apparent sex differences in behavior. *Journal of Experimental Social Psychology, 11*, 583–591.

Mary Crawford
Jeanne Marecek

Psychology Reconstructs the Female, 1968–1988*

Recent work on the psychology of gender is pluralistic, stemming from varied specialty areas within psychology, grounded in several intellectual frameworks, and reflecting a spectrum of feminist perspectives. This article is a critical appraisal of diverse approaches to the study of women and gender. It first describes prefeminist or "womanless" psychology, then analyzes four co-existing frameworks that have generated recent research. The four frameworks are: *Exceptional Women,* in which empirical research focuses on the correlates of high achievement for women, and women's history in the discipline is re-evaluated; *Women as Problem* (or *Anomaly*), in which research emphasizes explanations for female "deficiencies" (e.g., fear of success); the *Psychology of Gender,* in which the focus of inquiry shifts from women to gender, conceived as a principle of social organization that structures relations between women and men; and a (currently relatively undeveloped) *Transformation* framework that reflexively challenges the values, assumptions, and normative practices of the discipline. Examples of research programs within each approach are described, and the strengths and limitations of each approach are critically examined.

From: *Psychology of Women Quarterly,* 1989, *13,* pp. 147–165. Copyright © 1989 by Division 35, American Psychological Association. Reproduced with the permission of Cambridge University Press.

*This article was written while Mary Crawford was Jane Watson Irwin Visiting Professor of Psychology at Hamilton College and Jeanne Marecek was Fulbright Senior Lecturer at the University of Peradeniya, Sri Lanka. Order of authorship was determined alphabetically.

We thank Rhoda Unger for her comments on an earlier draft and the participants at the 1988 Nags Head Sex and Gender Conference for their lively discussion of the ideas in this article.

Correspondence may be addressed to either Mary Crawford, Department of Psychology, West Chester University, West Chester, PA 19383; or Jeanne Marecek, Department of Psychology, Swarthmore College, Swarthmore, PA 19081.

In 1968, Naomi Weisstein published a paper entitled *Kinder, Kirche, Küche as Scientific Law: Psychology Constructs the Female.*[1] Weisstein's paper presented one of the first formulations of the social construction of gender. It also documented biases, stereotypes, and fantasies in psychology's views of women. This work sets the stage for feminist efforts to reconstruct psychological knowledge about women and to develop a psychology of gender. These efforts have been rich and varied, with virtually every intellectual framework and every specialty area in psychology represented. Moreover, there is considerable diversity of opinion as to what questions are important and what forms inquiry should take. Rapid growth has left little time for critical reflection and dialogue. Yet, if the field is to mature rather than just expand, it is important that we critically engage our history.

Critical history examines the values of the field and makes value judgments about its past record. Creating such a history helps the field to develop a self-concept—a set of self-referential, self-regulating, and self-knowing structures (White in Bronfenbrenner, Kessel, Kessen, & White, 1986). Such a history will always be under revision, because the meaning of the past changes in accord with the shifts in perspective that take place as the present unfolds.

Michelle Fine's (1985) analysis of scholarship contained in *Psychology of Women Quarterly* and the *Signs* Review Essays by Mary Parlee (1975) and Nancy Henley (1985) are excellent examples of critical reflection, as are a number of more narrowly focused writings (e.g., Lykes & Stewart, 1986; Nieva & Gutek, 1981; Wallston, 1981). The goal of the critical history that we develop in this article is to examine the frameworks within which questions in the field are generated and to explore the political interests—both feminist and antifeminist—that different frameworks serve.

Not all scholarship on the psychology of women originates from a feminist perspective. Moreover, no single feminist perspective unifies all the work that is self-identified as feminist. An array of political stances is implicit in the scholarship of feminist psychologists (Hare-Mustin & Marecek, 1988; Marecek & Hare-Mustin, 1987). Not only do feminist psychologists differ in their politics, they also differ in the extent to which they believe that politics enter—or should enter—into their scholarly work. This diversity of approaches is reflected in the existence of two distinct organizations for feminist psychologists—the Association for Women in Psychology, founded in 1969 as an activist group outside the American Psychological Association (APA), the Division of the Psychology of Women, Division 35, representing the subfield within APA since 1973.

We organize feminist inquiry on the psychology of women and gender into four frameworks. Although frameworks have been proposed to characterize feminist curriculum revision (McIntosh, 1983; Schuster & Van Dyne, 1984) and scholarship in personality psychology (Torrey, 1987), this approach has not been used to organize and clarify approaches to the production of psychological knowledge about women. In this article we describe each conceptual framework and suggest the kinds of research that exemplify it. Although we present the frameworks in sequence, they are co-existing, interdependent, and mutually informing. Thus, we will give examples of current research developed within each. We evaluate the frameworks not in terms of their correctness, but rather in terms of their utility. Before developing our analysis, however, we will briefly recapitulate prefeminist or "womanless" psychology.

In "womanless" disciplines, women's experiences are thought to be too unimportant to be a focus of inquiry. So, for example, history has been taught as an account of men's public achievements, and literature as the writings of great male authors (McIntosh, 1983). In the psychology of the past 50 years, "womanlessness" was reflected in the disproportionate use of males as experimental subjects, in the failure to examine gender differences when both sexes were used as subjects, in the assumption that conclusions drawn from the study of male behavior applied to women, and more generally in the lack of attention to gender as a category of social reality. Several feminist critiques of research methodology have called attention to the practices of "womanless" psychology and its underlying assumption that women are uninteresting or unworthy of study (e.g., Grady, 1981; McHugh, Koeske, & Frieze, 1986).

Historically, much of psychological inquiry has been virtually "womanless," not only in its subject of inquiry, but in the place allowed women in the profession itself. Women did not have control over the resources needed for production of knowledge, and the topics and methods of accepted scholarship were defined in ways that were exclusionary at best and misogynist at worst (Lewin, 1984).

"Womanless" psychology not only omitted the consideration of women and women's experiences, it also authorized and validated the view that those activities in which men engage are the activities central to human life. It reaffirmed that the activities of women are "backstage" to the "real" action. For example, the landmark studies of achievement motivation were limited to male subjects (McClelland, Atkinson, Clark, & Lowell, 1953). Achievement was often defined narrowly to include only behaviors involved in market production; other forms of productivity and action were not considered useful to society.

Feminist psychology began with a recognition of the "womanless" state of the discipline and a basic consensus that women and gender must be integrated into theory and research. In what follows, we discuss the conceptual frameworks that feminists have devised to accomplish this integration.

Feminist Frameworks

Exceptional Women

The initial feminist critiques of the "womanless" state of various disciplines prompted a variety of responses. One response has been to retrieve evidence of women's efforts that had been expunged from the historical record. In a discipline such as history, this means including a sprinkling of female figures: Joan of Arc, Catherine the Great, Marie Curie, Dolley Madison, or Florence Nightingale. Often the personal foibles of the women are as much the focus of attention as their accomplishments.

In psychology, historical overviews may now feature Anna Freud or Karen Horney along with Wundt, Pavlov, Watson, Skinner, and Freud. More important, many women whose contributions to the history of psychology had gone unrecognized or been forgotten have been rediscovered (O'Connell and Russo, 1980, 1983; Russo & Denmark, 1987; Scarborough & Furumoto, 1987). The new subfield of the history of women in psychology is a vital one. Nonetheless, documenting the history of women's achievements in and of itself does not necessarily identify the needed changes in the current activities of the discipline.

The historical approach serves feminist interests by focusing attention on the "neglected foremothers" of psychology (Bernstein & Russo, 1974). This may instill confidence and courage in women undertaking careers in the field, a goal that is made explicit in discussions of these women as "role models" (O'Connell & Russo, 1980, 1983; Russo & Denmark, 1987). Moreover, the recognition of "great" women and the due consideration of their achievements contribute to a more accurate record of the discipline. But, a focus on "great" women may convey an underlying message that only exceptional women are capable of "real" achievement or are worthy of serving as role models. Such a focus also may deflect critical attention from the question of what is and is not to be considered an achievement.

The quest to rediscover the record of women's accomplishments is most useful when critical attention focuses on the social context of achievement. For example, Scarborough and Furumoto (1987) detailed not only the careers of successful women, but also of brilliant women who did *not* manage sustained achievement, and they analyzed the structural obstacles those women faced.

141

Russo and O'Connell (1980), O'Connell and Russo (1983, 1988), and Russo and Denmark (1987) discussed the impact of social factors such as employment opportunities, attitudes of male gatekeepers, and norms for familial relationships, as well as the effects of larger social movements. They also attempted to retrieve the history of minority women psychologists and discussed the reasons for their invisibility.

When accounts of the careers of exceptional women psychologists reveal exclusion and marginalization, these revelations can furnish a basis for a critique of the discipline (Russo & Denmark, 1987). Evelyn Fox Keller's (1983) biographical study of Barbara McClintock provides a ready example in the field of biology. The very absence of "exceptional" women in a discipline can be a catalyst for exploration of the structural, as opposed to personal, reasons for such absence. For example, Linda Nochlin's (1971) essay "Why are there no great women artists?" recognized and forcefully argued that exceptional achievement requires opportunities, training, financial backing, and recognition, as well as native ability.

Another feminist response to the "womanless" state of psychology has been to initiate research into the family backgrounds and personal characteristics of eminent or exceptional women. If the developmental experiences and personality traits that led to success could be pinpointed, then it might be possible to increase the number of successful women. Thus, the psychological study of exceptional women includes research on the characteristics of highly successful women, such as physicians (Lopate, 1968), corporate managers (Hennig & Jardim, 1981), academics, and scientists (Moulton, 1979). While it focuses some attention on women's contributions, this work may inadvertently reinforce a number of antifeminist views of women. First, it suggests that the only women of interest are those who do what has been traditionally considered "men's work." As in "womanless" psychology, the implication is that only "men's work" is of interest and social importance. Moreover, when research on exceptional women focuses on personal qualities, early experience, and family backgrounds as the determinants of accomplishment, it may reinforce the belief that success is solely the product of individual ability, determination or effort. Antifeminists may use such work to argue that women who do not pursue such careers (or who do not succeed spectacularly in them) either lack the "right stuff" to succeed or opt out of success by choice (e.g., Gilder, 1986).

The focus on exceptional women obviously moves beyond prefeminist psychology in a number of important ways. As scholarship on exceptional women has matured, interest has shifted from the search for personalistic explanations for women's success to the examination of structural factors that enhance some individuals' potential and block that of others. An underrepresentation of women in a discipline points to the importance of gender as a social and political category that influences the distribution of resources (Harding, 1986). Moreover, the experiences of women in psychology illuminate the social relations of the discipline, and the ways in which these social relations determine the processes by which knowledge is sought, validated, and disseminated (Morawski, 1987).

Women as Problem or Anomaly

When research is limited either to men or to a few special women, the production of knowledge is constrained. A broader consideration of women is typical of the approach we now turn to. In this framework, women are viewed as presenting psychology with a set of problems or anomalies. Feminist scholars who adopt this framework seek to explain the deficiencies or diminished accomplishments of some (or most) women in terms of social roles and learning rather than biological factors. Early formulations such as fear of success (Horner, 1970) and math anxiety (Tobias, 1978) are examples, as are recent formulations of an "imposter phenomenon" (Clance & Imes, 1978) and a "Cinderella complex" (Dowling, 1981). In these formulations, women's shortcomings are seen as arising from gender-related motives, fears, or self-concepts that cause a woman to act against her own best interests. (Although many of these constructs have been extended to men, their prototypical "victim" remains female.)

Work that focuses on deficiencies or lack of skills as the outcome of traditional gender-role socialization is another variant of the *Women as Problem* orientation. For example, women have been seen as deficient in crucial skills such as assertiveness or the ability to speak in an authoritative public style (Lakoff, 1973). The individual deficit model has also been influential in attempting to explain women's low career status, as Nieva and Gutek (1981) point out. Women managers have been represented as lacking in business acumen, leadership qualities, or the requisite interpersonal style, as overemotional and unmotivated to succeed.

Feminist approaches to women's psychological disorders often fit within the *Women as Problem* framework, partly because much traditional theorizing on personality fits within this framework (Torrey, 1987). A dominant line of feminist argument links psychological disorders prevalent among women to gender-role socialization. For example, stereotypically feminine traits such as dependency, fearfulness, a sense of helplessness, and excessive concerns about appearance are thought to be linked to disorders prevalent among women, such as agoraphobia, depression, and anorexia nervosa (Marecek, 1988; Widom, 1984). Feminist

therapists working within this framework conceive their clients as lacking certain skills or having negative or self-defeating self-concepts, attitudes, or behaviors. Therapy is seen as a regimen of "compensatory socialization" (Marecek & Hare-Mustin, 1987).

Research in this framework focuses on explanations for women's problems in terms of gender-role-related conflicts, such as role strain, role overload, and penalties for role violations. This approach emphasizes that incompatible demands placed on women may cause psychological conflict, guilt, or anxiety. The conflicts and strains of men's roles and the problems that stereotypic masculinity may cause to others are rarely topics of concern. For example, though the effect of women's labor force participation on their children is an issue of great concern to developmental psychologists, little or no concern has been expressed about the effects of men's commitment to paid work.

Examples of *Women As Problem* research are easy to generate. *Women As Problem* has been the dominant framework for the psychology of women for at least the past 10 years. Moreover, most of the "pop psych" offerings aimed at women are based on the premise that women have (or are) problems (Gervasio & Crawford, 1989; Worell, 1987).

It is important to consider the potential and the pitfalls of this framework by examining how it can serve various ideological interests. On the one hand, the *Women As Problem* framework serves feminist interests in several important ways. It focuses on ordinary women as well as on women who are special or eminent. Not only is a more representative view of women's experiences obtained, but more importantly, there is also an assumption that areas of experience that are important to women, such as domestic violence and menstruation, are worthy of study. The shift from the "inherent deficiency" model of prefeminist psychology to a "social

143

and cultural transmission" model is also a significant advance (Crawford, 1982). Moreover, with its insistence on socialization and gender-role prescriptions as sources of women's difficulties, this line of inquiry opens the way to a social critique.

But the *Women as Problem* framework has limitations as well. Perhaps the most serious of these, echoing the misogyny of prefeminist psychology, is that men remain the norm against which women are measured (Eichler, 1988). Any observed differences between women and men can be (and often are) interpreted as evidence of female deficiency, thus reinforcing existing gender politics. Women's behavior is seen as problematic *in comparison to men's behavior;* the goal of change efforts is often to help women attain stereotypically masculine behavior. Thus, for example, the concept of fear of success came to be used to explain women's deficiencies in achievement motivation (Horner, 1970). Lakoff's (1973) "women's language" was described in explicit contrast to the more forceful and effective style of men. Assertiveness training was prescribed as a remedy for alleged skill deficiencies in women, with the implicit promise of helping (some) women compete on equal terms with men by adjusting their speech patterns to be more like men's (Gervasio & Crawford, 1989). In each case, research subsequent to the original formulations raised serious questions as to whether a sex difference actually existed. Few psychologists are aware, for example, that there is no consistent evidence for a sex difference on the paper-and-pencil assertiveness inventories used in assertiveness research and training (Hollandsworth & Wall, 1977). Thus, the original observation of a "women's problem" may have been rooted in stereotypes that overstated the extent and universality of male-female difference (Lott, 1987a; Morawski, 1985). Moreover, bias is revealed in the asymmetry of interpretation. If the stereotypical female is problematically unassertive, why is the stereotypical male not problematically overassertive?

Even when an investigator explicitly contests the meaning of difference as deficiency, findings of difference remain problematic. For example, claims of a uniquely female moral sensibility or mode of thinking (Belenky, Clinchey, Goldberger, & Tarule, 1986; Gilligan, 1982) can be appropriated by those wishing to "confirm" that women do not (and cannot) think and act like men, and thus should be barred from positions of influence in the male world of public life (Crawford, 1989b; Mednick, 1987). Hare-Mustin & Marecek (1988) argued that work that frames gender as difference will always reach an impasse both in furthering our knowledge about gender and in bringing about political change. Whether the claim is that women are deficient, equal to (i.e., not different), or better than men, the governing presumption—that man is the referent and male behavior, the norm—remains the same.

A second limitation of the *Women as Problem* orientation is that it frequently stops short of the social critique that it invites. For example, "role conflict" is often regarded as an individual problem, not a social one; and each individual is encouraged to maximize her own "adjustment" by finding a personal solution to such problems as combining marriage, motherhood, and paid employment (Crawford, 1982). The cultural emphasis on autonomy from social influences and on individual responsibility for action frequently inclines psychologists toward viewing behavior in terms of personal, internal factors rather than external social ones (Fine, 1985; Hare-Mustin & Marecek, 1985). In addition, within this approach, it is difficult to conceptualize the diversity of women's experience except in terms of multiple problems. But representing Black or Hispanic, poor, lesbian, or disabled status only as part of an additive (or multiplicative) model of socialization deficits and role conflicts renders invisible the strengths that diverse socialization and life experiences may promote (Dill, 1979). It also lends itself with unfortunate ease to racist and other discriminatory interpretations.

Warnings of the antifeminist potential of the *Women As Problem* framework are not merely academic. Indeed, the most prominent examples of this framework are explicitly antifeminist. They focus on sex differences, specifically, on what are taken to be women's deficiencies or departures from the norm, but reach back to a long tradition of similar arguments about racial and ethnic differences. Biological explanations for such differences are proposed, usually based on correlational links between such factors as genes, hormones, neurochemistry, or brain structures, and the behaviors or characteristics in question (Bleier, 1986).

Another antifeminist variant of the *Women as Problem* framework focuses on women as causing or contributing to the difficulties of others. For example, as Caplan and Hall-McCorquodale (1985) showed, clinical studies of pathological behavior involve extensive mother-blaming. Mothers have been and continue to be implicated in psychopathologies ranging from arson to incontinence, drug abuse, infanticide, and bad dreams. Indeed, women's relationships with their families have been blamed repeatedly for social ills. Erikson (1964), for example, blamed Castro's revolutionary leanings on his mother's "grandiose maternality." Equality in marriage has been blamed, especially in the popular press, for male impotence, marital conflict, the rising divorce rate, and the decay of the social order (cf. Gilder, 1987).

Black women have been the focus of both racism and sexism in woman-blaming. Sociologists, psychiatrists, and social critics have accused women of color of castrating their husbands and sons because of their own lack of "femininity" and "healthy female narcissism" (Giddings, 1984). Moynihan (1965), Gilder (1987), and others attributed the social ills of the urban Black ghetto to its "matriarchial" social organization, a characterization repudiated by black feminist theorists (Hooks, 1981).

Is it possible to develop a psychology of women that does not rest on comparisons with men, but rather keeps women's experience as its focus? One area that would seem exempt from "difference" interpretation is research on experiences related to female physiology. Yet even childbirth is sometimes defined against men's activities in war as a "different" test of courage and bravery (Lott, 1987b, p. 188) and the experience of female orgasm is compared with males' (Wiest, 1977). Other areas of focus on women, such as lesbian relationships (Peplau, 1982), or use of humor and wit (Crawford, 1989a), or "ways of knowing" (Belenky et al., 1986) are subject to similar criticism. Although they originate in the impulse to understand *women's* experiences, the implicit or explicit reference group often remains men (or heterosexual couples). Lesbian couples, for example, are described as less sex-typed than heterosexual or gay male couples (Cardell, Finn, & Marecek, 1981); or their frequency of sexual activity is compared with that of these groups (Blumstein & Schwartz, 1983). Women's humor is understood as stemming from conversational goals that differ from those of men (Crawford, 1989a) or from their lower positions in a status hierarchy (Coser, 1960); women's ways of knowing are contrasted with men's (Crawford, 1989b). Nevertheless, to the extent that *Women as Problem* research can delineate aspects of women's experience that remain invisible in other frameworks, it contains the seeds of a rich psychology of women. Examples include work on women's friendships (Johnson & Aries, 1983; McCullough, 1987) and experiences in consciousness-raising groups (Kravetz, Marecek, & Finn, 1983).

The Psychology of Gender

This approach to feminist psychology shifts the focus of inquiry from women to gender, and from gender as difference to gender as social relations. That is, gender is conceived as a principle of social organization, which structures the relations, especially the power relations, between women and men (cf. Sherif, 1982; Stacey & Thorne, 1985).

The impetus for reframing the psychology of women as the psychology of gender originates in (and can also enrich) various projects of other phases. The biographies of eminent women in psychology, as well as in other sciences, reveal not only achievement but also exclusion and marginalization. Even when they "played by the rules," women were frequently denied full participation in the scientific community and the respect accorded to male scientists (Garrison, 1981; Keller, 1983; Russo & Denmark, 1987; Scarborough & Furomoto, 1987). Recognition of a similar dynamic in other arenas of public life invites a shift of attention from individual accomplishments to the structure and organization of the social systems in which individuals operate. In a similar fashion, the analyses of gender-role-related conflicts, an important contribution of the *Women as Problem* framework, prompt a conceptual shift from *role conflicts* (construed as individual problems) to *roles* (that is, gender relations) as social problems (Crawford, 1982).

While only a few psychological studies thus far conceive gender in this way, an increasing number of feminist psychologists and other social scientists are calling for such a conceptual shift. For example, Unger (1987) urged a shift from construing gender as a noun to construing it as a verb, following West and Zimmerman (1987), who speak of "doing" gender, rather than "having"

gender. That is, gender is thought of as a process, rather than a set of attributes. Deaux's (1984) review of a decade of psychological research on sex and gender concludes that research thus far has been limited by the "static nature of assumptions—that sex-related phenomena are best approached either through biological categories, via stable traits, or in terms of relatively stable stereotypic conceptions." In place of static constructs, Deaux urges psychologists to "deal with the *processes* involved . . . processes through which gender information is presented and acted upon" (p. 113). More recently, Deaux and Major (1987) have proposed a process model of gender in social interaction.

An example can best illustrate the promise of analyses that focus on how gender is produced by social structure and processes. Carol Brooks Gardner (1980) investigated "street remarks," comments passed between unacquainted individuals in public settings. Note that this study of ordinary people in everyday settings would probably not have been conceived within the *Exceptional Women* framework. Within the *Women as Problem* framework, researchers might have chosen to analyze street remarks directed at women as a function of the attractiveness, age, dress, or appearance of the recipient, thus suggesting that women are individually responsible for eliciting them. Instead, Gardner noted the types of street remarks men made, the positive and negative constructions given to them, women's strategies for dealing with them, and the outcomes of various conversational sequences. Her analysis focused on the functions that men's street remarks serve: they test the limits of women's capacity for expressive self-control; they reaffirm that a woman's physical appearance is an object of male scrutiny and approval; and, with hostility and threats of violence frequent in such interchanges, they serve to re-

146

iterate that women are at risk if they go un-escorted in public places.

Earlier, we observed that the *Exceptional Women* and the *Women as Problem* frameworks can overemphasize the individual and exaggerate self-determination and the power of personal effort. The *Psychology of Gender* framework, however, can run the opposite risk of overemphasizing the effects of the social structure. A view of gender-role conditioning as a global determinant of the experiences of all females may obscure the diversity of women's lives and the points of similarity between women's and men's lives. Not all women experience "role conflict," nor do all who experience it find it debilitating. Not all women speak and think in a "different voice." Some individuals resist the shaping forces of the social structure. In a sense, those individuals are, as Nancy Datan (1987) put it, "socialization failures." If we do not allow for the possibility of resistance to social forces or rebellion, our theories cannot explain the very existence of feminism. Moreover, the social structure does contain conflicting messages, including some that reinforce feminist values and actions (Lott, 1987b).

Gender is not the only axis along which social relations are organized. In some instances, similarities of class, age, or race may be as strong or stronger than gender similarities. In using gender as the lens through which to view the social structure, theorists must acknowledge that other lenses yield equally viable, though also partial, portrayals (Scott, 1985). A compelling example of the importance of recognizing interactions of gender, class, and race can be drawn from the feminist critique of violence against women. Feminists have pointed out that all women live with the threat of rape and have alleged the universality of victim-blaming. Yet, as Cole (1986) pointed out, victim-blaming interacts with both race and gender:

It is tempting to say that all women are bound by the recurring suggestion, innuendo, or outright assertion that whatever abuse they suffer, it is basically the woman's fault: "She shouldn't have been walking down that dark street"; or "If you wear a blouse like that, you're asking for it." Yet throughout U.S. history, there has been a glaring exception to this "rule"; it is the prevailing assumption that rape is most often committed by black men and that the victims are white women. In this case, blame is laid on the "over-sexed" black male. (p. 27)

An important difference between the *Psychology of Gender* framework and those previously described is that the conception of gender as a process cannot be readily accommodated within conventional methods of psychological research. When social organization and social relations are the subjects of inquiry, laboratory experiments are not necessarily the best means of study. Laboratory methods are designed to "decontextualize" the variables under study, that is, to isolate them from the contaminating influences of ongoing "real-life" processes. But gender is constructed and reconstructed through precisely these processes (Deaux & Major, 1987).

The *Psychology of Gender* framework is potentially valuable in over-coming the class, race, and ethnic biases in psychological research. It is easy to ignore (or "control") factors such as class, race, ethnicity, age, and disability, as well as gender, when basing a science largely on the behavior of college students in laboratory settings (Fine & Gordon, 1989). But once gender is conceptualized as a system of social relations, and methods are expanded to encompass that definition, other systems become both more visible and more amenable to study. Thus, a recent special issue of *Psychology of Women Quarterly* (Amaro & Russo, 1987) focused on the combined influences of gender and ethnicity on the psychological well-being of Hispanic women.

When scholars begin to question the adequacy of the discipline's most distinctive methods, they begin to look to other disciplines for fresh approaches. Thus, feminist psychologists are currently exploring methods from literary criticism (Crawford & Chaffin, 1986; Hare-Mustin & Marecek, 1988; Wetherell, 1986), symbolic anthropology (Bem, 1987), and sociology (Unger, 1987).

Feminism in psychology has not been limited to attempts to "remove sex bias from" or "add women to" an otherwise stable paradigm. Instead, there are incipient challenges to psychology's definition and normative practices. Disciplinary boundaries blur—but not without challenge and reassertion of disciplinary lines. For example, when we discuss Gardner's (1980) work on street remarks with other psychologists, a common reaction is that, although it is interesting research, it "isn't psychology," a judgment made on methodological grounds. Yet psychology does have a rich tradition on inquiry outside the positivist model of laboratory manipulation of isolated variables: field research, observational techniques, content analysis of open-ended responses, participant-observation, and case studies are a few examples.

Incipient challenges (both conceptual and methodological) are articulated and developed in the framework we turn to next. Intellectual ferment and a sense of broaching the unimagined characterize this fourth framework for feminist psychology.

Transformation

In this framework, attention focuses on the normative practices and philosophical premises of the discipline. This framework is in rudimentary stages in psychology of women and in psychology in general. Our notions of its scope and direction borrow heavily from the groundbreaking work of feminist philosophers and historians of science (e.g., Haraway, 1978; Harding, 1986; Merchant, 1989), whose challenge to basic tenets of science are applicable to psychology. In what follows, we indicate three of the issues that have concerned scholars working within this framework.

The myth of objectivity. The notion that facts exist apart from values, thus making it possible to obtain "value-free" knowledge (or practice therapy in value-free ways) is disputed. Because we necessarily speak, think, and perceive from a standpoint generated by our experience, position in the social hierarchy, and ideological commitments, objectivity is impossible to attain (Hartsock, 1985; Unger, 1983; Wallston, 1981). Empiricism, once thought to free our efforts to comprehend the world from bias, cannot do so. Indeed, claims of objectivity only serve to disguise the politics of meaning. From this vantage point, the value of feminist psychology is *not* that it is more objective than conventional psychology and thus better able to discover the "truth" about women's experience. Rather feminism holds the promise of helping psychology to be more self-conscious about its values and to change them as needed in order to promote equality and social justice.

The critique of the values of the discipline is also informed by work done in the other frameworks. For example, the biographies of "neglected fore-mothers" reveal that science is not the democratic community of ideas that is portrayed in our cultural myths, and point to the need to redefine the discipline to recognize the activities and contributions of women. Work on androgyny reveals the persistent reification of masculinity and femininity implicit in the concept of androgyny as well as other trait-based conceptions of gender (Lott, 1981; Morawski, 1985). Other work has analyzed key concepts in clinical theory from the standpoint of women's experience and shown them to be constructed from a masculinist point of view. Concepts that have been subjected to such critique include dependency (Lerner, 1983; Stiver, 1984), autonomy (Hare-Mustin & Marecek, 1985), and anger (Miller, 1983).

These endeavors serve to undermine the view that psychology is "objective" or value-free. Psychology, like any other mode of inquiry, rests on a set of background beliefs and assumptions. Psychology, like any discipline, actively, if covertly, selects its objects of study and devises a canon, in which the objects of study are ranked from more to less important. In a recent ranking of divisions of the American Psychological Association, the Division of the Psychology of Women (which ironically is one of the larger divisions) was perceived as 33rd out of 40 in importance and in the lowest category of interest (Harari & Peters, 1987).

A method is a theory. The methods of a discipline reflect certain values and assumptions about the phenomena under study. Methods limit what can be known about the phenomena. Feminists have criticized the methods of experimental psychology for context-stripping, that is, for isolating social phenomena from the situations in which they normally take place (Fine, 1985; Parlee, 1979; Sherif, 1979). The experimental paradigm has also been criticized for emphasizing discovery of universal (and static) laws of behavior. If one holds truth to be historically and culturally situated, then methods should focus on dynamic processes and regard historical and cultural influences not as

"nuisance variance" but as legitimate objects of study (Hoffnung, 1985).

The traditional research paradigm positions the experimenter as the expert and the subject as object of manipulation and observation. Such a paradigm is consonant with a mechanistic view of behavior. Some feminists have called for a revision of the research paradigm to one of mutual collaboration, in which the research participant is acknowledged as the primary interpreter of her or his experience and the research initiator is acknowledged as emotionally involved and as changed by the process of doing the research. As yet, there has been little movement in this direction in studies published in either feminist (Fine, 1985) or mainstream psychology journals (Fine & Gordon, 1989; Lykes & Stewart, 1986).

Critique of politics of psychology. Once psychology is seen as imbued with the values of the culture at large, then one can engage in debate as to the merits of those values. Feminists have been astute in identifying the gender politics of psychology: the assumption that the male is the norm and that women are deficient. Moreover, a critique of objectivity leads to a critique of the politics of psychology. Objectivity is a political tool of science: it is used to legitimize the expertise of social scientists and thus to buttress their power position in society.

One of the headiest developments in feminist theory is its social critique. Feminist philosophers, political theorists, and historians of science have debated the values of liberal humanism for feminist theory and praxis. Points of contention include the discourse on the self (Sherif, 1982); the extolling of individualism and autonomy over cooperation and collectivity (Hare-Mustin & Marecek, 1985); the focus on competing rights, rather than responsibilities, as the basis of moral behavior (Broughton, 1983;

Gilligan, 1982); and the equating of self-fulfillment with liberation from social restraints and freedom from obligation to others (Ehrenreich, 1983; Gervasio & Crawford, 1989). These ideological concerns have implications for how we construe gender, what strategies we devise to help women achieve equality, and whether we focus on individual "reformist" solutions or on collective, more revolutionary changes.

Psychology has participated in producing and reinforcing the ideology of liberal humanism. This is most readily apparent in various definitions of mental health, theories of personality, and modes of psychotherapy (cf. Wallach & Wallach, 1983), and in the persistent tendency to define mental health as a matter of individual characteristics, rather than collective conditions (Albee, 1981). It also is true of the way research issues are defined and constructed, for example how the self is conceived in research on identity and self-concept (Sampson, 1985).

We have described this phase in terms of its self-reflexive study of the values, assumptions, and normative practices of the discipline. But psychology (and psychology of women) cannot study only itself: self-scrutiny and self-criticism ideally should lead to a reconstructed discipline and new methods of inquiry. What would such inquiry look like?

It is difficult to imagine work so different from the "normal science" that most active feminist psychologists have been trained in. An attempt to specify exactly how the work of the future will proceed would be neither wise nor useful. We predict that the research within this framework will be characterized by the addition of sophisticated nonexperimental methods, recognition of the perspectives and personal involvements of both the investigator and the participants, and attention to and incorporation of social/political aspects of the work (Wallston, 1986).

An example of current work that has many of these characteristics is Kitzinger's (1986) study of lesbians' accounts of their lesbianism. Kitzinger used a modification of the Q-sort method to derive five general types of explanations or justifications in the women's accounts. Types of accounts included lesbianism as personal fulfillment and self-actualization; political choice; and "cross to bear." She then checked the validity of her interpretations by sharing them with the participants. She also included her own Q-sort in the results. Finally, she analyzed at length the potential gains and costs for the individual of maintaining each type of account, while acknowledging the validity of each account from the perspective of those who gave it. This research is more indebted to a social constructionist paradigm than to prefeminist "normal science."

Conclusion

Although the nature of written presentations forces us to present our frameworks in a linear sequence, we view them as co-existing. If they are related to each other at all sequentially, the sequence is circular rather than linear. The approaches are interactive and to some extent each is recursive on the others. Each approach can illuminate the assumptions of others and reveal how those assumptions permeate inquiry. All are well beyond "womanless" psychology. And, perhaps most important, each approach allows for work proceeding from feminist assumptions, as well as for work proceeding from antifeminist assumptions.

Because psychology is a cultural institution, doing psychological research is inevitably a political act. A central activity of feminist scholarship has been to draw attention to the politics of science. But this work has thus far been developed primarily for the biological sciences. By discussing the political and social implications of various psychologies of women and gender, we have attempted to show not that one approach is more feminist than the others, but rather that all have the potential for application in feminist and antifeminist ways. The multiplicity of approaches allows for healthy dialogue and cross-fertilization among them, and the reflexivity of the *Transformation* approach assures that the politics underlying the methods, topics, and governing assumptions of our scholarship are analyzed directly and self-consciously, rather than remaining unacknowledged.

Note

1. This paper has been published in several versions and reprinted a total of 30 times. See, for example, Weisstein (1969, 1970, 1971a, 1971b). It has become a classic in the field.

References

Albee, G. (1981). Prevention of sexism. *Professional Psychology, 12*, 20–28.

Amaro, H., & Russo, N. F. (1987). Hispanic women and mental health: Contemporary issues in research and practice. *Psychology of Women Quarterly, 11* (Special Issue), 391–535.

Belenky, M. F., Clinchey, B. M., Goldberger, N. R., & Tarule, J. M. (1986). *Women's ways of knowing: Development of self, voice, and mind.* New York: Basic.

Bem, S. L. (1987). Gender schema theory and the romantic tradition. In P. Shaver & C. Hendrick (Eds.), *Sex and gender* (pp. 251–271). Beverly Hills: Sage.

Bernstein, M. D., & Russo, N. F. (1974). The history of psychology revisited: Or, up with our foremothers. *American Psychologist, 29*, 130–134.

Bleier, R. (1986). Sex differences research: Science or belief? In R. Bleier (Ed.), *Feminist approaches to science* (pp. 147–164). New York: Pergamon.

Blumstein, P. W., & Schwartz, P. (1983). *American couples.* New York: William Morrow.

Bronfenbrenner, U., Kessel, F., Kessen, W., & White, S. (1986). Toward a critical social history of developmental psychology. *American Psychologist, 41*, 1218–1230.

Broughton, J. M. (1983). Women's rationality and men's virtues: A critique of gender dualism in Gilligan's theory of moral development. *Social Research, 50*, 597–642.

Caplan, P. J., & Hall-McCorquodale, I. (1985). Mother-blaming in major clinical journals. *American Journal of Orthopsychiatry, 55*, 345–353.

Cardell, M., Finn, S., & Marecek, J. (1981). Sex-role identity, sex-role behavior, and satisfaction in heterosexual, lesbian, and gay male couples. *Psychology of Women Quarterly, 5*, 488–494.

Clance, P. R., & Imes, S. A. (1978). The imposter phenomenon in high-achieving women: Dynamics and therapeutic intervention. *Psychotherapy: Theory, Research, and Practice, 15*, 241–247.

Cole, J. B. (Ed.). (1986). *All American women: Lines that divide, ties that bind.* New York: Free.

Coser, R. L. (1960). Laughter among colleagues: A study of the social functions of humor among the staff of a mental hospital. *Psychiatry, 23*, 8–95.

Crawford, M. (1982). In pursuit of the well-rounded life: Women scholars and family concerns. In M. Kehoe (Ed.), *Handbook for women scholars* (pp. 89–96). San Francisco: Americas Behavioral Research Corporation.

Crawford, M. (1989a). Humor in conversational context: Beyond biases in the study of gender and humor. In R. K. Unger (Ed.), *Representations: Social constructions of gender.* New York: Baywood.

Crawford, M. (1989b). Agreeing to differ: Feminist epistemologies and women's ways of knowing. In M. Crawford & M. Gentry (Eds.), *Gender and thought.* New York: Springer-Verlag.

Crawford, M., & Chaffin, R. (1986). The reader's construction of meaning: Cognitive research on gender and comprehension. In E. Flynn & P. Schweikart (Eds), *Gender and reading:*

Essays on reader, text, and context. Baltimore: Johns Hopkins University Press.

Datan, N. (1987, April). *Illness and imagery: Feminist cognition, socialization, and gender identify.* Paper presented at the Psychological Perspectives on Gender and Thought Conference, Hamilton College, Clinton, NY.

Deaux, K. (1984). From individual differences to social categories: Analysis of a decade's research on gender. *American Psychologist, 39*, 105–116.

Deaux, K., & Major, B. (1987). Putting gender into context: An interactive model of gender-related behavior. *Psychological Review, 94*, 369–389.

Dill, B. T. (1979). The dialectics of black womanhood. *Signs, 11*, 692–709.

Dowling, C. (1981). *The Cinderella complex.* New York: Pocket Books.

Ehrenreich, B. (1983). *The hearts of men: American dreams and the flight from commitment.* Garden City, NJ: Anchor Press/Doubleday.

Eichler, M. (1988). *Nonsexist research methods: A practical guide.* Winchester, MA: Allyn and Unwin.

Erikson, E. H. (1964). Inner and outer space: Reflections on womanhood. *Daedalus, 93*, 582–606.

Fine, M. (1985). Reflections on a feminist psychology of women. *Psychology of Women Quarterly, 9*, 167–183.

Fine, M., & Gordon, S. M. (1989). Feminist transformations of/despite psychology. In M. Crawford & M. Gentry (Eds.), *Gender and thought: Psychological perspectives* (pp. 146–174). New York: Springer-Verlag.

Gardner, C. B. (1980). Passing by: Street remarks, address rights, and the urban female. *Language and social interaction (Sociological Inquiry, 50)* 328–356.

Garrison, D. (1981). Karen Horney and feminism. *Signs: Journal of Women in Culture and Society, 6*, 672–691.

Gervasio, A. H., & Crawford, M. (1989). Social evaluations of assertiveness: A critique and speech act reformulation. *Psychology of Women Quarterly, 13*, 1–25.

Giddings, P. (1984). *When and where I enter: The impact of black women on race and sex in America.* New York: Morrow.

Gilder, G. (1986, September). Jobs: Women in the workforce. *The Atlantic*, p. 20.

Gilder, G. (1987). *Men and marriage.* Gretna, LA: Pelican.

Gilligan, C. (1982). *In a different voice: Psychological theory and women's development.* Cambridge, MA: Harvard University Press.

Grady, K. E. (1981). Sex bias in research design. *Psychology of Women Quarterly, 5*, 628–636.

Harari, H., & Peters, J. M. (1987). The fragmentation of psychology: Are APA divisions symptomatic? *American Psychologist, 42*, 822–824.

Haraway, D. (1978). Animal sociology and a natural economy of the body politic, Part II: The past is the contested zone: Human nature and theories of production and reproduction in primate behavior studies. *Signs: Journal of Women in Culture and Society, 4*, 37–60.

Harding, S. (1986). *The science question in feminism.* Ithaca, NY: Cornell University Press.

Hare-Mustin, R. T., & Marecek, J. (1985). Autonomy and gender: Some questions for therapists. *Psychotherapy, 23*, 205–212.

Hare-Mustin, R. T., & Marecek, J. (1988). The meaning of difference: Gender theory, postmodernism, and psychology. *American Psychologist, 43*, 455–464.

Hartsock, N. C. M. (1985). *Money, sex, and power.* Boston: Northeastern University Press.

Henley, N. (1985). Review Essay: Psychology and gender. *Signs: Journal of Women in Culture and Society, 11*, 101–119.

Hennig, M., & Jardim, A. (1981). *The managerial woman.* Garden City, NY: Anchor Press.

Hoffnung, M. (1985). Feminist transformation: Teaching experimental psychology. *Feminist Teacher, 2*, 31–35.

Hollandsworth, J. G., & Wall, K. E. (1977). Sex differences in assertive behavior: An empirical investigation. *Journal of Counseling Psychology, 24*, 217–222.

Hooks, B. (1981). *Ain't I a woman?* Boston: South End Press.

Horner, M. S. (1970). Femininity and successful achievement: A basic inconsistency. In J. M. Bardwick, E. Douvan, M. S. Horner, & D. Gutman (Eds), *Feminine personality and conflict* (pp. 45–74). Belmont, CA: Brooks/Cole.

Johnson, F. L., & Aries, E. J. (1983). The talk of women friends. *Women's Studies International Forum, 6,* 353–361.

Keller, E. F. (1983). *A feeling for the organism: The life and work of Barbara McClintock.* New York: Freeman.

Kitzinger, C. (1986). Introducing and developing Q as a feminist methodology: A study of accounts of lesbianism. In S. Wilkinson (Ed.), *Feminist social psychology: Developing theory and practice* (pp. 77–96). Philadelphia: Open University Press.

Kravetz, D., Marecek, J., & Finn, S. E. (1983). Factors influencing women's participation in consciousness-raising groups. *Psychology of Women Quarterly, 7,* 257–271.

Lakoff, R. (1973). Language and women's place. *Language and Society, 2,* 45–80.

Lerner, H. G. (1983). Female dependency in context: Some theoretical and technical considerations. *American Journal of Orthopsychiatry, 53,* 697–705.

Lewin, M. (Ed.). (1984). *In the shadow of the past: Psychology portrays the sexes.* New York: Columbia University Press.

Lopate, C. (1968). *Women in medicine.* Baltimore: Johns Hopkins University Press.

Lott, B. (1981). A feminist critique of androgyny: Toward the elimination of gender attributions for learned behavior. In C. Mayo & N. M. Henley (Eds), *Gender and nonverbal behavior* (pp. 171–180). New York: Springer-Verlag.

Lott, B. (1987a, August). *Masculine, feminine, androgynous, or human?* Paper presented at the meeting of the American Psychological Association, New York, NY.

Lott, B. (1987b). *Women's lives: Themes and variations in gender learning.* Monterey, CA: Brooks/Cole.

Lykes, M. B., & Stewart, A. S. (1986). Evaluating the feminist challenge to research in personality and social psychology: 1963–1983. *Psychology of Women Quarterly, 10,* 393–412.

Marecek, J. (1988). *Psychological disorders of women.* Unpublished manuscript, Swarthmore College.

Marecek, J., & Hare-Mustin, R. T. (1987, March). *Cultural and radical feminism in therapy: Divergent views of change.* Paper presented at the meeting of the American Orthopsychiatric Association, Washington, DC.

McClelland, D. C., Atkinson, J. W., Clark, R. A., & Lowell, E. (1953). *The achievement motive.* New York: Appleton-Century-Crofts.

McCullough, M. (1987, November). *Women's friendships across cultures: Black and white friends speaking.* Paper presented at meeting of the Speech Communication Association, Boston, MA.

McHugh, M., Koeske, R., & Frieze, I. H. (1986). Issues to consider in conducting nonsexist psychological research: A guide for researchers. *American Psychologist, 41,* 879–890.

McIntosh, P. (1983). *Interactive phases of curricular re-vision: A feminist perspective.* Working paper no. 124. Wellesley, MA: Wellesley College Center for Research on Women.

Mednick, M. T. S. (1987, July). *On the politics of psychological constructs: Stop the bandwagon—I want to get off.* Paper presented at the Third Interdisciplinary Congress on Women, Dublin, Ireland.

Merchant, C. (1980). *The death of nature.* New York: Harper & Row.

Miller, J. B. (1983). *The construction of anger in women and men.* Wellesley, MA: Stone Center.

Morawski, J. G. (1985). The measurement of masculinity and femininity: Engendering categorical realities. *Journal of Personality, 53,* 196–223.

Morawski, J. G. (1987, August). *Toward the unimagined: Feminism and epistemology in psychology.* Paper presented at American Psychological Association, New York, NY.

Moulton, R. (1979). Psychological challenges confronting women in the sciences. In A. M. Brisco, & S. M. Pfafflin (Eds.), *Expanding the role of women in the sciences* (pp. 321–335). New York: New York Academy of Sciences.

Moynihan, D. P. (1965). *The Negro family: The case for national action*. Washington, DC: U.S. Department of Labor.

Nieva, V. F., & Gutek, B. A. (1981). *Women and work: A psychological perspective*. New York: Praeger.

Nochlin, L. (1971). Why are there no great women artists? In V. Gornick & B. Moran (Eds.), *Woman in sexist society* (pp. 480–510). New York: Basic.

O'Connell, A. N., & Russo, N. F. (1980). Eminent women in psychology: Models of achievement. *Psychology of Women Quarterly, 5* (Special Issue), 1–144.

O'Connell, A. N., & Russo, N. F. (1983). *Models of achievement: Reflections of eminent women in psychology*. New York: Columbia University Press.

O'Connell, A. N., & Russo, N. F. (1988). *Models of achievement: Reflections of eminent women in psychology* (Vol. II). Hillsdale, NJ: Erlbaum.

Parlee, M. B. (1975). Review Essay: Psychology. *Signs, 1*, 119–138.

Parlee, M. B. (1979). Psychology and women. *Signs, 5*, 121–133.

Peplau, L. A. (1982). Research on homosexual couples: An overview. *Journal of Homosexuality, 8*, 3–8.

Russo, N. F., & O'Connell, A. N. (1980). Models from our past: Psychology's foremothers. *Psychology of Women Quarterly, 5*, 11–54.

Russo, N. F., & Denmark, F. L. (1987). Contributions of women to psychology. *Annual Review of Psychology, 38*, 279–298.

Sampson, E. E. (1985). The decentralization of identity: Toward a revised concept of personal and social order. *American Psychologist, 40*, 1203–1211.

Scarborough, E., & Furumoto, L. (1987). *Untold lives: The first generation of American women psychologists*. New York: Columbia University Press.

Schuster, M., & Van Dyne, S. (1984). Placing women in the liberal arts: Stages of curriculum transformation. *Harvard Educational Review, 54*, 413–428.

Scott, J. W. (1985, December). *Is gender a useful category of historical analysis?* Paper pre-sented at the meeting of the American Historical Association, New York, NY.

Sherif, C. (1979). Bias in psychology. In J. A. Sherman & E. T. Beck (Eds.), *The prism of sex: Essays in the sociology of knowledge* (pp. 93–133). Madison, WI: University of Wisconsin Press.

Sherif, C. (1982). Needed concepts in the study of gender identity. *Psychology of Women Quarterly, 6*, 375–398.

Stacey, J., & Thorne, B. (1985). The missing feminist revolution in sociology. *Social Problems, 32*, 301–316.

Stiver, I. P. (1984). *The meanings of ''dependency'' in female-male relationships*. Wellesley, MA: Stone Center.

Tobias, S. (1978). *Overcoming math anxiety*. New York: Norton.

Torrey, J. W. (1987). Phases of feminist re-vision in the psychology of personality. *Teaching of Psychology, 14*, 155–160.

Unger, R. K. (1983). Through the looking glass: No Wonderland yet? (The reciprocal relationship between methodology and models of reality). *Psychology of Women Quarterly, 8*, 9–32.

Unger, R. K. (1987, August). *The social construction of gender: contradictions and conundrums*. Paper presented at the meeting of the American Psychological Association, New York, NY.

Wallach, M. A., & Wallach, L. (1983). *Psychology's sanction for selfishness*. San Francisco: Freeman.

Wallston, B. S. (1981). What are the questions in psychology of women? A feminist approach to research. *Psychology of Women Quarterly, 5*, 597–617.

Wallston, B. S. (1986). *What's in a name revisited: Psychology of women versus feminist psychology*. Invited Address, Annual meeting of the Association for Women in Psychology, Oakland, CA.

Weisstein, N. (1968). *Kinder, Kirche, Küche as scientific law: Psychology constructs the female*. Boston: New England Free Press.

Weisstein, N. (1969). Woman as nigger. *Psychology Today, 3*, 20–23.

Weisstein, N. (1970). *Kinder, Kirche, Küche as scientific law: Psychology constructs the fe-

male. In R. Morgan (Ed.), *Sisterhood is powerful*. New York: Random House.

Weisstein, N. (1971a). Psychology constructs the female, or the fantasy life of the male psychologist. In M. H. Garskof (Ed.), *Roles women play: Readings toward women's liberation*. Belmont, CA: Brooks/Cole.

Weisstein, N. (1971b). Psychology constructs the female, or the fantasy life of the male psychologist (with some attention to the fantasies of his friends, the male biologist and the male anthropologist). *Journal of Social Education, 35*, 362–373.

West, C., & Zimmerman, D. H. (1987). Doing gender. *Gender and Society, 1*, 125–151.

Wetherell, M. (1986). Linguistic repertoires and literary criticism: New directions for a social psychology of gender. In S. Wilkinson (Ed.), *Feminist social psychology: Developing theory and practice* (pp. 77–96). Philadelphia: Open University Press.

Widom, C. S. (Ed.). (1984). *Sex roles and psychopathology*. New York: Plenum.

Wiest, W. M. (1977). Semantic differential profiles of orgasm and other experiences among men and women. *Sex Roles, 3*, 399–403.

Worell, J. 1987, August). *Support and satisfaction in women's close relationships*. Presidential address (Division 12, Section 4) presented at the meeting of the American Psychological Association, New York, NY.

Martha T. Mednick

On the Politics of Psychological Constructs: Stop the Bandwagon, I Want to Get Off*

ABSTRACT. Since the inception of the "new" era of feminist scholarship, several constructs have achieved prominence and popularity as explanations of women's behavior. These include fear of success, androgyny, and the notion of a different voice vis-à-vis moral development. It is argued that such popularity is more a political than an intellectual event. Furthermore, the case is made that genre of concepts deters rather than advances the goals of feminist psychology.

This article grew from discontent and from years of unease about the phenomenon of the extreme popularity of certain psychological concepts advanced to understand women. The concepts with which I am concerned

Martha Mednick, "On the politics of psychological constructs: Stop the bandwagon, I want to get off." *American Psychologist,* 1989, *44,* pp. 1118–1123. Copyright © 1989 by the American Psychological Association. Reprinted by permission.

*This article is based on a talk I delivered at the Third International Interdisciplinary Congress on Women, Dublin, Ireland, in July 1987. Many colleagues have helped to refine my ideas with their comments, as did the Dublin audience. I am most indebted to Myra Marx Ferree and Sandra S. Tangri, Helen Kearney, and three anonymous reviewers.

Correspondence concerning this article should be addressed to Martha T. Mednick, Department of Psychology, Howard University, Washington, DC 20059.

emerged during the past 20 years, as feminist psychologists were trying to rethink female behavior and to bring the psychological discipline to new levels of theory and research about women. There is no doubt that there has been substantial achievement. At the same time, however, it seems that certain of these ideas are so compelling and seductive that they take on a public and scholarly life of their own, one that is remote from their empirical and theoretical mooring and meaning. As I offer the following critique, I do not wish to be construed as debasing or dismissing this large body of work. My concern is with the extreme popularity of certain psychological concepts—with the phenomenon of the conceptual bandwagon. I wish to discuss why it happens and what the implications are for the work of feminist scholars and for feminist politics. These concepts, all of them developed by feminist psychologists, are very familiar and have been heavily researched and discussed in the psychological literature as well as in the lay literature and popular press.

Although such bandwagons eventually pass from the scene, they are part of a very influential reality for a significant period of time, and thus they have an effect. Scholarship is affected and inquiry stifled, if only because the development of alternative models is not as attractive as jumping on the bandwagon. Public views are affected, and because most of these ideas are offered as all-encompassing, simplistic solutions to the understanding of a social problem, they convey one-dimensional and even incorrect notions about what the problem is and how it can be solved. In the case of feminist scholarship, which originated and developed within the context of a widespread social movement, these issues take on particular significance.

My discussion will focus first on comments about bandwagon contructs: fear of success, androgyny, and Gilligan's "different voice" (Gilligan, 1982), with particular emphasis on the last. I will then turn to the meaning and implications of scholarly and public acceptance of such ideas and contrast these with alternative conceptual approaches that have not become bandwagon concepts. Finally, I will discuss the implications for women and feminist change, that is, politics.

Prominent Bandwagons

In the following review, my primary goal is not to debate scientific merit; indeed, the validity of the various ideas offered to explain female behavior has been extensively discussed in the feminist and mainstream psychological literature. There certainly is merit in much of this work. Theories about fear of success and androgyny stimulated research and thought, fostered "a new look" (Mednick, 1978; Mednick & Weissman, 1975), and provoked practitioners of major paradigms in psychology to take a closer look at the validity (particularly the external validity) of their theories and research. Still, although the issue of scientific merit must be separated from that of the bandwagon effect, the current scientific status of these concepts affects the nature of the questions to be raised in the remainder of my discussion, and so cannot be ignored.

I have selected "fear of success," "androgyny," and "different voice" because I perceive them to have been major bandwagons of the past two decades. It is my view that these three have been among the most heavily researched concepts, as well as the most visible to the public.

The concept of fear of success came along at the very beginning of the contemporary women's movement. Its public appearance followed closely the publication of *The Feminine Mystique* (Friedan, 1963) and the formation of the National Organization for Women. Indeed, as has been frequently noted, it was an idea whose time had come (Mednick, 1978, in press). It was enthusiastically embraced by feminist psychologists, researchers, and clinicians and was the subject of numerous lively discussions by achievement motivation researchers. However, after a while it began to get mixed reviews by researchers (feminist, as well as others; see Condry & Dyer, 1976; Henley, 1985), and interest ebbed. Nevertheless, the notion continues to attract professional and public attention. As recently as 1986, I was the invited discussant on a panel, sponsored by the women's section of the clinical division of the American Psychological Association that was entirely devoted to the question of women's "fears of success." The panelists were all clinical psychologists who spoke of their client's fears in the achievement arena (see Rothblum and Cole, 1987).

A popular advice book entitled, *Overcoming Fear of Success,* appeared in 1980 (Friedman, 1980) and was supplemented as recently as 1985 by a *Psychology Today* tape (Friedman, 1985). Furthermore, psychoanalysts have continued to embrace the idea as an explanation for clients' problems (Moulton, 1986), even after many researchers had discarded the concept on the basis of its problematic scientific status (Fleming, 1982). It refuses to be buried. It survives on intuitive appeal: It offers an explanation of why women have problems with accomplishment that is intuitively obvious, simple, and evidently very satisfying.

The concept of androgyny was advanced in the mid-1970s as the answer to the puzzle of gender; it represented a new look at conceptions about and measurement of masculinity and femininity. At that level, it was an excellent critique (Constantinople, 1973). It was the subject of considerable psychological research; at least three new scales were developed to measure it, and it spawned numerous dissertations (Bem, 1974; Bem & Lenney, 1976; Block, 1973; Spence & Helmreich, 1978). It was also widely discussed by feminist scholars in other social science disciplines and in the humanities (Heilbrun, 1973). Even more than the fear of success, it became a buzz word for the public and was personified in advertising, fashion, cosmetics for men, and rock musicians such as Boy George, Michael Jackson, and Prince. Although androgyny has not passed from the scene, it has not been very helpful, particularly in its popularized version, in solving the problem of gender. The fact that serious questions have been raised about its scientific merit, indeed, even by the authors of two of the most widely used measures of androgyny (Bem, 1981; see also Lott, 1987), has not impaired its survival as a bandwagon.

The current contender for the bandwagon title, and the one I wish to discuss in greater detail and to use as a foil for my points about politics, is Gilligan's (1982) concept of "a different voice." Gilligan presented her work as a critique of Kohlberg's conceptions of moral development, particularly with respect to purported sex differences in the ability to solve moral dilemmas (Kohlberg & Kramer, 1969). Gilligan argued that such differences are based on the irrelevance of Kohlberg's justice dilemmas to women. Arguing that women are oriented toward relatedness and men toward individuation and separation, she changed the moral development task to one involving relationships and scored women's responses from an interpersonal, caring perspective. This approach was the foundation of Gilligan's theory about a different moral voice. This idea has been widely and enthusiastically accepted by many feminist scholars in numerous disciplines, as well as by many writers, politicians, journalists, and the public. It is no doubt a conceptual bandwagon.

Turning first to questions of validity, I must note that Kohlberg's theory of moral development has been the subject of serious criticism at very fundamental levels. Some have argued that the stage/developmental/trait approach is not useful for behavioral prediction and have criticized the methodology (e.g., Gibbs & Schnell, 1985), whereas others, most notably philosophers, (Friedman, 1987), differ with Kohlberg's definition of the concepts of justice and morality. Such criticisms do not seem to have affected the enthusiasm for Gilligan's variation on Kohlberg's work, nor have recent discussions of the central question of sex differences by psychologists researching moral development have had any effect on Gilligan enthusiasts. It is on this issue that the merit of Gilligan's conceptualization clearly stands or falls.

Gilligan's book was reviewed by Colby & Damon (1983). Although they viewed Gilligan as eloquent and convincing in her presentation and deserving of attention, they concluded that the available data did not support her contention of a global dichotomy between the moral reasoning of men and women when the effects of occupation and education are controlled. They also argued that the abortion study (Gilligan's real-life dilemma) was not comparative, that is, did not include men, and that therefore one could not conclude anything about how men would have reacted to the dilemma.

A spate of articles has recently further addressed the basic question of sex differences. These articles have included qualitative reviews, quantitative reviews (i.e., meta-analyses), and empirical studies of hypotheses generated by Gilligan's theory (Friedman, Robinson, & Friedman, 1987; Gibbs, Arnold, & Burkhart, 1984; Luria, 1986; Thoma, 1986; Walker, 1984). There seems to be general agreement among moral development researchers that the presumed sex differences have not been supported. Moreover, Thoma (1986) found in his meta-analysis, a consistent difference, with women scoring *higher* than men on the Kohlberg measure. Thoma (1986) concluded,

> There is now considerable evidence that justice defined measures of moral reasoning are not biased against females. Further, there is little support for the notion that males are better able to reason about hypothetical dilemmas, or that moral reasoning is in some way a male domain. (p. 176)

It has also been shown that moral dilemmas that reflect Gilligan's perspective on female reasoning are solved no differently by men and women (Friedman et al., 1987; see also Lowery & Ford, 1986).

The many reviews, critiques, and questions have been long available to feminist researchers and scholars. For example, the feminist journal *Signs* published an interdisciplinary forum early in 1986 (Kerber et al., 1986) in which a number of scholars raised questions and concerns and cited some of the aforementioned criticism. *Signs* reaches a broad community of feminist scholars, and yet its publication of the aforementioned forum did not, and has not, dampened enthusiasm for a "different voice." Certainly it did not reach the public: Journalists, politicians, and our students are still embracing

the idea. The belief in a "different voice" persists; it appears to be a symbol for a cluster of widely held social beliefs that argue for women's difference, for reasons that are quite independent of scientific merit.

The "different voice" is part of a currently popular category of theories, sometimes referred to as cultural feminism (Scott, 1988), that argue for women's special, and even superior, nature. It fits in also with some feminists' efforts to revise psychoanalysis (Alpert, 1986; see also Belenky, Clinchy, Goldberger, & Tarule, 1986), which are particularly strong among many feminist therapists. Luria (1986) has tied Gilligan's work to Freudian and Ericksonian theory. Such theories link personality traits, such as relatedness and nurturance, to female anatomy and generally hold that women's fulfillment is possible only through maternal love or various sublimations thereof. These views place maximal emphasis on sex differences, direct the focus of explanation intrapsychically, and attribute causality either to biological/genetic factors, or to an early female socialization process with strong long-range effects. An intrapsychic emphasis places the burden of change *entirely* on the person and does not lead scientific inquiry to an examination of cultural, socioeconomic, structural, or contemporaneous situational factors that may affect behavior.[1]

---

1. I am here decrying dichotomous thinking and exaggeration of gender differences, but I want to be careful not to fall into the same trap. The focus on intrapsychic factors is perhaps less exclusive than I have indicated; moreover, in focusing on structure and situation, I do not believe that one can ignore personal history and development. Analyses must proceed on several levels with the goal of intregration. In any event, my main goal is to focus on the strong appeal of a view that, as shall be made clear, feeds into a cultural ideology about the meaning and significance of gender.

Alternatives to the Bandwagon: Minimalist Views

I will turn now to contrasting views that have been put forth by another group of feminist psychologists, generally social psychologists and others who have incorporated a concern with sociostructural factors into their thinking.

From the earliest days of development of a feminist psychology, theorists and researchers have decried falling into the trap of viewing women as a homogeneous mass (e.g., see Mednick, 1978). Lott (1987) recently reaffirmed such a view, as have most of the theorists and researchers who look at more than sex difference per se. Lott observed, for example, that women and men differ enormously in the conditions under which they live, most notably in their access to power and control of resources. It is conceivable that individuals' level of autonomy or relatedness may depend more on their position in the social hierarchy than on gender (Hare-Mustin & Maracek, 1986). Persons in power, for example, tend to focus on rules and rationality, whereas those with less power emphasize relatedness and compassion. In such a situation, individuals' behavior cannot be predicted from gender alone. An analysis in such structural terms would examine power differences between groups and "how these are related to economic, political, and other conditions." (Lott, 1987, p. 4). Wallston's (1987) remark is also apt: "When work on sex comparisons is equaled or exceeded by work on power and status, real strides will have been made in feminist social psychology" (p. 1037). Such views argue that women's behavior is a function of much more than a supposedly universal trait. The latter way of thinking by some political feminists has also been discussed by Eisenstein (1983) as a false universalism that leads to the incorrect perception of the situation of *all* women as the same.

Examples of psychological theorists who focus on social structure are Sherif (1979, 1982), who urged that gender must be studied in social and historical context; Eagley (1986, 1987), who presented a social role analysis of gender differences; Henley (1977, 1985), who examined language and nonverbal behavior within the framework of power relations in society; and Deaux and Major (1987), who proposed a model of proximal factors that determine behavioral differences and similarities between the genders. These views do not ignore differences (e.g., Eagley, 1987); they simply do not focus on sex alone as an explanatory concept. Of significance is their focus on contemporaneous situational factors or other social factors that create observed gender differences. These theorists acknowledge differences in gender behavior, and may even stress them (e.g., Eagley, 1987), but their analytic focus is less likely to be directed toward personal attributes. Such models of behavior are complex and thus less easily reduced, as is Gilligan's view and other women's nature models, to a simplistic, dichotomously presented, intuitively appealing, bandwagon construct.

A review by Major (1987) illustrates how the difference between the two views affects the problems studied and the choice of variables. Major was concerned with women's lesser sense of entitlement, that is, their acceptance of, and satisfaction with, smaller rewards than men. The conventional view has held that women feel less entitled than men do because they hold different values and preferences about work. Thus, women are said to be less interested in money than men are, more interested in comfort and interpersonal relationships, and thus not willing to do the kind of work that earns high pay. According to Major (1987), this focus on sex *differences* has negative consequences:

> This tendency to blame the victim may perpetuate occupational sex-segregation. . . . It is but a small step to argue that since women and men want or value different things, they might best be suited for different work organizations, different social organizations, and/or different family and social roles. (pp. 130–131)

In fact, as Major noted, there is little empirical evidence for such a sex difference. For example, when men and women are in the same high-prestige jobs, their values are identical, and their behavior is similar.

Proceeding from the view that situational factors and not just personal dispositions are important, Major and her colleagues demonstrated that women were capable of feeling as equally entitled as men under certain circumstances. For instance, when they were given social comparison information, women rewarded themselves more equitably than when they did not have this information. Major extended the discussion into the political realm by pointing out that it will be only through change in the structural variables that maintain the feeling of lesser entitlement that women's awareness of pay inequity will increase and thus lead to pressure for change. Such an outcome is not possible with the intrapsychic approach.

A study by Risman (1987) is also illustrative. She examined how family roles and gender differ in their influence on attitudes and behavior. She compared a group of widowed or deserted single fathers, living alone with young children, with a group of single mothers and with married mothers and fathers. She found that in some respects, the single fathers were more similar to the mothers in both groups than to the married

fathers. She interpreted this as raising serious doubts about arguments for women's (or men's) true nature and discussed reasons for the popularity of maximalist views that focus on maximum sex differences. In her words,

> Why has the individualistic perspective been so readily accepted not only by the lay public, but also by feminist social scientists? . . . The conservative view is that family relationships are the last refuge for self-determination and autonomy in an increasingly anonymous, profit-oriented society, and therefore should not be tampered with. (p. 25)

Thus, Risman observed, even radical social scientists have admonished feminists to refrain from a critique of the nuclear family because of its function as refuge from state domination. Such an argument also assumes that women are by nature, or by socialization, the appropriate persons to provide an emotional salve to workers and children, a view that Risman's study clearly contradicts. It seems that feminists, scholars, and others who embrace an individualistic perspective with a traditional view of women and espouse a romanticized glorification of feminine values are willing to forfeit what some regard as the most significant advance of feminist theory, "the capacity to analyze social processes through which individuals, cultural forms, and social systems are engendered" (Stacey, cited in Risman, 1987, p. 27).

My focus here is on the thinking and research of feminist psychologists, but as illustrated by Risman's work, feminist scholars of other disciplines have also struggled with the question of the locus of explanation. It is also important to recognize that any difference argument is ultimately rooted in psy-

161

chological research on cognitive and personality sex differences.

The feminist historian, Scott (1988), reminded us that historians cast the discussion in terms of equality versus difference. Scott's analysis of the social implications of the two viewpoints is instructive; the argument for difference provides a clear basis for intellectual inferiority and thus justifies social practices such as the denial of higher education to women (e.g., see Lewin, 1984; Shields, 1975).

Scott further pointed to the difference argument as precluding examination of individuality or of subgroups of individuals within the female category. Diversity is thus masked by the fact of oppositional categories (Scott, 1988). She argued for a more relativistic approach to categorical thinking, but she indicated that she realized the departure from categorical thinking would lead to a more difficult and more complex kind of theoretical modeling. Such modeling is not only harder to do, but it is also much more difficult to promulgate, particularly in those arenas in which social policy is made. Furthermore, if such models include social and historical context (as I believe they should), as well as analysis of social structure, more than personal change is involved. I contend that such an emphasis is much more of a threat to powerful interests and institutions than the realm of discourse that focuses on personal change.

Conceptual Bandwagons, Society, and Politics

Now I will consider society, politics, and the question of why "the different voice" became a bandwagon. Scott's (1988) work has already led to the germ of the answer. I believe that the phenomenon is complex, psychological as well as political, and I have looked to several kinds of explanation. I will offer a brief discussion of each and close with a few remarks on the implications of these bandwagons for social change.

Part of the explanation of easy acceptance by the public and even by scholars may lie in the well-documented tendency to underestimate the role of situations as determinants of a person's behavior and to overestimate the importance of personal or dispositional factors, that is, "the fundamental attribution" error (Watson, de Bortali-Tregerthon, & Frank, 1984). Complementary to this tendency, and perhaps even more significant, is a general inclination to base explanations for one's own behavior on personal experience rather than on a consideration of facts, that is, science (Brigham, 1986). Decision theory research also has shown that people do not behave "rationally"; that is, they do not use reality information but, in fact, construct simplified models of the world for directing their own behavior. All the concepts that have been bandwagons have lent themselves to such construction because of their intuitive appeal and easy connection to personal experience.

Because they connect to the very salient, influential, cultural belief system about gender, bandwagon constructs have been particularly tenacious in their hold on the public and scholarly minds. There is a strong belief in sex differences, particularly those congruent with stereotypes (Deaux & Major, 1987; Greeno & Maccoby, 1986).

A philosophical analysis of gender and morality presented by Friedman (1987) very nicely separates the question of the lack of scientific foundation for sex differences in moral development from that of the strongly held conviction that they exist. She reviewed the evidence that "gender differences are alive and well at the level of popular perception i.e., both men and women on average, still conceive of women and men as differently moralized" (see also, Greeno & Maccoby, 1986). Furthermore, Friedman noted, "different voice" is resonant with gender stereotypes about the qualities of women and men and fits with social expectations about gender specialization. Greeno and Maccoby (1986) also made the point that evidence for the difference *stereotype* is strong, whereas evidence for an actual difference is less clear. They observed:

> It seems almost philistine to challenge the nature of her evidence. Many women readers find that the comments by women quoted in Gilligan's book resonate so thoroughly with their own experience that they do not need any further demonstration of the truth of what is being said . . . *intuitively* we feel that Gilligan must be right. . . . (but) . . . a warning: Women have been trapped for generations by people's willingness to accept their own intuitions about the truth of gender stereotypes. (p. 315)

These analyses speak to the paradox of different voice, that is, why so many continue to accept the concept in the face of its weak scientific status.

In sum, the simplicity of such ideas is appealing; such gender dichotomy confirms stereotypes and provides strong intuitive resonance. We need to add one more element: The consequences are attractive in the current political and intellectual climate. We are now faced with the question of the impli-

cations of "different voice" and similar scholarly ideas for feminist social change.[2]

Throughout the 1980s we have been in the throes of the social conservative movement's effective push for its social agenda. The agenda to which I refer has been described by Klatch (1988) in her study of activist conservative movement women. She delineated two groups, social conservatives and laíssez faire conservatives. The social conservative group is the one of concern to this analysis. This group is defined by Klatch (1988) as one with a strong belief in the family as the center of the world; the family's role as a moral authority is viewed as essential to the taming of the harsher, baser instincts intrinsic to human nature. The corollary of this is a strict belief in gender role division. Women's role is to support men and a strong family through altruism and self-sacrifice. Klatch quoted from a lecture given at a Moral Majority conference by one of its leaders.

> Women's nature is other-oriented. . . . To the traditional woman, self-centeredness remains as ugly and sinful as ever. The less time women spend thinking about themselves, the happier they are. . . . Women are ordained by their nature to spend time meeting the needs of others (pp. 676–677)

The social conservatives were in their ascendance, as was the Reagan revolution, at about the time Gilligan's book appeared. I am not arguing that Gilligan herself is a conservative or that she sees her theory in this light. Still it fell on fertile soil as far as its public acceptance was involved. Recall that Schafley's Eagle Forum and other right wing women's groups established a strong foothold in pivotal agencies, especially those concerned with the so-called "women's/family agenda," such as Health and Human

---

2. I must note that the view presented here does not consider the issue of the devaluation of that which is associated with women's role and nature. Such views are found in almost all cultures and can only change when the *tasks* that men and women do, and the social contexts in which they are conducted, are reevaluated—not "women's nature."

Services and the Department of Education. Scott's (1988) analysis of the Sears decision certainly supports the assertion that a maximalist/difference model is readily used in support of a conservative agenda.

It is my view that the different voice/maximalist view, even though professed by feminists who are not in agreement with the rightist agenda, nevertheless attained its popularity because it meshed so easily with the pro-family women's nature ideology that has become the dominant public rhetoric. As I have demonstrated, arguments for women's instrinsic difference, whether innate or deeply socialized, support conservative policies that, in fact, could do little else but maintain the status quo vis-à-vis gender politics.

Although maximalist feminist scholars are probably aware of the need for structural change in society, their individualistic theories simply do not incorporate the social side of the equation. The "different voice/woman's special nature" views came along at a time when feminists were losing at the political level and had not yet developed strategies for dealing with such losses. I see these theories about women as a legitimization of a change of focus from sociopolitical analysis and action to the personal. It was apparently easier to turn from social action and to think about women's nature, even a better, glorified nature, than to continue to try to change society in the face of loss and resistance.

One unfortunate outcome of this trend has been the growth of a mental health, rather than a social change, movement (Kahn & Jean, 1985), an approach that stresses self-help and self-development. One example of such focus has been research on and use of assertiveness training. Crawford and Gervasio (1989) have offered a critique of the assertiveness literature from a social perspective, noting its emphasis on interpersonal challenge rather than on

encouraging people to work for individual and social equality on a political level. . . . Women's situation includes unequal access to economic power. . . . Assertive training aimed at women blames women for being victims of sexism and diverts attention from its dynamics. (p. 31)

The focus on personal change diverts scholarship and action away from questions that could be directed toward an understanding of the social foundations of power alignments and inequity. Of course, a society that is resistant to feminist inspired change will welcome such a focus on personal change. I believe that as political feminists and as feminist scholars, we should be suspicious of such facile acceptance of ideas, even when feminists are the authors.

Finally, I conclude with the following quotation from *After the Second Sex: Conversations With Simone De Beauvior* (Schwarzer, 1984):

We are being given the illusion that woman can accomplish anything today and that it is her fault if she does not. It all goes hand in hand with this so-called *new femininity—with an enhanced status for traditional feminine values,* such as woman and her rapport with nature, woman and her maternal instinct, woman and her physical being. . . . This renewed attempt to pin women down to their traditional role, together with a small effort to meet some of the demands made by women,—that's the formula used to try and keep women quiet. And, unfortunately, as one can see from the tragic results, it is a really successful approach. Even women who call themselves feminists don't always see through it. Once again women are being defined in terms of "the other," once again they are being made into the "second sex." (p. 103, emphasis added)

References

Alpert, J. (1986). *Psychoanalysis and women: Contemporary reappraisals.* New York: Erlbaum, Analytic Press.

Belenky, M. F., Clinchy, B. M., Goldstein, N. R., & Tarule, J. M. (1986). *Women's ways of knowing: The development of self, voice, and mind.* New York: Basic Books.

Bem, S. L. (1974). The measurement of psychological androgyny. *Journal of Consulting and Clinical Psychology, 42,* 155–162.

Bem, S. L. (1981). Gender schema theory: A cognitive account of sex typing. *Psychological Review, 88,* 354–364.

Bem, S. L., & Lenney, E. (1976). Sex-typing and the avoidance of cross-sex behavior. *Journal of Personality and Social Psychology, 33,* 48–54.

Block, J. H. (1973). Conceptions of sex role: Some cross-cultural and longitudinal perspectives. *American Psychologist, 28,* 512–526.

Brigham, J. C. (1986). *Social psychology.* Boston: Little, Brown.

Colby, A., & Damon, W. (1983). Listening to a different voice: A review of Gilligan's *In a different voice. Merrill-Palmer Quarterly, 29,* 473–481.

Condry, J. C., & Dyer, S. L. (1976). Fear of success: Attribution of cause to the victim. *Journal of Social Issues, 32,* 63–83.

Constantinople, A. (1973). Masculinity-feminity. An exception to a famous dictum. *Psychological Bulletin, 80,* 389–407.

Crawford, M., & Gervasio, A. H. (1989). Social evaluations of assertiveness: A critique and speech act reformulation. *Psychology of Women Quarterly, 13,* 1–26.

Deaux, K., & Major, B. (1987). Putting gender into context: An interactive model of gender-related behavior. *Psychological Review, 94,* 369–384.

Eagly, A. H. (1986). Some meta-analytic approaches to examining the validity of gender-difference research In J. Hyde & M. C. Unn (Eds.), *The psychology of gender: Advances through meta-analysis* (pp. 159–177). Baltimore, MD: Johns Hopkins University Press.

Eagly, A. H. (1987). *Sex differences in social behavior: A social-role interpretation.* Hillsdale, NJ: Erlbaum.

Eisenstein, H. (1983). *Contemporary feminist thought.* Boston: G. K. Hall.

Fleming, J. (1982). Projective and psychometric approaches to measurement: The case of fear of success. In A. J. Stewart (Ed.), *Motivation and society: A volume in honor of David C. McClelland* (pp. 63–95). San Francisco: Jossey-Bass.

Friedan, B. (1963). *The feminine mystique.* New York: Dell.

Friedman, M. (1980). *Overcoming fear of success.* New York: Seaview.

Friedman, M. (1985). *Overcoming fear of success* (Tape No. 20284). Brooklyn, NY: Psychology Today Tapes.

Friedman, M. (1987). Beyond caring: The de-moralization of gender. In M. Hanen & K. Nielson (Eds.), *Science morality, & feminist theory. Canadian Journal of Philosophy, 13* (Suppl).

Friedman, W. J., Robinson, A. B., and Friedman, B. L. (1987). Sex differences in moral judgments? *Psychology of Women Quarterly, 11*(1), 37–46.

Gibbs, J. C., Arnold, K. D., & Burkhart, J. E. (1984). Sex differences in the expression of moral judgment. *Child Development, 55,* 1040–1043.

Gibbs, J. C., & Schnell, S. V. (1985). Moral development versus socialization, *American Psychologist, 40,* 1071–1080.

Gilligan, C. (1982). *In a different voice: Psychological theory and women's development.* Cambridge, MA: Harvard University Press.

Greeno, C. G., & Maccoby, E. E. (1986). How different is the "different voice"? *Signs: Journal of Women in Culture and Society, 11,* 310–316.

Hare-Mustin, R., & Maracek, J. (1986). Autonomy and gender: Some questions for therapists. *Psychotherapy, 23,* 205–212.

Heilbrun, C. G. (1973). *Toward a recognition of androgyny.* New York: Harper-Colophon.

Henley, N. (1977). *Body politics.* Englewood Cliffs, NJ: Prentice-Hall.

Henley, N. (1985). Psychology and gender. *Signs: Journal of Women in Culture and Society, 11,* 104–119.

Kahn, A., & Jean, P. J. (1985). Integration and elimination or separation and redefinition. *Signs: Journal of Women in Culture and Society, 8,* 659–671.

Kerber, L., Greeno, C., Maccoby, E., Luria, Z., Stack, C., & Gilligan, C. (1986). On *In a different voice*: An interdisciplinary forum. *Signs: Journal of Women in Cultural and Society, 11,* 304–333.

Klatch, R. (1988). Coalition and conflict among women of the new right. *Signs: Journal of Women in Culture and Society, 13,* 671–694.

Kohlberg, L., & Kramer, R. (1969). Continuities and discontinuities in childhood and adulthood moral development. *Human Development, 12,* 93–120.

Lewin, M. (Ed.). (1984). *In the shadow of the past: Psychology portrays the sexes.* New York: Columbia.

Lott, B. (1987, August). Feminist, masculine, androgynous or human. Paper presented at the meeting of the American Psychological Association, New York City.

Lowery, C. R., & Ford, M. R. (1986). Gender differences in moral reasoning: A comparison of the use of justice and care orientations. *Journal of Personality and Social Psychology, 50,* 777–783.

Luria, Z. (1986). A methodological critique. *Signs: Journal of Women in Culture and Society, 11,* 316–321.

Major, B. (1987). Gender, justice and the psychology of entitlement. In P. Shaver & C. Hendrick (Eds.), *Review of personality and social psychology: Vol. 7, Sex and gender* (pp. 124–148). Beverly Hills: Sage.

Mednick, M. T. (1978). Psychology of women: Research issues and trends. *New York Academy of Science Annuals, 309,* 77–92.

Mednick, M. T. (in press). Fear of success. In H. Tierney (Ed.), *Women's studies encyclopedia.* Westport, CT: Greenwood.

Mednick, M. T., & Weissman, H. (1975). The psychology of women—selected topics. *Annual Review of Psychology, 26,* 1–18.

Moulton, R. (1986). Professional success: A conflict for women. In J. C. Alpert (Ed.), *Psychoanalysis and women: Contemporary reappraisals* (pp. 161—181). New York: Erlbaum, Analytic Press.

Risman, B. J. (1987). Intimate relationships from a micro-structural perspective. *Gender and Society, 1,* 6–32.

Rothblum, E. D., & Cole, E. (Eds.). (1987). Treating women's fear of failure [Special issue]. *Women and Therapy, 6*(3).

Schwarzer, A. (1984). *After the second sex: Converservations with Simone DeBeauvior.* New York: Pantheon.

Scott, J. (1988). Deconstructing equality versus difference: On the uses of post-structuralist theory. *Feminist Studies, 14,* 33–50.

Sherif, C. W. (1979). Bias in psychology. In J. A. Sherman & E. T. Beck (Eds.), *The prism of sex: Essays in the sociology of knowledge* (pp. 93–134). Madison: University of Wisconsin Press.

Sherif, C. W. (1982). Needed concepts in the study of gender identity. *Psychology of Women Quarterly, 6,* 375–398.

Shields, S. (1975). Functionalism. Darwinism, and the psychology of women: A study in social myth. *American Psychologist, 30,* 739–754.

Spence, J. T., & Helmreich, R. L. (1978). *Masculinity and femininity.* Austin: University of Texas Press.

Thoma, S. (1986). Estimating gender differences in the comprehension and preferences of moral issues. *Developmental Review, 6,* 165–180.

Walker, L. J. (1984). Sex differences in the development of moral reasoning: a critical review. *Child Development, 55,* 677–691.

Wallston, B. S. (1987). Social psychology of women and gender. *Journal of applied and social psychology, 17,* 1025–1050.

Watson, D. L., de Bortali-Tregerthan, G., & Frank, J. (1984). *Social psychology: Science and application.* Glenview, IL: Scott, Foresman.

Women's Place in Psychology: New Directions

Recent scholarship, reflected in the readings included in this book, suggests the emergence of importantly different ways of understanding knowledge and history, and urges a re-evaluation of how history is approached. The reassessment suggested here must include at least two dimensions. First, historians of psychology are charged to reconsider how we do history: What are our sources; how sensitive are we to contextual forces shaping historical events; what is the aim of history, ceremonial or critical; how aware are we of our own biases, our own imbeddedness in context? Second, we are challenged to reconsider what counts as history, what are the criteria by which we select ideas and individuals as worthy of inclusion in the stories of psychology's evolution.

These readings also suggest that the time may be auspicious for this re-viewing of the history of psychology. The discipline appears in many ways to be primed for serious self-reflection, perhaps culminating in a new understanding of the meaning of psychology as a discipline. Numerous avenues of thought seem to point to a "crisis" in psychology (e.g., Caplan & Nelson, 1973; Gadlin & Ingle, 1975; Howard, 1985; Koch, 1981; Wallston & Grady, 1985). Such discussion is reminiscent of the uncertainty that Kuhn (1970) argues portends a paradigm shift. Among the voices raised to encourage such a shift are those whose work has challenged psychology's paradigmatic foundation in positivism (e.g., K. Gergen, 1973, 1985; K. Gergen & Morawski, 1980; M. Gergen, 1988; Scarr, 1985; Toulmin & Leary, 1985).

At the same time that psychology confronts such demands for self-reflection, events in the broader society compel a reassessment of many of the concepts that psychology has long addressed. Among these is gender. A fundamental re-construction of the meaning of gender is underway in this society, and this emerging new knowledge cannot help but affect psychology. We see the impact of this process on psychology's subject matter, where concerns with gender have stimulated the development of entire fields of study and have radically altered interpretations of human behavior and experience in a wide range of arenas. The impact is also felt in the discipline's methodology, as criticism of traditional methods has focused on the gender bias inherent in much of psychological research and theory (e.g., Crawford & Marecek, 1989; O'Connell, 1978;

Pepleau & Conrad, 1989; Sherif, 1979; Spence, 1981; Unger, 1981; Wallston & Grady, 1985; Wittig, 1985).

Re-Constructing Histories of Psychology

Thus, we face a confluence of events which may collectively create fertile soil for the emergence of a new approach to the history of psychology, based on thoughtful challenges to traditional paradigms. Such a history will attend to context, recognizing the inextricable imbeddedness both of historical events and of the writing of history. And it will be inclusive rather than exclusive, broadening the parameters of psychology's self-definition to incorporate the lives and work of psychologists who have been marginalized by more traditional accounts.

Demographic shifts within psychology magnify the importance of our moving toward this new history. Women's growing majority among undergraduate and graduate students renders the absence of appropriate models for their intellectual and professional development increasingly problematic. Women are still disproportionately represented among the applied specialties (O'Connell & Russo, 1988; Russo & Denmark, 1987), where they provide a plethora of direct services to people in need of psychological care. Unfortunately, unless we reconsider what we judge as historically noteworthy, contributions to psychological practice (where women predominate) will continue to go largely unnoticed by a discipline committed to positivist research as the key criterion for eminence and historical merit. The discounting of applied psychology by the discipline's histories means that some of the most important work in psychology—including its most direct impact on human lives—remains marginalized, invisible, and devalued. It is incumbent upon the institutions that educate future psychologists to see that the broad scope of psychology is not narrowed by its histories to focus on research to the exclusion of application. Attempts to create histories that are contextual and inclusive will contribute to this goal.

The Impact of Re-Placing Women

If the process of re-shaping histories of psychology is successful in integrating women and their work, what will this mean for psychology as a discipline? Will psychology-including-women be a different sort of psychology than that which has marginalized them? Do women approach psychology differently, so that incorporating them and their work will significantly alter the nature of the field—its subject matter, its methods, its priorities, its understanding of and impact upon the human experience?

Recently, a number of psychologists have suggested that women do, in fact, relate to the world in strikingly different ways than do men, and that women's distinctive modes of being affect every aspect of their life and work (e.g., Belenky, Clinchy, Goldberger and Tarrule, 1986; Chodorow, 1978; Gilligan, 1982; Keller, 1985; Miller, 1976). Women, this position argues, are more relational and less individualistic, lean toward cooperative rather than competitive problem solving, base their moral judgements on interpersonal caring rather than on individual rights, value subjective and intuitive knowledge over (or at least equally with) analytic and rational ways of knowing, learn through connection with rather than objective separation from the subject of interest.

If these arguments are valid, then women surely approach psychology differently; the psychology done by women differs markedly from the psychology that has constituted our histories, psychology done largely by men. The topics women deem central would differ, as would their methodologies, the conclusions drawn, the implications and application of their work. Women would be more interested in understanding through connection and applying that understanding to caring roles than in an objective search for abstract truth whose application to human experience is unclear.

This image of psychology significantly altered through the infusion of women's ways of being may be empowering to women who envision an important role for themselves in the field. In contrast to the usual devaluation of female qualities, this approach urges that traditionally "feminine" traits be cherished as the more humane of human attributes. It implies, thus, that the very best of psychology can be done by women expressing their essential nature. In addition, such a vision may act as a stimulant for psychology as a whole to re-think its priorities, asking what role the field should play in human experience.

However, others urge caution, pointing to the theoretical and empirical limitations of such formulations and to the possibly detrimental consequences of their too-easy acceptance. The article by Mednick in this book raises many of these issues, and others can be found sprinkled through the literature on gender (e.g., Hare-Mustin & Marecek, 1988; Kahn & Yoder, 1989; Lott, 1988; Westkott, 1988). In particular, these analyses highlight the assumption of essential sex differences which underlie such theories, reminding us that arguments for essential sex differences are not new but old, and have historically consistently been used to restrict women's opportunities. Further, these critics argue, the argument for essential differences distracts from the demonstrable reality that behavior is a function not of sex but of context. We ignore this reality at our peril, they insist, for the focus on internal explanations of behavior distracts us from the social action necessary to the improvement of women's situation. These and other questions challenge the utopian vision of a society (and a discipline) made more humane by the growing presence and recognition of women.

Yet, the controversy is not so simply settled. It is true that women's place in psychology has been markedly different from men's. It is true that women (in the main) have participated in different roles as psychologists; have raised different questions, especially about gender equity; and have worked to unpack the assumptions which have heretofore shaped psychology in women-exclusive ways. There is no doubt that women's greater presence and visibility is changing the face of psychology. Is that because women are inherently different in how they approach the questions raised by psychology? Or has their marginal position (the context) shaped their different perspective on the field? Would men, if marginalized, approach psychology as women do now? Do other marginalized groups approach psychology in a manner similar to women?

Looking to the Future

The answers to such complex questions as the meaning of gender and its relation to psychology will not be immediately forthcoming. For our purposes, the essential initial act is to raise the questions. Of this much we can be sure: the consequences of re-placing women in psychology will be profound and complex; this is already demonstrably the case. The change process is a veritable study in the social construction of knowledge—our "knowledge" about the meaning of gender and our "knowledge" about the meaning of psychology. Both understandings are presently in flux, and this generation of students may well bear witness to the emergence of new "truth" in both domains.

Psychology is at a crossroads, where the opportunity to reevaluate the direction of the discipline intersects with invigorating changes in our understanding of gender. We must be attentive both to the changes these events bring to psychology and to the possibilities they reveal. Among those possibilities is the opportunity to transform histories of the discipline in ways that will encourage further expansion in scope and more inclusive definitions of merit. This process promises finally to create histories of psychology that reflect its myriad applications and the diversity of its practitioners.

STUDENT EVALUATION OF READINGS

Once again you are asked to provide feedback about the value of the readings in *Section III* and the *Conclusion* in furthering your understanding of the process and impact of re-placing women in psychology's history. This form will provide your instructor with information both about your reaction to the various readings and about elements of the readings which might be unclear, confusing, or seemingly in conflict with material you've encountered elsewhere. Your responses will also serve as a basis for future revisions of the book, so your input will help other students, as well. Your thoughtful responses will, as always, be greatly appreciated.

1. **Please rate each of the readings from 1 to 5 on the following dimensions:** (1 = poor; 3 = average; 5 = exceptional)

	Lott	Crawford and Marecek	Mednick	Concl.
a. Clearly written, readable	____	____	____	____
b. Presents new information I'd not found elsewhere	____	____	____	____
c. Stimulated my interest in topics it raised	____	____	____	____
d. Caused me to re-think ideas I'd held previously	____	____	____	____

2. **To what extent do these readings fulfill the following aims:** (1 = not helpful; 3 = moderately helpful; 5 = extremely helpful)

	Lott	Crawford and Marecek	Mednick	Concl.
a. Helps to clarify how histories are shaped by context	____	____	____	____
b. Helps to explain women's invisibility in histories of psychology	____	____	____	____
c. Is useful as a basis for re-placing women in psychology	____	____	____	____

3. **Briefly explain what you believe is the strongest point of each reading:**

   Lott:

   Crawford and Marecek:

   Mednick:

   Conclusion:

4. **Briefly explain what you believe is the greatest shortcoming of each reading:**

Lott:

Crawford and Marecek:

Mednick:

Conclusion:

5. Are there any areas where you see conflicts or disagreements between these readings and material presented in your text or in lectures?

6. Do you have any other comments about these readings?

REVIEW QUESTIONS

As with earlier review questions in this book, these questions are intended to encourage thoughtful analysis and synthesis of the concepts raised by the readings in *Section III* and the *Conclusion*. They strive both to integrate these notions with earlier readings here and to suggest connections with material in your text.

I. Lott's article suggests a reciprocal influence between feminist research and social and personality psychology.
   a. What are the elements of this reciprocity; how can each benefit from the other?
   b. Select an item (a theory, a construct, a piece of research) from your mainstream psychology (your text, other course work or research, etc.) and explain how this item might be enhanced by the qualities of feminist research discussed by Lott.
   c. Reciprocally, where in the feminist orientation described by Lott do you detect the influence of mainstream approaches (as discussed in your text)?

II. Crawford and Marecek trace the treatment of gender in the psychological literature over two decades.
   a. This article was selected because it provides a constructionist historical analysis of psychology's treatment of gender. Explain how this is so.
   b. Explain how this article is in keeping with or divergent from Furumoto's recommendations for a "new history."
   c. If the part of your text that deals with this period (1968–1988) had incorporated the issues raised by Crawford & Marecek, how would it be different—not simply what additional names would be added, but how would it be fundamentally different in structure or character?

III. Mednick's article discusses how the acceptance of psychological constructs is shaped by socio-political forces.
   a. Explain how Mednick's analysis shows the dialectic nature of the social construction of truth: psychological constructs reflect broader social context and at the same time help to shape that context.
   b. What parallels do you see between Mednick's comments about contemporary psychology and Shields' assertion that turn-of-the-century science "played handmaiden to social values"?
   c. It is not only ideas about gender that are susceptible to the influence of social beliefs on science. Identify a concept from your text which you believe reflects the influence of the social context in which it emerged, and explain how you see context as shaping this concept.

IV. The structure of this book has provided an idea of how knowledge and history are shaped by context, and how context has acted to exclude women and their work from psychology's histories.

 a. What do you think about the potential for re-constructing histories of psychology to incorporate women and their work? What would it require in the way of re-defining psychology and its criteria for merit?

 b. Does it matter? What impact would it have (on the discipline, on students, on the public's view of psychology, etc.) for psychology's women to be visible in psychology's histories?

 c. How has the perspective on knowledge and history offered here influenced your response to your regular text? Select an item from your text and discuss the contrast between how you would have viewed it before and how you now see it, having been introduced to the constructionist perspective.

Resources for Re-Placing Women in Psychology: History, Constructionism, and Gender Theory

Resources for Re-Placing Women in Psychology: History, Constructionism, and Gender Theory

Acker, Joan, Barry, Kate, & Esveld, Joke. (1983). Objectivity and truth: Problems in doing feminist research. *Women's Studies International Forum, 4,* 423–435.

Aiken, Susan H., Karen, Dinnerstein, Myra, Lensink, Judy, & MacCorquedale, Patricia. (1987). *Changing our minds: Feminist transformations of knowledge.* Albany: State University of New York Press.

Alic, Margaret. (1986). *Hypatia's heritage: A history of women in science from antiquity through the nineteenth century.* Boston: Beacon Press.

Anderson, John E. (1956). Child development: An historical perspective. *Child Development, 27,* 181–196.

Ballou, Patricia K. (1986). *Women: A bibliography of bibliographies.* Boston: G. K. Hall.

Belenky, Mary F., Clinchy, Blythe M., Goldberger, Nancy R., & Tarrule, Jill M. *Women's ways of knowing: The development of self, voice and mind.* New York: Basic Books.

Benjamin, Ludy T., Jr. (1974). Prominent psychologists: A selected bibliography of biographical sources. *JSAS Catalog of Selected Documents in Psychology, 4,* 1.

Benjamin, Ludy T., Jr., & Heider, Kathryn L. (1976). History of psychology in biography: A bibliography. *JSAS Catalog of Selected Documents in Psychology, 6,* 61, Manuscript No. 1276.

Benjamin, Ludy, T., Jr. (1980). Women in psychology: Biography and autobiography. *Psychology of Women Quarterly, 5,* 140–144.

Benjamin, Ludy T., Jr. (1981). *Teaching history of psychology: A handbook.* New York: Academic Press.

Benjamin, Ludy T., Jr. (1988). *A history of psychology: Original sources and contemporary research.* New York: McGraw-Hill.

Berger, Peter L., & Luckmann, Thomas. (1967). *The social construction of reality.* New York: Doubleday.

Bernard, Jessie. (1964). *Academic woman.* University Park, PA: Pennsylvania State University Press.

Bernstein, Maxine D., & Russo, Nancy F. (1974). The history of psychology revisited: Or, up with our foremothers. *American Psychologist, 29,* 130–134.

Bleier, Ruth. (1986). *Feminist approaches to science.* New York: Pergammon.

Bohan, Janis S. (1990). Social constructionism and contextual history: An expanded approach to the history of psychology. *Teaching of Psychology, 17,* 82–89.

Bohan, Janis S. (1990). Contextual history: A framework for re-placing women in the history of psychology. *Psychology of Women Quarterly, 14,* 213–228.

Boring, E. G. (1951). The woman problem. *American Psychologist, 6,* 679–682.

Boring, E. G. (Ed.). (1952). *A history of psychology in autobiography* (Vol. 4). Worcester; MA: Clark University Press.

Boring, E. G., & Lindsey, Gardner. (1966). *A history of psychology in autobiography.* (Vol. 5). New York: Appleton-Century-Crofts.

Brodsky, Annette, & Hare-Mustin, Rachel T. (1980). *Women and psychotherapy: An assessment of research and practice.* New York: Guillford.

Bronstein, Phyllis, & Quina, Kathryn. (1988). *Teaching a psychology of people: Resources for gender and sociocultural awareness.* Washington, D.C.: American Psychological Association.

Brumberg, Joan J., & Tomes, Nancy. (1982). Women in the professions: A research agenda for American historians. *Reviews in American History, 10,* 275–296.

Brush, Stephen G. (1974). Should the history of science be rated X? *Science, 183,* 1164–1172.

Bryan, Alice L., & Boring, E. G. (1944). Women in American psychology: Prolegemenon. *Psychological Bulletin, 41,* 447–454.

Bryan, Alice L., & Boring, E. G. (1946). Women in American psychology: Statistics from the OPP Questionnaire. *American Psychologist, 1,* 71–79.

Bryan, Alice L., & Boring, E. G. (1947). Women in American psychology: Factors affecting their professional careers. *American Psychologist, 2,* 3–20.

Burman, Erica. (1990). Differing with deconstruction: A feminist critique. In Ian Parker & John Shotter (Eds.), *Deconstructing social psychology* (pp. 208–220). London: Routledge.

Caplan, Nathan, & Nelson, Stephen D. (1973). On being useful: The nature and consequences of psychological research on social problems. *American Psychologist, 28,* 199–211.

Cates, Judith N. (1970). Women in psychology: Report of the Subcommittee on Women of the Committee on Equal Opportunity in Psychology. Washington D.C.: American Psychological Association.

Chodorow, Nancy. (1978). *The reproduction of mothering.* Berkeley: University of California Press.

Collingwood, R. G. (1946). The a priori impossibility of a science of man. In R. G. Collingwood, *The idea of history* (pp. 205–231, 315–320). New York: Oxford University Press.

Committee on Women in Psychology. (1988). *Women in the American Psychological Association.* Washington, D.C.: American Psychological Association.

Crawford, Mary, & Gentry, Margaret (Eds.). (1989). *Gender and thought: Psychological perspectives.* New York: Springer.

Crawford, Mary, & Maracek, Jeanne. (1989a). Feminist theory, feminist psychology: A bibliography of epistemology, critical analysis, and applications. *Psychology of Women Quarterly, 13,* 477–491.

Crawford, Mary, & Marecek, Jeanne. (1989b). Psychology reconstructs the female, 1968–1988. *Psychology of Women Quarterly, 13,* 147–165.

Danzinger, Kurt. (1990). The social context of research practice and the history of psychology. In William Baker, Michael Hyland, Rene Vantlezewijk & Syke Terwee (Eds.). *Recent trends in theoretical psychology, Vol. III* [Proceedings of the 3rd Biennial Conference of the International Society for Theoretical Psychology, April 17–21, 1989]. New York: Springer Verlag.

Deaux, Kay. (1984). From individual differences to social categories: Analysis of a decade's research on gender. *American Psychologist, 39,* 105–116.

Denmark, Florence L. (1979). Women in psychology in the United States. *Annals of the New York Academy of Sciences, 323,* 65–78.

Denmark, Florence L. (1980). Psyche: From rocking the cradle to rocking the boat. *American Psychologist, 35,* 1057–1065.

Denmark, Florence. (1983). Integrating the psychology of women in to introductory psychology. *G. S. Hall Lectures* (Vol. 3, pp. 37–71). Washington DC: American Psychological Association.

Denmark, Florence L., Russo, Nancy F., Frieze, Irene H., & Sechzer, Jeri A. (1988). Guidelines for avoiding sexism in psychological research: A report of the Ad Hoc Committee on Non-sexist Research. *American Psychologist, 43,* 582–585.

Douvan, Elizabeth. (1976). The role of models in women's professional development. *Psychology of Women Quarterly, 1,* 5–20.

Ehrenreich, Barbara, & English, Diedra. (1978). *For her own good: 150 years of experts' advice to women.* New York: Anchor Press.

Eichenbaum, Louise, & Orbach, Susie. (1983). *Understanding women: A feminist psychoanalytic approach,* New York: Basic Books.

Fausto-Sterling, Anne. (1985). *Myths of gender.* New York: Basic Books.

Fee, Pamela. (1986). Critiques of modern science: The relationship of feminism to other radical epistemologies. In Ruth Bleier (Ed.), *Feminist approaches to science* (pp. 42–56). New York: Pergammon.

Fernberger, Samuel W. (1932). The American Psychological Association: A historical summary, 1892–1930. *Psychological Bulletin, 29,* 1–89.

Flax, Jane. (1980). (87). Postmodernism and gender relations in feminist theory. *Signs, 12,* 621–643.

Flax, Jane (1990). *Thinking fragments: Psychoanalysis, feminism and postmodernism in the contemporary west.* Berkeley: University of California Press.

Furumoto, Laurel. (1985). Placing women in the history of psychology course. *Teaching of Psychology, 12,* 203–206.

Furumoto, Laurel. (1987). On the margins: Women and the professionalization of psychology in the United States, 1890–1940. In Mitchell G. Ash and William R. Woodward (Eds.), *Psychology in twentieth century thought and society* (pp. 93–113). Cambridge: Cambridge University Press.

Furumoto, Laurel. (1988a). The new history of psychology. In Ira S. Cohen (Ed.), *G. Stanley Hall lecture series,* Vol. 9, (pp. 9–34).

Furumoto, Laurel. (1988b). Shared Knowledge: The experimentalists, 1904–1929. In Jill G. Morawski (Ed.), *The rise of experimentalism in American psychology,* (pp. 94–113). New Haven, CT: Yale University Press.

Furumoto, Laurel, & Scarborough, Elizabeth. (1986). Placing women in the history of psychology: The first generation of American women psychologists. *American Psychologist, 41,* 35–42.

Gadlin, Howard, & Ingle, Grant. (1975). The one-way mirror: The limits of experimental self-reflection. *American Psychologist, 30,* 1003–1009.

Gergen, Kenneth. (1973). Social psychology as history. *Journal of Personality and Social Psychology, 26,* 309–320.

Gergen, Kenneth. (1985). The social constructionist movement in modern psychology. *American Psychologist, 40,* 266–275.

Gergen, Kenneth. (1988). Feminist critique of science and the challenge of social epistomology. In Mary M. Gergen (Ed.), *Feminist thought and the structure of knowledge* (pp. 27–48). New York: New York University Press.

Gergen, Kenneth. (1990). Toward a postmodern psychology. *The Humanistic Psychologist, 18,* 23–34.

Gergen, Mary M. (1988a). *Feminist thought and the structure of knowledge.* New York: New York University Press.

Gergen, Mary M. (1988b). Toward a feminist metatheory and methodology in the social sciences. In Mary M. Gergen (Ed.), *Feminist thought and the structure of knowledge,* (pp. 87–102). New York: New York University Press.

Gilligan, Carol. (1982). *In a different voice: Psychological theory and women's development.* Cambridge, MA: Harvard University Press.

Goldstein, Elyse. (1979). Effect of same-sex and cross-sex role models on subsequent academic productivity of scholars. *American Psychologist, 34,* 407–410.

Guthrie, Robert J. (1976). *Even the rat was white.* New York: Harper and Row.

Haber, Barbara (1978). *Women in America: A guide to books.* Boston: G. K. Hall.

Harding, Sandra. (1986). *The science question in feminism.* Ithaca, New York: Cornell University Press.

Harding, Sandra, & Hintikka, Merrill (Eds.). (1983). *Discovering reality: Feminist perspectives on metaphysics, epistemology, methodology, and the philosophy of science.* Boston: D. Reidel.

Harding, Sandra, & O'Barr, Jeanne F. (Eds.). (1987). *Sex and scientific inquiry.* Chicago: University of Chicago Press.

Hare-Mustin, Rachel, & Marecek, Jeanne. (1988). The meaning of difference: Gender theory, postmodernism, and psychology. *American Psychologist, 43,* 455–464.

Hare-Mustin, Rachel, & Marecek, Jeanne. (1990). *Making a difference: Psychology and the construction of gender.* New Haven, CT: Yale University Press.

Henle, Mary. (1976). Why study the history of psychology? *Annals of the New York Academy of Sciences, 270,* 14–20.

Howard, George, S. (1985). The role of values in the science of psychology. *American Psychologist, 40,* 255–265.

Hymowitz, Carol, & Weissman, Michelle. (1978). *A history of women in America.* New York: Bantam Books.

Kahn, Arnold & Yoder, Janice. (1989). The psychology of women and conservatism: Rediscovering social change. *Psychology of Women Quarterly, 13,* 417–432.

Keller, Evelyn F. (1985). *Reflections on gender and science.* New Haven, CT: Yale University Press.

Koch, Sigmund. (1959). The nature and limits of psychological knowledge: Lessons of a century qua science. *American Psychologist, 36,* 257–269.

Krawiec, T. S. (1972, 1974, 1978) *The psychologists* (3 Vols.). New York: Oxford University Press.

Kuhn, Thomas. (1970). *The structure of scientific revolutions.* Chicago: University of Chicago Press.

Kuhn, Thomas. (1977). *The essential tension: Selected studies in scientific tradition and change.* Chicago: University of Chicago Press.

Langland, Elizabeth & Gove, Walter, (Eds.). (1981). *A feminist perspective in the academy: The difference it makes.* Chicago: University of Chicago Press.

Lather, Patti. (1990). Postmodernism and the human sciences. *The Humanistic Psychologist, 18,* 64–84.

Lerner, Gerda. (1979). *The majority finds its past.* New York: Oxford University Press.

Lewin, Miriam (Ed.). (1984). *In the shadow of the past: Psychology portrays the sexes.* New York: Columbia University Press.

Lincoln, Yvonna, & Guba, Egon. (1985). *Naturalistic inquiry.* Beverly Hills, CA: Sage.

Lindzey, Gardner (Ed.). (1973). *A history of psychology in autobiography* (Vol. 6). Englewood Cliffs, New Jersey: Prentice Hall.

Lindzey, Gardner (Ed.). (1980). *A history of psychology in autobiography* (Vol. 7). San Francisco: Freeman.

Lott, Bernice. (1985a). The devaluation of women's competence. *Journal of Social Issues, 41,* 43–60.

Lott, Bernice. (1985b). The potential enrichment of social/personality psychology through feminist research and vice versa. *American Psychologist, 40,* 155–164.

Lott, Bernice. (1988). Separate spheres revisited, *Contemporary Social Psychology, 13,* 55–62.

Lykes, M. Brinton, & Stewart, Abigail J. (1986). Evaluating the feminist challenge to research in personality and social psychology: 1963–1983. *Psychology of Women Quarterly, 10,* 393–412.

Marecek, Jeanne (Ed.). (1989). Theory and method in feminist psychology [special issue]. *Psychology of Women Quarterly, 13* (4).

Mattfield, Jacquelyn, A., & Van Aben, Carol G. (Eds.). (1965). *Women and the scientific professions.* Cambridge, MA: M.I.T. Press.

Mednick, Martha T. (1989). On the politics of psychological constructs: Stop the bandwagon, I want to get off. *American Psychologist, 44,* 1118–1123.

Miller, Jean Baker. (1976). *Toward a new psychology of women.* Boston: Beacon Press.

Morawski, Jill G. (1985). The measurement of masculinity and feminity: Engendering categorical realities. *Journal of Personality, 53* (2), 196–223.

Morawski, Jill G. (1988). Impossible experiments and practical constructions: The social bases of psychologists' work. In Jill G. Morawski (Ed.), *The rise of experimentalism in American psychology,* (pp. 72–93). New Haven, CT: Yale University Press.

Morawski, Jill G. (1990). Toward the unimagined: Feminism and epistemology in psychology. In Rachel Hare-Mustin & Jeanne Marecek (Eds.), *Making a difference: Psychology and the construction of gender* (pp. 150–201). New Haven, CT: Yale University Press.

Napoli, Donald S. (1981). *Architects of adjustment: The history of the psychological profession in the U.S.,* Port Washington, New York.

Nicholson, Linda J. (Ed). (1990). *Feminism/Postmodernism.* New York: Routledge.

Nowell-Smith, P. H. (1977). The constructionist theory of history. *History and Theory, Studies in the Philosophy of History, 16,* 1–28.

O'Connell, Agnes N. (Chair, APA Division 35 Task Force on Women doing Research). (1978). Gender-specific barriers to research in psychology. *JSAS Catalog of Selected Documents in Psychology, 8,* Ms. No. 1753.

O'Connell, Agnes N., & Russo, Nancy F. (Eds.). Eminent women in psychology: Models of achievement. [special issue]. *Psychology of Women Quarterly, 5* (1).

O'Connell, Agnes N., & Russo, Nancy F. (1983). *Models of achievement: Reflections of eminent women in psychology.* (Vol. I), New York: Columbia University Press.

O'Connell, Agnes N., & Russo, Nancy F. (1988). *Models of achievement: Reflections of eminent women in psychology* (Vol. 2). Hillsdale, NJ: Lawrence Erlbaum.

O'Connell, Agnes N., & Russo, Nancy F. (1990). *Women in psychology: A biobibliographic sourcebook.* New York: Greenwood Press.

Ogilvie, Marilyn B. (1986). *Women in science: Antiquity through the nineteenth century: A biographical dictionary with annotated bibliography.* Cambridge, MA: MIT Press.

O'Leary, Virginia E., Unger, Rhoda K., & Wallston, Barbara S. (Eds.). (1985). *Women, gender, and social psychology.* Hillsdale, NJ: Lawrence Erlbaum.

Over, Ray. (1983). Representation, status, and contributions of women in psychology: A bibliography. *Psychological Documents,* Ms. No. 2573.

Palmieri, Patricia A. (1983). Here was fellowship: A social portrait of academic women at Wellesley College, 1895–1920. *History of Education Quarterly, 23,* 195–214.

Parker, Ian, & Shotter, John (Eds.). (1990). *Deconstructing social psychology.* London: Routledge.

Pepleau, Letetia, & Conrad, Eva. (1989). Beyond non-sexist research: The perils of feminist methodology in psychology. *Psychology of Women Quarterly, 13,* 379–400.

Polkinghorne, Donald. (1983). *Methodology for the human sciences: Systems of inquiry.* Albany: State University of New York Press.

Raven, Susan, & Weir, Alison. (1980). *Women of achievement: 35 centuries of history.* New York: Harmony Books.

Reinharz, Shulamit, Bombyk, Marti, & Wright, Janet (1983). Methodological issues in feminist research: A bibliography of literature in women's studies, sociology and psychology. *Women's Studies International Forum, 16,* 437–454.

Rosenberg, Rosalind. (1982). *Beyond separate spheres: Intellectual roots of modern feminism.* New Haven, CT: Yale University Press.

Rosenberg, Rosalind (1988). The limits of access: The history of coeducation in America. In John M. Faragher & Florence Howe (Eds.). *Women in higher education in American history* (pp. 107–128). New York: Norton.

Rossiter, Margaret W. (1982). *Women scientists in America: Struggles and strategies to 1940.* Baltimore: The Johns Hopkins University Press.

Russo, Nancy. (1982). *Resources for teaching the history of women in psychology.* Washington, D.C.: Office for Women's Programs, American Psychological Association.

Russo, Nancy, & Denmark, Florence L. (1987). Contributions of women to psychology. *Annual Review of Psychology, 38,* 279–298.

Sassan, Georgia. (1980). Success anxiety in women: A constructivist interpretation of its source and significance. *Harvard Educational Review, 50* (1), 13–24.

Sayers, Janet. (1986a). *Sexual contradictions: Psychology, psychoanalysis, and feminism.* London: Tavistock.

Sayers, Janet. (1986b). Sexual identity and difference: Psychoanalytic perspectives. In Sue Wilkinson (Ed.), *Feminist social psychology* (pp. 25–38). Philadelphia: Open University Press.

Sayers, Janet. (1990). Psychoanalytic feminism: Deconstructing power in theory and therapy. In Ian Parker & John Shotter (Eds.), *Deconstructing social psychology* (pp. 196–207).

Scarborough, Elizabeth, & Furumoto, Laurel. (1987). *Untold lives: The first generation of American women psychologists.* New York: Columbia University Press.

Scarborough, Elizabeth. (1988). The history of psychology course. In Phyllis A. Bronstein & Kathryn Quina, (Eds.), *Teaching a psychology of people: Resources for gender and sociocultural awareness* (pp. 88–93). Washington, D.C.: American Psychological Association.

Scarr, Sandra. (1985). Constructing psychology: Making facts and fables for our time. *American Psychologist, 40,* 499–512.

Scott, Joan W. (1988). Deconstructing equality versus difference: On the uses of post-structuralist theory. *Feminist Studies, 14,* 33–50.

Searing, Susan E. (1986). Further readings on feminism and science. In Ruth Bleier (Ed.), *Feminism and science* (pp. 191–195). New York: Pergammon.

Sears, Robert R. (1975). Your ancients revisited: A history of the child development movement. In E. Mavis Hetherington (Ed.), *Review of child development research.* (Vol. 5, pp 1–73). Chicago: University of Chicago Press.

Senn, Milton L. (1975). Insights on the child development movement in the United States. *Monographs of the Society for Research in Child Development, 40,* (3–4, Serial No. 16), pp. 1–106.

Sexton, Virginia S. Women in American psychology: An overview. *Journal of International Understanding,* 1974, *9,* pp. 66–77.

Sherif, Carolyn W. (1979a). Bias in psychology. In Julia Sherman & Evelyn T. Beck (Eds.), *The prism of sex: Essays in the sociology of knowledge* (pp. 93–133). Madison: University of Wisconsin Press.

Sherif, Carolyn W. (1979b). What every intelligent person should know about psychology and women. In Eloise C. Snyder (Ed.), *The study of women: Enlarging perspectives on social reality* (pp. 143–183). New York: Harper and Row.

Sherif, Carolyn W. (1981). Needed concepts in the study of gender identity. *Psychology of Women Quarterly, 6,* 375–398.

Sherman, Julie A., & Beck, Evelyn T. (Eds.). (1979). *The prism of sex: Essays in the sociology of knowledge.* Madison: University of Wisconsin Press.

Shields, Stephanie A. (1975a). Functionalism, Darwinism, and the psychology of women. *American Psychologist,* 739–754.

Shields, Stephanie A. (1975b). Ms. Pilgrim's progress: The contribution of Leta Stetter Hollingworth to the psychology of women, *American Psychologist, 30,* 852–857.

Shields, Stephanie A., & Mallory, Mary E. (1987). Leta Stetter Hollingworth speaks on "Columbia's Legacy." *Psychology of Women Quarterly, 11,* 285–300.

Sicherman, Barbara, & Green, Carol H. (1980). *Notable American women, the modern period: A biographical dictionary.* Cambridge: Harvard Belknap.

Siegal, Patricia J., & Finley, Kay T. (1985). *Women in the scientific search: An American biobibliography, 1724–1979.* Metuchen, NJ: Scarecrow Press.

Simeone, Angela. (1987). *Academic women: Working towards equality.* South Hadley, MA: Bergin and Garvey.

Solomon, Barbara M. (1985). *In the company of educated women: A history of women and higher education in America.* New Haven, CT: Yale University Press.

Spence, Janet. (1981). Changing conceptions of men and women: A psychologist's perspective. In Elizabeth Langland & Walter Gove (Eds.), *A feminist perspective in the academy: The difference it makes* (pp. 130–148). Chicago: University of Chicago Press.

Stevens, Gwendolyn, & Gardner, Sheldon. (1982). *The women of psychology,* Vols. I and II. Cambridge, MA: Schenkman.

Stevens, Gwendolyn & Gardner, Sheldon. (1985). Psychology of the scientist: LIV. Permission to excel: A preliminary report of influences on eminent women psychologists. *Psychological Reports, 57,* 1023–1026.

Stocking, George W. (1965). On the limits of "presentism" and "historicism" in the historiography of the behavioral sciences. *Journal of the History of the Behavioral Sciences, 1,* 211–218.

Strouse, Jean (Ed.). (1985). *Women and analysis: Dialogues on psychoanalytic views of feminity*. Boston: G. K. Hall.

Sweeney, Patricia E. (1950). *Biographies of American women: An annotated bibliography*. Santa Barbara, CA: ABC-CLIO, Inc.

Terris, Virginia. (1900). *Women in America: A guide to information sources*. Detroit: Gale Research Co.

Tingley, Elizabeth, & Tingley, Donald F. (1981). *Women and feminism in American history: A guide to information sources*. Detroit: Gale Research Co.

Torrey, Jane W. (1987). Phases of feminist re-vision in the psychology of personality. *Teaching of Psychology, 14*, 155–160.

Toulmin, Stephen. (1982). The construal of reality: Criticism in modern and postmodern science. *Critical Inquiry, 9*, 93–111.

Toulmin, Stephen & Leary, David. (1985). The cult of empiricism in psychology, and beyond. In Sigmund Koch & David Leary (Eds.), *A century of psychology as science* (pp. 594–617). New York: McGraw Hill.

Trecker, Janice L. (1974). Sex, science and education. *American Quarterly, 26*, 352–366.

Unger, Rhoda K. (1981). Sex differences: Historical perspectives and methodological implications. *Developmental Review, 1*, 187–206.

Unger, Rhoda K. (1982). Advocacy versus scholarship revisited: Issues in the psychology of women. *Psychology of Women Quarterly, 7*, 5–17.

Unger, Rhoda K. (1983). Through the looking glass: No wonderland yet! (The reciprocal relationship between methodology and models of reality). *Psychology of Women Quarterly, 8*, 9–32.

Unger, Rhoda K. (1985a). Epistemological consistence and its scientific implications. *American Psychologist, 40*, 1413–1414.

Unger, Rhoda K. (1985b). Explorations in feminist methodology: Surprising consistencies and unexamined conflicts. *Imagination, Cognition, and Personality, 4*, 359–403.

Unger, Rhoda K. (1988). Psychological, feminist, and personal epistemology: Transcending contradiction. In Mary M. Gergen (Ed.), *Feminist thought and the structure of knowledge.* (pp. 124–141). New York: New York University Press.

Unger, Rhoda K. (1989a). *Representations: Social constructions of gender*. Amityville, NY: Baywood.

Unger, Rhoda K. (1989b). Sex, gender, and epistemology. In Mary Crawford & Margaret Gentry (Eds.), *Gender and thought: Psychological perspectives* (pp. 17–35). New York: Springer.

Viney, Wayne, & Wertheimer, Michael L. (1979). *History of psychology: A guide to information sources*. Detroit: Gale Research Co.

Walker, Lenore E. (1991). The feminization of psychology. *Psychology of Women: Newsletter of Division 35, APA, 18* (2), 1, 4.

Wallston, Barbara S. (1981). What are the questions in psychology of women: A feminist approach to research. *Psychology of Women Quarterly, 5*, 597–617.

Wallston, Barbara S., & Grady, Kathleen. (1985). Integrating the feminist critique and the crisis in social psychology: Another look at research methods. In Virginia E. O'Leary, Rhoda K. Unger, & Barbara S. Wallston (Eds.), *Women, gender, and social psychology* (pp. 7–33). Hillsdale, NJ: Lawrence Erlbaum.

Wallston, Barbara S. (1987). Social psychology of women and gender. *Journal of Applied Psychology, 17,* 1025–1050.

Walsh, Mary R. (1977). *Doctors wanted: No women need apply. Sexual barriers in the medical profession 1835–1975.* New Haven, CT: Yale University Press.

Walsh, Mary R. (1985). Academic professional women organizing for change: The struggle in psychology. *Journal of Social Issues, 41,* 17–27.

Watson, Robert I. (1974, 1976). *Eminent contributors to psychology: A bibliography of primary references,* (2 Vols.). New York: Springer Publishing Company.

Weisstein, Naomi. (1968). *Kinder, Kirche, Küche as scientific law: Psychology constructs the female.* Boston: New England Free Press.

Weisstein, Naomi. (1971). Psychology constructs the female, or the fantasy life of the male psychologist (with some attention to the fantasies of his friends, the male biologist and the male anthropologist). *Journal of Social Education, 35,* 362–373.

West, Candace, & Zimmerman, Don H. (1987). Doing gender. Gender and Society, *1,* 125–151.

Westkott, Marcia. (1986). *The feminist Legacy of Karen Horney.* New Haven, CT: Yale University Press.

Westkott, Marcia. (1988). Female relationality and the idealized self. Unpublished manuscript, University of Colorado, Boulder.

Wilkinson, Sue (Ed.). (1986). *Feminist social psychology: Developing theory and practice.* Philadelphia: Open University Press.

Wittig, Michele. (1985). Metatheoretical dilemmas in the psychology of gender. *American Psychologist, 40,* 800–811.

Zita, Jacquelyn N. (1988). The feminist question of the science question of feminism. *Hypatia, 3,* 157–168.

Zuckerman, Harriett, & Cole, Jonathan. (1975). Women in American science. *Minerva, 13,* 82–102.

Biographical Information Sources: Selected Women of Psychology

Selected Women of Psychology

The following women have been selected to represent the variety and significance of women's work in psychology and to include a range of historical periods. Each woman is identified by simple (and necessarily incomplete) descriptors of her work. The numbers preceding the names are used as a key to the bibliography which follows. A given woman's number in this list will appear in the bibliography in front of each reference which deals with her life and/or work. For example, references which discuss Anne Anastasi are preceded with a number 1. This format will allow you easily to locate readings about a particular woman of interest to you.

Key:

Contemp = Contemporary psychologist, currently working

Pioneer = Very early woman psychologist (major work prior to 1920)

PSA = Psychoanalytic Theory/Practice

	Name	Primary Area of Work
1.	Anne Anastasi	Individual Differences, Psychometrics
2.	Sandra Bem	*Contemp*—Gender, Androgyny
3.	Marie Bonaparte	*PSA*
4.	Charlotte Buhler	Humanistic Psychology
5.	Mary Calkins	*Pioneer*—Self Psychology, Paired Associates Technique
6.	Nancy Chodorow	*Contemp*—Gender, *PSA,* Mothering
7.	Mamie Phipps Clark	*Contemp*—Developmental Psychology, Racism
8.	Florence Denmark	*Contemp*—Social Psychology, Feminist Psychology
9.	Helene Deutsch	*PSA,* Psychology of Women
10.	Dorothea Dix	Mental Health Reformer
11.	June Etta Downey	*Pioneer*—Aesthetics, Personality Measurement
12.	Anna Freud	Child and Adolescent *PSA*
13.	Eleanor Jack Gibson	Experimental Psychology, Perception
14.	Carol Gilligan	*Contemp*—Moral Development, Gender
15.	Florence Goodenough	Developmental Psychology
16.	Edna Heidbredder	Theory, History of Psychology, Cognition
17.	Mary Henle	*Contemp*—History, Gestalt Psychology
18.	Leta Hollingworth	*Pioneer*—Sex Differences, Giftedness
19.	Karen Horney	*PSA,* Object Relations
20.	Barbel Inhelder	Cognitive Development
21.	Mary Cover Jones	Behaviorism, Behavior Therapy
22.	Grace Kent	Clinical Practice, Clinical Research
23.	Melanie Klein	*PSA,* Object Relations
24.	Christine Ladd-Franklin	*Pioneer*—Color Vision, Mathematics
25.	Eleanor Maccoby	Child Development, Gender
26.	Margaret Mahler	*PSA,* Object Relations

27. Myrtle McGraw — Child Development, Nature/Nurture
28. Martha Mednick — *Contemp*—Social Psychology, Gender
29. Jean Baker Miller — *Contemp*—*PSA*, Psychology of Women
30. Maria Montessori — Early Childhood, Educational Psychology
31. Lois Barclay Murphy — Social Psychology, Child Development
32. Anna Roe — Occupational Psychology
33. Virginia Satir — Family Dynamics/Therapy
34. Carolyn Wood Sherif — Social Psychology, Feminist Psychology
35. Janet Taylor Spence — Experimental Psychology, Gender
36. Leona Tyler — Individual Differences, Clinical Psychology
37. Barbara Wallston — (d. 1987)—Social Psychology, Feminist Psychology
38. Margaret Floy Washburn — *Pioneer*—Comparative Psychology
39. Helen (Thompson) Woolley — *Pioneer*—Sex Differences
40. Bluma Zeigarnik — Field Theory (Zeigarnik Effect)

Biographical Information Sources for
Selected Women of Psychology

The following references discuss one or more of the "**Selected Women of Psychology**" listed above. To locate references about a particular woman, simply scan the left hand column for the number of her listing on that list.

For example, Anne Anastasi is number 1 on the list of Selected Women of Psychology. To find references about her life and work, scan the numbers here for a number 1; the corresponding reference discusses Anastasi.

Women Covered	Citation
3, 9, 12, 13 . .	Alexander, Franz, Eisenstein, Samuel, & Grotjohn, Martin. (Eds.). (1966). *Psychoanalytic pioneers*. New York: Basic Books.
1	Anastasi, Anne. (1980). Autobiography. In Gardner Lindzey (Ed.), *A history of psychology in autobiography* (vol. 7, pp. 1–37). San Francisco: W. H. Freeman.
11	Anderson, John E. (1933). June Etta Downey (1875–1932). *American Journal of Psychology, 45,* 362–363.
18	Benjamin, Ludy T. (1975). The pioneering work of Leta Hollingworth in the psychology of women. *Nebraska History, 56,* 493–505.
1, 4, 9, 15, . . 17, 19, 22, 23, 25, 31, 34, 35, 36, 40	Bernstein, Maxine D., & Russo, Nancy F. (1974). The history of psychology revisited: Or, up with our foremothers. *American Psychologist, 29,* 130–134.
3	Bertin, Celia. (1982). *Marie Bonaparte: A life.* New Haven, CT: Yale University Press.
10	Browne, William J. (1969). A psychiatric study of the life and work of Dorothea Dix. *American Journal of Psychiatry, 126,* 335–341.
3, 9, 19	Buckley, Nellie L. (1982). Women psychoanalysts and the theory of feminine development: A study of Karen Horney, Helen Deutsch and Marie Bonaparte. Ph. D. Dissertation, University of Chicago.
5	Calkins, Mary W. (1930). Autobiography. In Carl Murchinson (Ed.), *A history of psychology in autobiography* (vol. 1, pp. 31–62). Worcester, MA: Clark University Press.
38	Dallenbach, Carl M. (1940). Margaret Floy Washburn: 1871–1939. *American Journal of Psychology, 53,* 1–5.
4, 7, 12, 15, . . 22, 25, 34, 35, 39	Denmark, Florence L. (1980). Psyche: From rocking the cradle to rocking the boat. *American Psychologist, 35,* 1057–1065.
1	Denton, Laurie. (1987). The rich life and busy times of Anne Anastasi. *APA Monitor,* October, 10–12.
9	Deutsch, Helene. (1973). *Confrontations with myself.* New York: Norton.

12 . . . . Dyer, Raymond. (1983). *Her father's daughter: The work of Anna Freud.* New York: Aronson.

16 . . . . Evans, Rand B. (1986). Edna Heidbredder: 1890–1985. *Cheiron Newsletter, 13*,(1), 5–6.

12 . . . . Fine, Reuben. (1985). Anna Freud (1895–1982). *American Psychologist, 40,* 230–232.

5 . . . . Furumoto, Laurel. (1979). Mary Whiton Calkins (1863–1930): Fourteenth president of the American Psychological Association. *Journal of the History of the Behavioral Sciences, 15,* 346–356.

16 . . . . Furumoto, Laurel. (1980a). Edna Heidbreder: Systematic and cognitive psychologist. *Psychology of Women Quarterly, 5,* 94–102.

5 . . . . Furumoto, Laurel. (1980b). Mary Whiton Calkins (1863–1930). *Psychology of Women Quarterly, 5,* 55–68.

38 . . . . Furumoto, Laurel & Scarborough, Elizabeth. (1987). Placing women in the history of comparative psychology: Margaret Floy Washburn (1871–1939) and Margaret Morse Nice (1883–1974). In Ethel Tobach (Ed.), *Historical perspectives and the international status of comparative psychology* (pp. 103–117). Hillsdale, NJ: Lawrence Erlbaum.

30 . . . . Fynne, Robert J. (1924). *Montessori and her inspirers.* New York: Longmans, Green.

19 . . . . Garrison, Dee. (1981). Karen Horney and feminism. *Signs: Journal of Women in Culture and Society, 6,* 672–691.

13 . . . . Gibson, Eleanor J. (1980). Autobiography. In Gardner Lindzey (Ed.), *A history of psychology in autobiography* (vol. 2, pp. 239–271). San Francisco: W. H. Freeman.

38 . . . . Goodman, Elizabeth S. (1979). Margaret Floy Washburn: ''A complete psychologist.'' *APA Monitor,* Dec., 3, 16.

5, 11, 18, . . . *Great American Scientists.* (1961). Englewood Cliffs, NJ: Prentice Hall.
24, 38, 39

24 . . . . Green, Judy. (1987). Christine Ladd-Franklin (1847–1930). In Louise S. Gristein & Paul J. Campbell (Eds.), *Women of mathematics* (pp. 121–128). New York: Greenwood.

23 . . . . Grosskurth, Phyllis. (1986). *Melanie Klein: Her world and her work.* New York: Knopf.

7 . . . . Guthrie, Robert. (1976). *Even the rat was white.* New York,: Harper & Row.

18 . . . . Haber, Louis. (1979). *Women pioneers of science.* New York: Harcourt Brace Jovanovich.

15 . . . . Harris, Dale B. (1959). Florence L. Goodenough: 1886–1959. *Child Development, 30,* 305–306.

4 . . . . Havighurst, Robert J. (1974). Charlotte Buhler: 1893–1974. *Human Development, 17,* 377–378.

5 . . . . Heidbreder, Edna. (1972). Mary Whiton Calkins: A discussion. *Journal of the History of the Behavioral Sciences, 8,* 56–68.

17 . . . . Henle, Mary. (1986). An American adventure [autobiography]. In Mary Henle, *1979 and all that: Essays in the theory and history of psychology* (pp. 238–240). New York: Columbia University Press.

16 . . . . . . Henle, Mary. (1987). Edna Heidbreder (1890–1985). *American Psychologist,* *42,* 94–95.

18 . . . . . . Hollingworth, Harry L. (1943/1990). *Leta Stetter Hollingworth.* Boston: Anker Press. (Ludy Benjamin & Stephanie Shields, Editors of re-issue).

18 . . . . . . Hollingworth, Leta Stetter. (1940). *Prairie years* [autobiography]. New York: Columbia University Press.

19 . . . . . . Horney, Karen. (1980). *The adolescent diaries of Karen Horney.* New York: Basic Books.

20 . . . . . . Inhelder, Barbel. (1989). Autobiography. In Gardner Lindzey (Ed.), *A history of psychology in autobiography* (pp. 209–243). Palo Alto, CA: Stanford University Press.

23 . . . . . . Isaacs, Susanna. (1961). Obituary: Melanie Klein, 1882–1960. *Journal of Child Psychology and Psychiatry, 2,* 270–281.

3 . . . . Jackson, D. Joyce (1987). Contributions to the history of psychology: XLIII. A tribute to Princess Marie Bonaparte. *Psychological Reports, 60,* 1231–1240.

5, 11, 18, . . . James, Edward T., James, Janet W., & Boyer, Paul S. (Eds.). (1971). *Notable*
24, 38, 39   *American women, 1607–1950: A biographical dictionary* (3 vols.). Cambridge, MA: Harvard Bellknap.

24 . . . . . . Kass-Simon, Gabriele, & Farnes, Patricia (Eds.), (1990). *Women of science: Righting the record.* Bloomington: Indiana University Press.

19 . . . . . . Kelman, Harold. (1954). In memoriam: Karen Horney, MD. *American Journal of Psychoanalysis, 14,* 5–7.

19 . . . . . . Kelman, Harold. (1973). *Feminine Psychology: Karen Horney, MD.* New York: W. W. Norton.

19 . . . . . . Kelman, Norman. (1953). Karen Horney, MD: 1885–1952. *Psychoanalytic Review, 40,* 191–193.

23 . . . . . . King, Pearl H. M. (1983). The life and work of Melanie Klein in the British Psychoanalytic Society. *International Journal of Psychoanalysis, 64,* 251–260.

30 . . . . . . Kramer, Rita. (1976). *Maria Montessori: A biography.* New York: G. P. Putnam.

30 . . . . . . Liotta, Elena. (1986). Maria Montessori (1870–1952): In memoriam. *History of Psychology, 18,* 43–48.

27 . . . . . . Lipsitt, Lewis P. (1990). Myrtle B. McGraw (1899–1988). *American Psychologist, 45,* 977.

12 . . . . . . Lustman, Seymour L. (1967). The scientific leadership of Anna Freud. *American Psychoanalytic Association Journal, 15,* 810–827.

25 . . . . . . Maccoby, Eleanor. (1989). Autobiography. In Gardner Lindzey (Ed.), *A history of psychology in autobiography* (pp. 291–335). Palo Alto: Stanford University Press.

10 . . . . . . Marshall, Helen E. (1937). *Dorothea Dix, a forgotten Samaritan.* Chapel Hill: University of North Carolina Press.

38 . . . . . . Martin, Mabel F. (1940), The psychological contributions of Margaret Floy Washburn. *American Journal of Psychology, 53,* 7–18.

38 . . . . . . McCurdy, Harold. (1940). Memories of Margaret Floy Washburn. *Vassar Alumnae Magazine, 25,* 3–4.

27 . . . . McGraw, Myrtle B. (1990). Memories, deliberate recall, and speculations [autobiography.] *American Psychologist, 45,* 934–937.

34 . . . . Mednick, Martha T., & Russo, Nancy F. (1983). Carolyn Wood Sherif: Brilliant scholar, gifted teacher, cherished friend. *Psychology of Women Quarterly, 8,* 3–8.

21 . . . . Mussen, Paul, & Eichorn, Dorothy. (1988). Mary Cover Jones (1896–1987). *American Psychologist, 43,* 818.

3 . . . . Nacht, S. (1963). Marie Bonaparte (1882–1962). *International Journal of Psychoanalysis, 44,* 516–517.

5, 11, 18 . . . *Notable American Women, 1607–1950: A biographical dictionary.* (1971). Edward T. James (Ed.). Cambridge, MA: Belknap.

4, 15, 19, . . . *Notable American Women: The modern period: A biographical dictionary.*
24, 38, 39 (1980). Barbara Sicherman & Carol H. Green (Eds.). Cambridge, MA: Belknap.

19 . . . . O'Connell, Agnes N. (1980). Karen Horney: Theorist in psychoanalysis and feminine psychology. *Psychology of Women Quarterly, 5,* 81–94.

5, 16, 19, . . . O'Connell, Agnes N., & Russo, Nancy F. (Eds.). (1980). Eminent women in
21, 31, 32, 38 psychology: Models of achievement [special issue]. *Psychology of Women Quarterly, 5.*

7, 17, 27, . . . O'Connell, Agnes N., & Russo, Nancy F. (1983). *Models of achievement:*
31, 34 *Reflections of eminent women in psychology.* New York: Columbia University Press.

1, 8, 28, ... O'Connell, Agnes N., & O'Connell, Nancy F. (1988). *Models of*
35, 36 *achievement: Reflections of eminent women in psychology,* Vol. II. Hillsdale, NJ: Lawrence Erlbaum.

1, 2, 4, 5, . . . O'Connell, Agnes N., & Russo, Nancy F. (1990). *Women in psychology: A*
7, 8, 13, 15, *bio-bibliographic sourcebook.* New York: Greenwood.
16, 18, 20,
24, 25, 34,
35, 36, 38

37 . . . . O'Leary, Virginia E. (1988). Barbara Strudler Wallston (1943–1987). *American Psychologist, 43,* 817.

12 . . . . Peters, Uwe H. (1985). *Anna Freud: A life dedicated to children.* New York: Schoken.

38 . . . . Pillsbury, Walter. (1940). Margaret Floy Washburn (1871–1939). *Psychological Review, 47,* 99–109.

18 . . . . Poffenberger, Albert T. (1940). Leta Stetter Hollingworth: 1886–1939. *American Journal of Psychology, 53,* 299–301.

21 . . . . Pomerleau, Cynthia. (1984). Mary Cover Jones. *Women and Health, 9,* 1–3.

5 . . . . Pratola, Stephanie. (1974). Up with our foremother. *American Psychologist, 29,* 780.

19 . . . . Quinn, Susan. (1987). *A mind of her own: The life of Karen Horney.* New York: Summit.

9 . . . . Roazen, Paul. (1974). Helene Deutsch, 1884–1982. *American Journal of Psychiatry, 140,* 497–499.

9 . . . . Roazen, Paul. (1985). *Helene Deutsch: A psychoanalyst's life.* New York: Summit.

18, 24, 38, . . Rosenberg, Rosalind. (1982). *Beyond separate spheres: Intellectual roots of* 39 *modern feminism.* New Haven, CT: Yale University Press.

11, 15, 18, . . Rossiter, Margaret W. (1982). *Women scientists in America: Struggles and* 38, 39 *strategies to 1920.* Baltimore, MD: The Johns Hopkins University Press.

19 . . . . . . Rubins, Jack L. (1978). *Karen Horney: Gentle rebel of psychoanalysis.* New York: Dial Press.

37 . . . . . . Russo, Nancy F. (1990). Barbara Strudler Wallston: Pioneer of contemporary feminist psychology, 1943–1987. *Psychology of Women Quarterly, 14,* 277–287.

23 . . . . . . Sayers, Janet. (1989). Introduction to *Feminine Character* by Melanie Klein. London: Routledge.

24 . . . . . . Scarborough, Elizabeth. (1988). Christine Ladd-Franklin (1847–1930): In memoriam. *History of Psychology, 20,* 55–56.

5, 24, 38, . . . Scarborough, Elizabeth, & Furumoto, Laurel. (1987). *Untold lives: The first* 39 *generation of American women psychologists.* New York: Columbia University Press.

23 . . . . . . Segal, Hanna. (1979). *Melanie Klein.* New York: Bruner/ Mazel.

34 . . . . . . Shaffer, Leigh S., & Shields, Stephanie A. (1984). Carolyn Wood Sherif (1922–1982). *American Psychologist, 3,* 176–179.

22 . . . . . . Shakow, David. (1974). Grace Helen Kent. *Journal of the History of the Behavioral Sciences, 10,* 275–280.

18 . . . . . . Shields, Stephanie A. (1982). Ms. Pilgrim's progress: The contributions of Leta Stetter Hollingworth to the psychology of women. *American Psychologist, 30,* 852–857.

18, 39 . . . . . Shields, Stephanie A. & Mallory, Mary E. (1987). Leta Stetter Hollingworth speaks on ''Columbia's Legacy.'' *Psychology of Women Quarterly, 11,* 285–300.

30 . . . . . . Standing, E. Mortimer. (1984). *Maria Montessori.* New York: New American Library.

26 . . . . . . Stephansky, Paul E. (Ed.). (1988). *The memoirs of Margaret Mahler.* New York: Free Press.

1, 3, 4, 5, . . . Stevens, Gwendolyn, & Gardner, Sheldon. (1982). *The women of psychology,* 7, 8, 10, 11, *Vol. I: Pioneers and innovators; Vol. II: Expansion and refinement.* 12, 13, 15, 16, Cambridge, MA: Schenkman. 17, 18, 19, 20, 21, 22, 23, 24, 25, 26, 28, 30, 31, 32, 33, 34, 35, 36, 38, 39

3, 9, 19 . . . . Strouse, Jean. (1985). *Women and analysis: Dialogues on psychoanalytic views of femininity.* Boston, MA: G. K. Hall.

10 . . . . . . Sweeney, Patricia E. (1950). *Biographies of American women: An annotated bibliography.* Santa Barbara, CA: ABC-CLIO, Inc.

3, 9, 12, 19, . .   Thompson, Nellie L. (1987). Early women psychoanalysts. *International*
23, 26   *Review of Psycho-Analysis, 14,* 391–407.

10 . . . .   Tiffany, Francis. (1980). *Life of Dorothea Lynde Dix.* Boston: Houghton-Mifflin.

19, 23 . . . . .   Uglow, Jennifer S. (Ed.). (1982). *The international dictionary of women's biography.* New York: Continuum.

19, 23, 30 . . .   Uglow, Jennifer S. (1989). *The continuum dictionary of women's biographies.* New York: Continuum.

11 . . . .   Uhrbrock, Richard S. (1933). June Etta Downey: 1875–1932. *Journal of General Psychology, 9,* 351–364.

5 . . . .   Updike, Donald B. (1931). *In memoriam: Mary Whiton Calkins, 1863–1930.* Boston: Marymount Press.

11 . . . .   Van Horn, Christina, & Furumoto, Laurel. (1985). June Etta Downey: The psychologist, the poet, and the person. Paper presented at meetings of the Rocky Mountain Psychological Association, Tucson, AZ.

10 . . . .   Viney, Wayne, & Bartsch, Karen. (1984). Dorothea Lynde Dix: Positive or negative influence on the development of treatment for the mentally ill. *Social Sciences Journal, 21,* 71–82.

10 . . . .   Viney, Wayne, & Zorich, Steven. (1982). Contributions to the history of psychology, XXIX: Dorothea Dix and the history of psychology. *Psychological Reports, 50,* 211–218.

38 . . . .   Washburn, Margaret Floy. (1932). Some reflections [autobiography]. In Carl Murchinson (Ed.), *History of psychology in autobiography* (Vol. 2, pp. 333–359). Worcester, MA: Clark University Press (Reprinted 1961, NY: Russell & Russell).

19 . . . .   Westkott, Marcia. (1986). *The feminist legacy of Karen Horney.* New Haven, CT: Yale University Press.

10 . . . .   Wilson, Dorothy C. (1975). *Stranger and traveler: The story of Dorothea Dix, American reformer.* Boston: Little, Brown.

21 . . . .   Wolpe, Joseph. (1988). Mary Cover Jones (1896–1987). *Journal of Behavior Therapy and Experimental Psychiatry, 19,* 3–4.

24 . . . .   Woodworth, Robert S. (1930). Christine Ladd-Franklin. *Science, 71,* 307.

38 . . . .   Woodworth, Robert S. (1948). Margaret Floy Washburn: 1871–1939. *Biographical memoirs of the National Academy of Sciences* (vol. 25, pp. 273–295). Washington, DC: National Academy of Sciences.

12 . . . .   Young-Bruehle, Elizabeth. (1988). *Anna Freud: A biography.* New York: Summit.

5, 11, 15, . . .   Zusne, Leonard. (1975). *Names in the history of psychology: A biographical*
18, 24, 30   *sourcebook.* Washington, DC: Hemisphere.

4, 5, 10, 11, . .   Zusne, Leonard. (1984). *Biographical dictionary of psychology.* Westport,
12, 15, 18,   CT: Greenwood.
19, 22, 23,
24, 30

2, 15, 19, . . .   Zusne, Leonard. (1987). *Eponyms in psychology: A dictionary and*
22, 24, 30,   *biographical sourcebook.* Westport, CT: Greenwood.
35, 40